Gender and the Information Revolution in Africa

edited by Eva M. Rathgeber and Edith Ofwona Adera

INTERNATIONAL DEVELOPMENT RESEARCH CENTRE
Ottawa • Cairo • Dakar • Johannesburg • Montevideo • Nairobi • New Delhi • Singapore

Published by the International Development Research Centre
PO Box 8500, Ottawa, ON, Canada K1G 3H9

© International Development Research Centre 2000

Legal deposit: 1st quarter 2000
National Library of Canada
ISBN 0-88936-903-8

The catalogue of IDRC Books and this publication may be consulted online at http://www.idrc.ca/booktique.

CONTENTS

CONTENTS

FOREWORD

On the occasion of the 40th anniversary of the United Nations Economic Commission for Africa, the African Centre for Women organized a conference, African Women and Economic Development: Investing in Our Future (28 April to 1 May 1998). One of the major themes of the conference was "African women and the information age: a rare opportunity." In plenary and working-group sessions, the issues discussed included ways to make policies on information and communication technologies (ICTs) relevant to women, ICTs as tools for democratization, the impact of ICTs on women's work, and building women's capacity to make use of these technologies. The contributors to this book played a key role in the discussions of this theme.

Conference participants recommended priority areas for action, stressing the need to disseminate information to women and policymakers on the potential impact of ICTs on women in Africa, to spark women's interest in having their voices heard in this debate, and to improve opportunities for women to become ICT literate. In the information age, women risk becoming stereotyped in the manner of traditional media and failing to become the creators of information. Conference participants also recognized the usefulness of categorizing female users and conducting a needs assessment to establish the priorities of various groups, such as businesswomen, rural producers, parliamentarians, and health-care providers. Because women carry out roughly two-thirds of all the agricultural tasks in Africa, they can certainly benefit from ICTs for agricultural applications. Businesswomen and female artisans can reach markets throughout the world, as the World Bank-initiated "virtual *souk*" (virtual market) project demonstrated during the conference.

According to statistics from the United Nations Educational, Scientific and Cultural Organization, the vast majority of women in Africa are still illiterate (as of 1995, the figure was 54% for women older than 15), and even today, most girls are not receiving more than primary education (in 1996, 45% of students enrolled in first-level schooling in Africa were girls, but many of them did not even complete this level). So how can they be expected to operate within an emerging new knowledge-based world order? On the threshold of a new millennium, most African women have not entered the information age. What does this mean for the future of Africa? The contributors to this book have addressed the question of the role of education and women's access to, and understanding of, ICTs. Knowledge can help to increase options and choices in one's life, but an information infrastructure is also needed. This includes physical infrastructure, as well as a minimal level of knowledge and skills to make use of the equipment. New technologies may also offer women opportunities in distance learning, which is more flexible than traditional educational approaches. In policy formulation, it is also important to consider youth's access to knowledge of ICTs, computers, and their use.

Conference participants also discussed the potential importance of ICTs in the development of democratic systems of governance and in facilitating women's input into decision-making structures. An open society, with free access and flow of information, promotes a culture of participatory government. Exchanging information with other countries and regions of the world, in turn, strengthens the position of countries in the globalization process. Strategies for integrating a gender perspective in ICT policies in Africa are an essential first step to enabling women's voices to be heard.

One of the actions recommended by conference participants was to develop tools for ownership to ensure long-term commitment and sustainability. Nowadays, information can be created more easily than before; however, we cannot lose sight of the question of who has access to information. Control of information is often a source of power. Women must not miss the chance to create, use, and access information to improve their lives and participate in the economic, political, and social life of their communities and countries.

The aim of this book is to raise awareness among policymakers and civil society of what is at stake for women in the information age. It makes a strong case for ensuring that gender is an issue and ultimately aims to take the discussions and recommendations of the conference one step further and stimulate action at the policy level.

Josephine Ouedraogo
Director, African Centre for Women
United Nations Economic Commission for Africa
Addis Ababa, Ethiopia
June 1999

Acknowledgments

The relationship between the use of information and communication technologies (ICTs) and gender remains largely unexplored, both in Africa and elsewhere. Much of the original conceptualization that provided terms of reference for most of the chapters of this volume came from the Gender Working Group that met in Nairobi in November 1997. Members of the group included Nidhi Tandon of Abantu for Development; Gillian Marcelle, then of the United Nations University Institute for New Technologies; Nancy Hafkin of the United Nations Economic Commission for Africa (ECA); Liz Levey of the Ford Foundation; Hilda Tadria of ECA; Anriette Esterhuyzen of SANGONeT; Ruth Ochieng of ISIS–Women's International Cross Cultural Exchange; Suzanne Drouilh of Nairobi; Fatoumata Sow of Dakar; Tina James of the International Development Research Centre (IDRC), Johannesburg; and John Baraza, Edith Ofwona Adera, and Eva Rathgeber of IDRC, Nairobi. During 2 days of animated discussion, this group identified a number of key research issues related to ICTs and gender.

EXECUTIVE SUMMARY

Eva M. Rathgeber and Edith Ofwona Adera

Most of the chapters in this volume were presented at an international conference, African Women and Economic Development: Investing in Our Future, which was held from 28 April to 1 May 1998, in Addis Ababa, Ethiopia, and hosted by the United Nations Economic Commission for Africa to mark its 40th anniversary. This collection examines the current and potential impact of the explosion of information and communication technologies (ICTs) in Africa, focusing on the gender dimensions and analyzing the extent to which the revolution is serving women's needs and preferences. The book argues that it is not enough for women to be simply passive participants in the development and dissemination of ICTs in Africa. They must also be decision-makers and actors in the process of using the new ICTs to accelerate African economic, social, and political development.

The chapters in this volume address three broad topics: the current state of ICT and telecommunications policy in Africa; sectoral applications of ICTs in agriculture, education, and governance (democratization); and, finally, some current practical experiences in Africa.

In the opening chapter, Nancy Hafkin presents an historical perspective on the emergence and convergence of the themes "gender and development" and "ICTs and development" to develop a clearer understanding of the analysis of gender and ICTs in Africa. She points out that the decade of the 1970s adopted the theme "women in development" (WID), which emphasized a home, family, and social-welfare approach. This approach saw women as passive recipients of development benefits. However, the 1980s saw the addition of the empowerment approach, which stressed the need for women's access to productive resources, such as land, labour, and capital (credit, education, and training). Concerns began to emerge about the effects of new technologies on women's economic and social roles, and debates began to focus on gender gaps in technology. It was generally held that technologies are gender neutral and that their use is equally available to men and women. Information technology remained a specialized tool, and there

ix

was no thought of questioning its relevance or potential benefits for African women (nor indeed any women) at that time.

Hafkin observes that the application of science and technology (S&T) to development became institutionalized at the regional level in Africa at about the same time as WID was emerging as a new development focus. However, it was only in the early 1980s that the first real interest in the relationship between gender and S&T for development began to emerge in Africa. The focal points for these activities were generally in women's programs, rather than in S&T units. In the initial years, emphasis was on encouraging young girls to stay in school and study S&T. Hafkin identifies the emergence of the field of development information in the late 1970s, contributing to the creation of a stronger link between ICTs and gender. Governments were encouraged to systematize development-information management to make it an effective tool for decision-makers and planners.

Hafkin also notes that with the emergence of the economic forces of globalization, which rely heavily on communications technology, ICTs have become increasingly important as tools to accelerate social and economic development. The Global Knowledge Conference, held in Toronto in 1997 (GK97), was critical in focusing the discussion of gender and ICTs on differential access and patterns of use. GK97 gave women a platform to advocate an increase in women's share of the benefits of the ICT revolution and to argue for "connectivity for all."

Writing on the ICT challenge for Africa, Eva Rathgeber examines the current status of the telecommunications sector in the continent. She points out that although many African countries are experiencing some extension and modernization of their telecommunication networks, sub-Saharan Africa's overall teledensity is still less than 1 line per 200 people. African countries have responded to these challenges with varying results. A growing number are opening the telecommunication sector to private investors. Rathgeber focuses on the need to ensure that the future development of the telecommunications sector takes into account social issues in general and gender issues in particular. She observes that most African countries, with the notable exception of South Africa, have given little attention to formulating ICT policies to provide the sector with an overall structure for development and growth. She argues that such policies are needed to develop a well-coordinated pattern of development that has specific goals, seizes opportunities, and makes the best use of government, donor, and private-sector investments.

Rathgeber argues that if women are to participate fully in all aspects of ICT development, then ICT policies must include a gender dimension. She stresses that in promoting the spread of ICTs to less advantaged regions of each country, one must make a distinction between the attitudes and needs of male and female users. It is evident that highly targeted efforts are needed to involve women and ensure that their needs are integrated into ICT policies. Rathgeber discusses the potential of ICTs to improve or make an impact on the lives of African women and argues that men's and women's attitudes, needs, and perspectives on ICTs are likely to differ. This suggests a reconceptualization of the use of ICTs as tools for African development and a reorganization of existing knowledge and information bases.

Writing on strategies to include a gender perspective in African ICT policy, Gillian Marcelle argues that both women and men in Africa should have the opportunity to benefit from ICTs. She notes that ensuring equitable treatment for men and women will require concerted efforts and involve considerable demands on the institutional capacities of policymakers. She maps out the current state of national ICT policy-making in Africa and provides a brief historical review of the landmarks in African ICT policy-making. She also examines closely the process of ICT policy-making in four African countries, Mozambique, Senegal, South Africa, and Uganda; provides details of the policy-making apparatus used in each of these countries; assesses the challenges facing their policy-makers; and reviews their successes. She concludes with recommendations and actions for various sets of actors in ICT policy and implementation.

Marcelle also suggests that African governments take steps in five key areas: (1) define and specify measurable goals and objectives for the ICT sector and ICT applications, taking into account rural women and their needs as potential beneficiaries of ICTs; (2) create the necessary institutional structure to develop and steer a vision of national ICT development and include representatives of women's organizations and experts in gender and development issues in policy formulation; (3) secure advice and strengthen technical expertise in ICT-related fields; (4) develop consultative mechanisms to ensure that all key stakeholders are actively involved in policy formulation, implementation, and review; and (5) improve capacity to review policy objectives, monitor and evaluate programs, and respond to changes occurring in the technological and socioeconomic environment.

Hilda Munyua begins her chapter by identifying some of the key problems facing women in the agricultural sector in Africa, including cultural, social, economical, legal, and educational handicaps and a lack of appropriate and usable information that could help them improve their farming activities. Munyua notes that a lack of reliable and comprehensive information is a major hindrance to agricultural development. Unfortunately, this has received inadequate attention in most African countries, especially in rural areas, where 70–80% of the African population still resides. Munyua notes that women's information needs include further knowledge of agricultural production, processing, marketing, decision-making, trade laws, and the natural-resource base. They also need to exchange information on indigenous knowledge, and they require appropriate ICTs to access vital information efficiently and cost-effectively. She points out that the media play a major role in delivering agricultural messages, with radio being the main source of information for many people in rural areas. Nonetheless, she argues that where appropriate, satellite, solar, and fibre-optic technologies, which are now in use for computers, telephones, and facsimile, should be tapped to enable rural female farmers to access further information. She advocates using such modern ICTs concurrently with traditional ones.

She sees the establishment of rural telecentres as an effective way to move forward. These can provide rural female farmers, female leaders, and others with access to a range of services, including electronic mail, the World Wide Web, electronic networks, news groups, listservs, teleconferencing, CD-ROMs, and distance learning. Munyua looks at some policy implications of the broader use of ICTs. She notes that if female farmers are to have access to, and to benefit from, the information available, then supportive policies and regulations that empower women must be developed, adequate resources must be allocated, tele-communication infrastructure must be provided, and an awareness of the potential of ICTs for development must be cultivated. She argues that women must be involved in decision-making processes to ensure that the new telecommunications systems in various countries meet their needs and constraints.

Munyua emphasizes that the content of the information must be relevant to the requirements of rural women and that existing information should be re-packaged in appropriate format, size, and language and be affordable. This may create jobs, reduce rural–urban migration, and help reverse the brain drain in many countries in Africa. Also required are institutional strengthening and capacity-building. In particular, women should have the technical capability to handle the technologies as they become available; hence, a strong argument can be made for providing adequate, relevant training.

Drawing on the anglophone African experience and writing on the theme of reconceptualizing education for production, use, and management of ICTs,

Cathy-Mae Karelse notes that although ICTs can be used by various groups in society to promote their social causes, the position of most women in Africa distances them from these technologies. In addition, she says women are absent from S&T courses and programs and seldom found in senior management or policy-making positions. Nonetheless, she points out, it is widely acknowledged that women generate local knowledge systems and possess significant information for development. However, experience has shown that when ICTs are introduced into these contexts, women are seldom invited to enter the negotiations regarding the use of the ICTs, which further undermines women's status. The ICT sector is male dominated, and women on the ground do not have easy access to these technologies for their own organizational and information needs.

However, attention is increasingly paid to the various ways ICTs can be used to improve women's social status, as well as their involvement in the information society. Karelse sees education as a key component in developing the human-resource capacity to participate in the information society. Education programs must be directed to developing both gender equity and equality. She stresses that training must also prepare women for various levels of participation in the global information society, including management positions. Women must develop skills to design and shape information systems appropriate to their needs. She suggests that the private sector can assist by emphasizing the participation of women in their own information-infrastructure development. Karelse suggests that telecentres and multipurpose centres in the rural sector can serve as important conduits for women to gain access to further training and resources.

Fatimata Seye Sylla, writing on the same theme and drawing on the francophone African experience, points to the importance of ICTs as tools for exchanging information worldwide and the need to train African children to master and use these new tools. She notes that previous experience showed that girls are less attracted than boys to S&T subjects, whether in the formal- or the informal-education system. For this reason, girls are likely to suffer a disadvantage in the use of ICTs. Sylla analyzes the causes of such disparities and proposes ways of attracting more girls to the use of ICTs. She argues that women and girls must be given the appropriate background and training, which will ultimately help them to prepare training materials that reflect their interests and take account of their specific needs. The use of ICTs in educational establishments throughout Africa must also be popularized. Sylla also suggests that women can open websites to generate and make accessible a wide range of relevant information, using appropriate software and equipment. Sylla outlines roles for various stakeholders, including those in the private sector, who might invest in the manufacture and local assembly of ICTs, in production and dissemination of teaching materials, in training, and in employment. She suggests that telecommunications companies reduce connection costs for women for specific periods to provide an incentive. Finally, the state should play a pioneering role with policy commitments to the implementation of the proposals.

Solange Mienje Momo advocates the expansion of women's access to ICTs. She analyzes the situation of African women within their sociocultural context, noting the progress that has been made on improving the status of women worldwide since the first women's conference in Mexico in 1975. However, stagnation, if not decline, in this progress marked the 1985–95 period, because of its economic, political, and social turbulence. Momo outlines women's information needs and analyzes their participation in the use and management of ICTs. She emphasizes that the first stage of any process of change must be the acquisition of knowledge, whether the change is socioeconomic, cultural, political, or legal. Efficient information flow, she says, is an integral part of development. Momo provides examples of successful initiatives to increase women's access to ICTs in Burkina Faso, Burundi, and Uganda and concludes by urging governments to facilitate women's access to information and allow them to actively contribute to economic development.

Aida Opoku-Mensah provides an overview of the emergence of civil society in Africa, outlining the level of participation of women in the electoral process. She notes that the participation of women, as full and equal partners with men, in key decision-making processes (particularly in politics and governance) has not yet been achieved. However, she argues that ICTs have the capacity to greatly enhance people's participation in the democratic process in developing countries, and in many instances they are already doing so. She cautions that although the ICTs may provide new opportunities for social and political dialogue, they may also increasingly disenfranchise already marginalized people as the gap between the information rich and the information poor widens. Who gains access to ICT resources in many countries will depend to a large extent on the effectiveness of government policies.

Opoku-Mensah provides insights, glimpses, and examples of how ICTs are being used throughout the continent to empower women and improve the protection of their rights. She notes that new technologies have characteristics similar to those of alternative media and are well-suited to the needs of women's networks because they are decentralized and horizontal. She examines the potential

xiv

of ICTs to contribute to the advancement of women and illustrates how fairly affordable computer-mediated communications, such as e-mail, Internet, hypertext, and hypermedia, have infinitely facilitated networking, research, training, and the sharing of ideas and information. She emphasizes the need to develop imaginative approaches to overcome the difficulties of weak infrastructure, actively promote training in rural areas, and find the ways and means to interface new and old media technologies for women who have no access to computers or electricity. She concludes with recommendations on the ways the main actors in society, namely, governments, women's groups, and international organizations, can enhance the use of ICTs.

Finally, Shanyisa Anota Khasiani gives an overview of the experience and ongoing lessons learned in a project on women and governance in two rural districts of Kenya. The project's overall objective was to build on existing infrastructure in community-based resource centres to provide the women of the communities with the ability to generate, access, and use civic information to enhance their participation in governance. Khasiani tests the hypothesis that community-based resource centres with ICTs can play a pivotal role in giving Kenyans, especially Kenyan women, information about the electoral process. The project's aims were to enhance women's interaction and generate, store, and promote the exchange of strategic information to enable women to make informed decisions and participate effectively in the electoral process in the long term.

The project has already developed information, education, and communication materials to demystify ICTs and demonstrate the potential for women to use ICTs to become more involved in governance, including both effectively participating in electoral politics and responding to their own information requirements in their daily activities. She identifies civic education and small-scale enterprise as two priority areas for intervention. Khasiani concludes by highlighting key challenges facing the project, including repackaging information to make it more relevant, addressing the cultural dimension within indigenous communication systems, diffusing fairly new technologies in the study areas, solving infrastructure problems, and meeting the impacts of the ongoing liberalization of the telecommunications environment (policy).

Together, these essays provide an overview of a number of compelling issues in the wider use and acceptance of ICTs in Africa. They specifically underscore the importance of giving special attention to the needs, priorities, and perspectives of women. Information is the universally acknowledged linchpin of development, and several of the papers stress the paucity of any type of information available to rural women. They see the new ICTs as having the potential to redress this information imbalance, but they also stress the importance of making information directly relevant to the needs of rural women, whether in agriculture, health, microenterprises, or other sectors. This will involve careful selection and repackaging, often repackaging into local languages.

Most of the authors further emphasize that unless policies are well thought out and unless targeted training is provided, the ICT revolution currently sweeping the world is likely to bypass the majority of African women. Women must become involved in ICT policy formulation, and the starting point for participation in this process will be to make women aware of the importance of the information revolution. Women must understand their own information needs and develop sufficient technical knowledge to be credible advocates of their views in policy debate. Finally, the authors provide numerous examples of ongoing ICT initiatives, many of them started by African women's organizations. These initiatives illustrate the varied potential of these technologies to empower women.

Chapter 1

CONVERGENCE OF CONCEPTS: GENDER AND ICTS IN AFRICA

Nancy J. Hafkin

A concern for gender and development emerged on the international scene in the 1970s. As this concern matured, linkages developed between this and other major development concerns — science and technology (S&T), development information, and, most recently, information and communication technologies (ICTs) — as a focus in the development community. Only in the last 5 years have two concepts begun to converge: that of ICTs and development and that of gender and development (until the late 1980s, women in development [WID]). The critical mass of activity in this area in Africa has taken place only in the past 2 years.

This chapter looks at the ways these themes have emerged and converged historiographically and thereby develops a clearer understanding of the analysis of gender and ICTs in Africa.

Women in development

Nearly 25 years ago, the field of WID (as it was then known) was beginning to take on an institutional and operational form in Africa; 1975 marked the first United Nations-organized world conference on women: the International Women's Year conference in Mexico City. Of all the regions of the world represented at this conference, only Africa had a regional program at that time — the Women's Programme of the United Nations Economic Commission for Africa (ECA), started in 1971 and based in Addis Ababa. The tremendous energy from the conference led to the declaration of the United Nations Decade for Women, 1976–85. In the United Nations in Africa, this energy transformed the existing unstructured program of activities for women into the African Training and Research Centre for Women (ATRCW) in 1975, a unit within the Social Development Division of ECA (Snyder and Tadesse 1995).

ATRCW began working in the area of WID with a focus on women's economic and political roles in the context of human-resource development. Before this, numerous programs had been directed to helping women in the African region. However, before ATRCW, the emphases had been on

- A home and family approach, which most often followed a Western, almost Victorian, home-economics model; and

- A social-welfare approach, which saw women as passive recipients of development benefits and emphasized family planning because of women's reproductive roles.

Both of these earlier approaches virtually ignored women's economic roles and paid no attention to women's empowerment, because that was felt to be irrelevant to women.

From its founding, ATRCW's approach to women in Africa emphasized human-resource development, based on

- Recognition of women's productive roles as active participants in the economy; and

- Identity of the goals of human-resource development and the goals of development in general (the full participation of women is essential to development).

In the early 1980s, the addition of the empowerment approach complemented these elements. It stressed the need for women's access to productive resources. With the empowerment approach, ATRCW took the view that women had had autonomy and authority in precolonial Africa but lost these in colonial times and did not regain them in the postindependence era, when political life began to follow Western models of patriarchy. Women now talk of how empowerment has in many ways restored their former status (Hafkin and Bay 1976). In the 1980s, the productive resources of Africa were the classic land, labour, capital, credit, education, and training. By the mid-1990s, however, when ICTs became an important productive resource, gender analysts turned their attention to finding ways to ensure women's access to ICTs.

Technology concerns in WID

Ester Boserop's very important book *Woman's Role in Economic Development* (Boserop 1970) stressed that new technologies introduced in Africa, as well as in other developing areas, had been generally displacing the labour of women. Her research marked the beginning of the intellectual examination of the effects of new technologies on women's jobs and the opening of debates about gender gaps in technology. It also moved beyond the view generally held at that time that technologies are gender neutral and that their use is equally available to men and women. Despite Boserop's seminal work, governments and many development agencies continued to adhere to the view that technology is gender neutral, that there is no such thing as gender-based technology (despite obvious societal gender differences), and that the arrival of technology is an unquestionable panacea.

Early in the work of the ECA Women's Programme, concern emerged about the relationship between technology and women's economic and social roles. In its first years, the ECA Women's Programme attempted to look at the relationship between women and technology, publishing, for example, "The Impact of Modern Life and Technology on Women's Economic Role: Implications for Planning" (ECA–FAO–SIDA 1972). The crowning piece in this area was the landmark publication of Marilyn Carr's *Appropriate Technology for African Women* (Carr 1977). However, because information technology remained a specialized tool of computer programmers in the world of mainframes and mini-computers, whose numbers in Africa were highly limited, there was no interest at that time in raising questions about its relevance to African women.

S&T for development

Applications of S&T for development took on institutional forms at the regional level in Africa in the 1970s, at about the same time as WID was emerging as a major development focus. In 1973, the ECA Conference of Ministers responsible for economic development and planning adopted the S&T component of the African Strategy for Development and approved the African Regional Plan for the Application of Science and Technology to Development. This was to be implemented by the Intergovernmental Committee of Experts for Science and Technology for Development. This committee has met biennially since the mid-1970s.

S&T examines the gender element

By the early 1980s, the first concerns about the relationship between gender and S&T for development began to emerge in Africa. The leaders were the International Development Research Centre (IDRC), the United Nations Educational, Scientific and Cultural Organization (UNESCO), and the United Nations Development Programme (UNDP). They each worked with ECA to develop projects in Africa in this area. The institutional focal points of these activities were generally in the women's programs, rather than in the S&T units. In the initial years, emphasis was on encouraging young girls to stay in school and study S&T.

A significant publication in this area in the late 1980s was Patricia Stamp's *Technology, Gender, and Power in Africa* (Stamp 1989), which examined the relationship between gender and technology in Africa. It was published following a meeting in 1989, organized jointly by the Rockefeller Foundation and IDRC, on Gender, Technology and Development: a Diagnosis of Available Literature. In the foreword to the book, Eva M. Rathgeber remarked on one of the key findings of the meeting, that "for most women in the developing world, technology has failed" (Rathgeber 1989, p. vii). This was thought to stem from the fact that technologies are not gender neutral but rather are value laden from beginning to end and that most technologies destined for women in Africa have been produced by Western men who do not understand the social, economic, or cultural contexts for use of these technologies.

In addition to expounding the view that technology, to date, had generated negative consequences for women in Africa, Stamp (1089) brought together an analysis of WID research, feminist political economy, and the vast literature on technology transfer. She felt that no one had conceptualized the relationship between gender and technology. On the positive side, however, she noted that when women in Africa accepted technology transfer, these technologies empowered them; and that women's organizations and the social structure reconfigured themselves to the requirements of the new technologies.

Although the relationship had not been conceptualized, Stamp (1989) delineated 10 issues in the relationship between gender and technology in Africa. Three of these issues are especially relevant to gender and ICTs:

- Governments and development agencies treat technologies as neutral, value-free tools and assume that the adoption of these technologies will naturally lead to development;

- Governments and development agencies tend to ignore women's relationships to technology; and

- Women have unequal access to development resources (of which information has, at the end of the 20th century, come to be regarded as primary, equivalent to land and capital).

In the 1990s, the field of gender and S&T for developing countries in general and Africa in particular has matured. The actors have become almost too numerous to list. *Missing Links* (UNCSTD–GWG 1995) contains a 25-page bibliography of publications on gender and S&T in developing countries. The following are notable among the platforms, organizations, and institutions involved:

- Agenda 21, the recommendations of the United Nations Conference on Environment and Development (in 1992);

- The Fourth World Conference on Women (Beijing) Platform for Action (in 1995);

- The gender activities of the Science in Africa Programme of the American Association for the Advancement of Science;

- The Board on Science and Technology for International Development of the US National Research Council;

- The Forum of African Women Educationalists, for their innovative program to teach S&T to girls in Africa;

- IDRC;

- The International Federation of Institutes for Advanced Study, through their Gender, Science and Development Programme;

- Intermediate Technology for Development Group, through its Africa Office;

- The International Gender, Science and Technology Information Map (WGST 1998);

- The International Research and Training Institute for the Advancement of Women;

- The International Women's Tribune Center;

- The Third World Organisation of Women in Science and Technology, which promotes the role of women in science and development in the South (its 1999 meeting in Johannesburg was notable for the amount of attention paid to gender and ICTs in Africa);

- UNESCO, particularly through *World Science*;

- The S&T programs of the United Nations Development Fund for Women (UNIFEM); and

- The social-exclusion studies of the United Nations University Institute for New Technologies, in Maastricht.

The emergence of development information

In the late 1970s, another development area emerged in Africa that would contribute to the linkage of gender and ICTs for development information. Again, IDRC contributed significantly to the intellectual origins of the work in this area. In 1975, IDRC began work on DEVSIS, a database of indexed and abstracted development information linked to the MINISIS software for bibliographic information management and using Hewlett–Packard minicomputers.[1] Developing regions were encouraged to adopt this system of information management for decision-makers and planners. With assistance from IDRC, as well as from UNESCO and UNDP, the Pan African Documentation and Information System came into existence at ECA in Addis Ababa in 1979. (In 1987, the name was changed to the Pan African Development Information System (PADIS) to reflect the expansion of its scope beyond that of a bibliographic database.) From its origins, the link with S&T was explicit: the system was to include both S&T and socioeconomic information. Also, from its origin, the link between development information as a field and ICTs was implicit: the system's success was tied to both computers and communication satellites (which, unfortunately, would not

---

[1] Mention of a proprietary name does not constitute endorsement of the product and is given only for information.

become available for development-information communication networks in Africa for another 20 years). However, these elements were not emphasized, nor was there any explicit articulation for ICTs as tools for development until 1990, when the personal-computer revolution began to reach Africa.

Women and development information

The first African regional effort to link gender, development information, and information technology came in 1989, when ATRCW and PADIS at ECA (with the support of UNIFEM and the Ford Foundation) organized an Expert Group Meeting on the Establishment of a Data Bank on Women in Development in Africa. The meeting brought together men and women from some 25 African countries (from Tunisia, to Ethiopia, to Mozambique, to Senegal) from non-governmental organizations (NGOs) and public-sector organizations dealing with information on WID. The need to use information technology was explicit both in the background papers ("Model for the Establishment of a Data Bank and Women's Information Network for Africa") and in the country papers.[2] Regrettably, despite intense interest during the meeting, the necessary funding was never raised to establish the network. However, the work of the expert group has been taken up again in the late 1990s by the Gender in Africa Information Network, with its Information and Communication Technology Working Group, under the leadership of the African Gender Institute at the University of Cape Town. This network, coordinated by Jennifer Radloff, is a major promoter of using ICTs to empower women through the dissemination of information on gender and development. Its electronic discussion list (gain@lists.sn.apc.org) is extremely active, informative, and stimulating.

IDRC further articulated the relationship between gender and development information in *Gender and Information: A Strategy for Integrating Gender Issues into the Work of the Information Sciences and Systems Division* (IDRC 1993).

ICTs emerge as major theme in S&T

With the emergence of globalization, which is essentially based in communications, ICTs did not remain a subset of S&T but became the more important field by the mid-1990s, almost eclipsing the work done in the previously larger main field. Increasingly, scholars and practitioners were looking at ways to use these

---

[2] Expert Group Meeting on the Establishment of a Data Bank on Women in Development, Addis Ababa, 15–19 May 1989 (unpublished). The papers, which are a rich source of information, are in the PADdev database, available from UNECA, P.O. Box 3001, Addis Ababa, Ethiopia; fax: +251 1 51 05 12; e-mail: eca-info@un.org.

new tools to accelerate social and economic development and produce sustainable development. The definitive book on this subject, covering all aspects of the field, has been Robin Mansell and Uta Wehn's *Knowledge Societies — Information Technology for Sustainable Development* (Mansell and Wehn 1998), which comes directly out of the S&T-for-development milieu. (The authors are both associated with the Science Policy Research Unit of the Institute of Development Studies, University of Sussex, in the United Kingdom.)

The first linkages between gender and ICTs for development started with the work of NGONET, in preparation for the United Nations Conference on Environment and Development's Earth Summit, in Rio, 1992. NGONET's aim was to use ICTs to give women and groups from the South a chance to use an innovative process of information exchange to express their views to a global development forum. In 1993, NGONET inspired the creation of the Women's Programme of the Association for Progressive Communications (APC), which played a similar role for the Beijing World Conference on Women in 1995 (APC 1997). The APC Women's Programme was based on solid analysis of feminist perspectives on technology and communications; its emphasis was on giving women the experience of ICTs. The APC Women's Programme defined itself as a global initiative to facilitate women's access to, and use of, computer communications. Its main task was to "demystify" ICTs for women.

Despite an almost routine linking of gender with other development issues by this time, this did not happen easily with ICTs. In 1995, the Commission on Science and Technology for Development (UNCSTD) of the United Nations Conference on Trade and Development, through its Advanced Technology Assessment System, published the volume *Information Technology for Development* (United Nations 1995). Although its stated aim was to deal, *inter alia*, with the social impacts of the diffusion and application of information technology and comprehensively cover the field of information technology for development, the book made no mention of gender issues. This was surprising, as it did consider such topics as unemployment, marginalization, and economic and social exclusion, which have very important gender dimensions. Furthermore, in 1993, shortly after its founding, UNCSTD had adopted the theme of gender as one of those it would address over the next 2 years.

Geoffrey Oldham, the farsighted member of UNCSTD who proposed the inclusion of gender, noted that the suggestion was adopted only after much debate, as many members of UNCSTD thought that gender had little to do with S&T. Professor Oldham subsequently chaired UNCSTD's Gender Working Group (GWG). The GWG made extensive recommendations to governments, international organizations, NGOs, and the private sector on implementing policies to promote a more gender-equitable approach to S&T (UNCSTD–GWG 1995).

The emergence of gender and ICTs

In 1995, *Missing Links* (UNCSTD–GWG 1995) provided the first comprehensive documentation of the links between gender and ICTs with specific reference to developing countries. In an article by IDRC's Gender and Information Working Group (GIWG), "Information as a Transformative Tool: The Gender Dimension," the IDRC team (led by Martha Stone) argued that acquiring information and knowledge is the first step to change and underlined the growing role of ICTs in this process:

> The flow of information and the associated information and communication technologies (ICTs) constitute a fundamental component of science and technology (S&T). Advances in ICTs are having an increasingly profound effect on the landscape of human activity.
>
> IDRC–GIWG (1995, pp. 267–268)

Having established this, the GIWG stated that the information revolution had essentially bypassed women and that information-society literature had been conspicuously silent on gender issues. With regard to developing societies, the GIWG said that little research had been done to address the circumstances of women. The gender and information dimension of S&T for development had also been absent from discussions at international forums.

The GIWG proceeded to define the major points of intersection between ICTs and gender, S&T, and development. ICTs can be said to

- Influence the content and mechanisms whereby women (and men) in developing countries learn about S&T;

- Constitute an increasingly significant component of S&T — ICTs have the potential to enhance the ability of women (and men) to learn, interact, and participate; and

- Have profound implications for women (and men) in terms of employment, education, training, and other aspects of productive life.

The first two points show that the GIWG was still making the arguments for both ICTs and gender as valid topics for research and policy within the S&T framework, which remained predominant at this time.

The GIWG's conclusion was that the new ICTs had the potential to strengthen the role of women as both participants in development and beneficiaries of it, following which it made extensive recommendations for the participation of women in an information society, as well as suggestions for research and policy in developing countries (IDRC–GIWG 1995).

The Global Knowledge Conference, held in Toronto, 1997 (GK97) and organized by the World Bank and the Government of Canada, was also very important to the promotion of a link between gender and ICTs. When the agenda for this conference was first drawn up, virtually no references were made to gender. However, as gender emerged as a vital theme in the electronic discussion list that preceded the conference (one of the first examples of the impact of electronic democracy!), its organizers quickly responded by giving substantial space to the gender issue throughout the conference. GK97 gave women a platform to advocate an increase in their share in the benefits of the information-technology revolution and to argue for "connectivity for all."

Gender and ICTs in Africa

The first operational activities associating gender and ICTs in Africa appeared in widely scattered parts of the continent in 1995 and 1995, in Kenya, South Africa, and Senegal. These activities predated the fifth World Conference on Women in Beijing, where most of the African ICT activists were involved. The activities all had an NGO base and an association with the APC Women's Programme. These included the activities of Environment, Development, Action (ENDA) - Dakar, Eco News Africa, and SANGONeT, which are well documented in this volume.

As women began to articulate the issues for the region, as in this volume, the arguments paralleled those used to encourage the participation of the region as a whole in the information age: that the information age offers opportunities to African women to catch up technologically and leapfrog over other developments they had missed and that if African women do not participate in it, they will find themselves further marginalized (Knight 1995). They also argued for women's recognition of the importance of ICTs on the basis of their need for empowerment, inclusion in ICT human-resource development, and access to the new technologies (Marcelle 1997). Arguments were also made about the value of these tools in strengthening women's economic and political roles. Rather than simply accepting and using the tools as they became available, it was suggested that African women use and transform them to create an information society to accommodate their needs, aspirations, and vision (Marcelle 1999).

In 1996, the ECA Conference of African Ministers responsible for economic and social development and planning adopted the African Information Society Initiative (AISI). Gender concerns were explicitly set out, with the idea that women were both users and providers of information and the idea that gender cut across all of AISI's major themes: policy, infrastructure, connectivity, human-resource development, and content creation. ECA and its partners in AISI implementation (Partnership for Information and Communication Technologies in Africa [PICTA] [ECA 1996]) have undertaken significant gender-focused activities through the theme of democratizing access to the information society, a major theme of AISI (see also the AISI 1993; PICTA 1998).

The area in the linkage of gender and ICTs that has received the least attention in Africa to date is the role of women in the information economy — the jobs and economic opportunities created by ICTs, whether used in the primary information sector (telecommunications and informatics industry, software, libraries, etc.) or used to enhance productivity and growth in other sectors. In other regions of the world, the information economy has opened up employment and entrepreneurial opportunities for women (for example, in information processing, teleworking, and rental of telephones, as with Grameen Telecommunications). However, in Asia, the advent of ICT-related industries has slotted women into low-paid jobs with long hours (Mitter and Rowbotham 1995). Outside the most visible spheres of penetration, in which women are much more likely to be secretaries using computers than systems analysts and programmers, the examples in Africa are not widespread enough to have economic significance (that is, the women in Ghana and Senegal who own and operate phone shops and the woman in Malawi who owns an Internet service provider company). Although the topic of the possibilities for development of a knowledge-based economy in Africa is yet to be explored in any depth, either in its gender dimension or overall, it remains an important one for the future.

Including the publication of this volume, there is now a critical mass of activities on gender and ICTs in Africa. The ECA 40th Anniversary Conference on African Women and Economic Development: Investing in Our Future presented the issue to more than 1 000 decision-makers and planners from Africa and reached even more through the Afr-fem electronic discussion list that both preceded and continued after the conference.

After a resolution of the April 1998 World Conference on Telecommunications Development, the International Telecommunication Union (ITU) established a gender and telecommunications working group, in which African issues were well represented (Women'sNet 1999). The Gender in African Information Network continues to grow as a force attracting women to the use of ICTs (GAIN 1998). Numerous projects are under way as part of the telecentre movement to see that the new information mechanisms provide access for women and meet their needs in Africa. Notable in this area are the efforts of IDRC's Acacia Initiative, which works with the South African Universal Service Agency to establish telecentres in South Africa, with particular attention to the needs and participation of women. The Center for Information Society and Development in Africa has an active gender working group that conducts training, with Abantu for Development, on women, connectivity, and ICT policy issues. At the conclusion of the ECA conference, the APC issued a communiqué underlining what it regarded as the key issues on gender and ICTs in Africa (APC 1988). These issues were

- *Enabling environment* — Women and other members of civil society need to join forums to convince policymakers of the importance of an enabling environment in which communication and communication technologies can flourish;

- *ICTs in education* — ICTs must be part of the curriculums for girls and boys everywhere in Africa from an early age;

- *Content production* — Men and women should be encouraged to develop content relevant to their interests and needs;

- *Information facilitators* — Owing to the growing complexity of the technology, information facilitators are needed to interface with communities to help them meet their information needs; and

- *Private-sector commitment to sustainable development* — As a vital partner in extending connectivity in Africa, the private sector needs to realize the importance of access to ICTs for all groups in society, including women.

These issues identify the salient areas in which much work continues to be done to ensure that women in Africa are able to use ICTs for their own economic and social benefit.

What is the future of ICTs for women in Africa? Many have credited the new technologies with great liberating potential. The Internet has been described as gender neutral (so long as the author uses initials instead of a first name or a gender title) and a participation-promoting technology with the ability to transcend hierarchy and patriarchy. Women in rural communities can make links from the local to the global in their work, provided they have access to ICTs in terms of both the technologies and the tools to use them (which include both computer and major-language literacy). The vision is that women in Africa will take advantage of this medium, fitting it into their economic, social, and cultural context, to empower themselves. Certainly, the African women at Beijing have provided many examples of this (through Women'sNet), and more stunningly innovative uses are coming out of Africa every month, such as the ECO News Africa project. It uses solar-powered FM radios to assist pastoral women in the Ilaramatak-Orkonerei community of Simanjiro District, Tanzania, in sharing indigenous knowledge and practices.

The converse side of the argument is that the new technologies are not gender neutral. Women in Africa will find them difficult to access, and they will not have the time, the tools, or the income to master them. As men become more conscious of the power and global dominance of these tools, they will act more to ensure that men dominate their use and become dominant in the information economy derived from the use of these tools. The pessimistic view sees ICTs as new tools to enforce and exacerbate social inequality. Left alone, societal forces will prevail, and women will get left behind.

Without the efforts of the women whose writings are included in this book and those of the activists working diligently to put these tools into the hands of women across the region, the pessimistic scenario may become reality. However, women and women's organizations are becoming more aware of the importance of ICTs for empowering women. One of the pioneers of these activities, Marie-Hélène Mottin-Sylla, of ENDA-Dakar, won a global award for her efforts to bring electronic connectivity to women in francophone Africa. In early 1999, the Gates Foundation approved a grant for WomenConnect!, a project worth 1 million US dollars. The aim of WomenConnect! is to provide connectivity to rural women in Africa, with particular attention to women working on issues in health and environmental protection. Through the activism of individuals, groups, and institutions such as the Gates Foundation, women in Africa can and will exploit these technologies to meet their needs and improve the quality of their lives.

References

AISI (African Information Society Initiative). 1999. African Information Society Initiative. United Nations Economic Commission for Africa, Addis Ababa, Ethiopia. Internet: www.bellanet.org/partners/aisi

APC (Association for Progressive Communications). 1997. Findings—global networking for change: experiences from the APC Women's Programme. APC, San Francisco, CA, USA.

——— 1998. APC Africa communique, 4 June 1998. APC, San Francisco, CA, USA.

Boserop, E. 1970. Woman's role in economic development. St Martin's Press, London, UK.

Carr, M. 1977. Appropriate technology for African women. African Training and Research Centre for Women, Addis Ababa, Ethiopia.

ECA (United Nations Economic Commission for Africa). 1996. The African Information Society Initiative (AISI): a framework to build Africa's information and communication infrastructure. ECA, Addis Ababa, Ethiopia. Internet: www.bellanet.org/partners/aisi/more/aisi

ECA–FAO–SIDA (United Nations Economic Commission for Africa; Food and Agriculture Organization of the United Nations; Swedish International Development Authority). 1972. The impacts of modern life and technology on women's economic role: implications for planning. ECA, Addis Ababa, Ethiopia.

GAIN (Gender in Africa Information Network). 1998. Report of a Gender in Africa Information Network (GAIN) workshop for the information and communication technology technical group. GAIN, Cape Town, South Africa.

Hafkin, N.J.; Bay, E.G. 1976. Women in Africa: studies in social and economic change. Stanford University Press, Stanford, CA, USA.

IDRC (International Development Research Centre). 1993. Gender and information: a strategy for integrating gender issues into the work of the Information Sciences and Systems Division. IDRC, Ottawa, ON, Canada.

IDRC–GIWG (International Development Research Centre Gender and Information Working Group). 1995. Information as a transformative tool: the gender dimension. *In* United Nations Commission on Science and Technology for Development Gender Working Group, ed., Missing links: gender equity in science and technology for development. IDRC, Ottawa, ON, Canada. pp. 163–172.

Knight, P.; Baranshamajee, E.; Booshlog, E.R.; Brajovic, V.P.; Clemant-Jones, R.A.; Hawkins, R.J. 1995. Increasing Internet connectivity in sub-Saharan Africa — issues, options and World Bank group role. World Bank, Washington, DC, USA.

Mansell, R; Wehn, U. 1998. Knowledge societies — information technology for sustainable development. Oxford University Press, Oxford, UK.

Marcelle, G.M. 1997. Using information technology to strengthen African women's oganisations. Abantu for Development, London, UK.

——— 1999. Creating an African women's cyberspace. *In* Mitter, S., ed., Social exclusion in the information society. Routledge, London, UK. (In press.)

Mitter, S.; Rowbotham, S. 1995. Women encounter technology: perspectives of the Third World. Routledge, London, UK.

PICTA (Partnership for Information and Communication Technologies). 1998. PICTA. United Nations Economic Commission for Africa, Addis Ababa, Ethiopia. Internet: www.bellanet.org/partners/picta

Rathgeber, E. 1989. Foreword. *In* Stamp, P., Technology, gender, and power in Africa. International Development Research Centre, Ottawa, ON, Canada. pp. vi–xi.

Snyder, M.C.; Tadesse, M. 1995. African women and development: a history. Zed, London, UK.

Stamp, P. 1989. Technology, gender, and power in Africa. International Development Research Centre, Ottawa, ON, Canada.

UNCSTD–GWG (United Nations Commission on Science and Technology for Development Gender Working Group), ed. 1995. Missing links: gender equity in science and technology for development. International Development Research Centre, Ottawa, ON, Canada.

United Nations. 1995. Information technology for development. United Nations, New York, NY, USA.

WGST (Women in Global Science and Technology). 1998. International gender, science and technology information map. WGST, Grifton, ON, Canada. Internet: www.wigsat.org/GSTPMap.html

Women'sNet. 1999. Women'sNet. SANGONeT, Johannesburg, South Africa. Internet: www.womensnet.org.za

Chapter 2

WOMEN, MEN, AND ICTS IN AFRICA: WHY GENDER IS AN ISSUE

Eva M. Rathgeber

During the past decade, global communications have changed dramatically, as a result of the increased use of information and communication technologies (ICTs). It has been widely acknowledged that the new ICTs have the potential to democratize national and international systems to an extent that no political movement has achieved. For the first time, a clear opportunity is afforded for individuals and populations outside the centre to have a significant influence and to ensure that their ideas and perspectives are taken into account by decision-makers in their own countries and indeed that their views become part of world thinking. For the first time, Africans living in remote areas can bring their perspectives, viewpoints, and experience to the global marketplace of ideas and knowledge. The most prominent and revolutionary feature of ICTs is their ability to eliminate the barriers of time and space, which have effectively silenced millions of people. However, if Africans are to become fully integrated into the global communication revolution, they require a basic level of technical knowledge and, even more dauntingly, an initial financial investment in the new technologies. At the national level, there is the need to create and maintain an adequate telecommunications infrastructure, and at the community or personal level, there is the need to invest in the purchase and maintenance of personal computers.

ICTs depend on good telephone connections, and this continues to be an elusive goal in many African countries. The status of the telecommunications sector in Africa is examined in this chapter, which then focuses on the need to ensure that social issues in general and gender issues in particular are taken into

NB: The views expressed in this chapter are my own and not necessarily those of the International Development Research Centre. I am grateful to Nancy Hafkin, Maureen O'Neil, and Eglal Rached for comments on an earlier version.

account in the further development of this sector. It is argued that ICTs have the
potential to improve or make an impact on the lives of African women but that
it is not enough for women simply to be passive participants in the development
and wide dissemination of these technologies in Africa. Women in Africa must
also be decision-makers and actors in the process of using the new ICTs to accelerate development. This chapter suggests that men's and women's attitudes, needs,
and perspectives on ICTs are likely to differ and that it is important to take account of the specific needs of women. A reconceptualization of the use of ICTs
as tools for African development may therefore be necessary, along with a reorganization of existing knowledge and information, and this implies a potential new
role for African universities and research institutions. Finally, this chapter discusses a number of relevant activities already under way in various parts of sub-
Saharan Africa (SSA).

The globalized economy

Even while the economies of many countries have grown Africa has become
increasingly marginalized in the 1990s. For the most part, the continent has lagged
behind in the process of economic globalization that has swept up other regions
of the world, including the so-called emerging regions, such as Latin America and
parts of Asia. To a significant extent, this has been due to Africa's poor infrastructure, including its telecommunications infrastructure, and its lower availability of
skilled labour. The continent's comparative advantage in labour costs, which might
have been a substantial attraction to international investors in earlier decades, has
become less significant with the emergence of the new ICTs.

　　　This is true for at least three reasons. First, the effective use of ICTs depends on the availability of skilled labour. Second, ICTs have eliminated the need
for some types of labour-intensive work. Third, ICTs have directly contributed to
job fragmentation, whereby large portions of work can be completed in different
parts of the world. The newly industrialized countries of Asia were quick to recognize and take advantage of globalization, and they offered attractive opportunities
to foreign investors, not the least of which were their excellent infrastructure and
educated labour force. The World Bank identified East Asia's capacity to produce
ICTs as a significant factor in its economic growth. Indeed, by 1995, ICTs
accounted for more than 25% of all exports from East Asian economies (Crede
and Mansell 1998). Similarly, United Nations figures suggest that more than 50%
of the gross domestic product of the countries of the Organisation for Economic
Co-operation and Development now comes from the knowledge industry (ECA
1998).

During the 1990s, the research and development (R&D) of transnational corporations has become increasingly internationalized, being characterized by rapid exchange of information and innovations via satellite. Also, production processes have become fragmented because information can be quickly transferred from one location to another. For example, many American firms now contract out routine data-processing work to countries like India or Barbados, which have advanced telecommunications infrastructures and highly skilled labour but much lower operating costs. Some have denounced these processes of globalization as another stage of imperialism. However, if globalization is interpreted as another stage of imperialism, it is even more pernicious than its predecessors, as it co-opts large numbers of people living in developing countries and makes distinctions among individuals based on education, skills, and access to ICTs, rather than on the simple centre–periphery or other geographical paradigms of an earlier age. Globalization has created new outsiders in the metropole, just as it has created new insiders in the periphery.

Nonetheless, access to ICTs offers new economic and social opportunities. At the end of the 20th century, Africa faces the challenge of using these opportunities constructively, rather than remaining passive and allowing ICTs to become another instrument of foreign domination. This was aptly summarized by Henry Chasia, the Kenyan deputy secretary-general of the International Telecommunication Union (ITU). In a speech at Arlington, Virginia, in September 1998, he noted that "the information economy is not an economy of dependency. It is a democratizing economy in which each one of us is free to contribute his or her talents and be compensated for it in an open global bazaar" (Chasia 1998).

African responses

The European Union, Japan, and the United States still dominate global telecommunications. In 1995, they shared 74% of world revenues from telecommunications (Crede and Mansell 1998). Africa has tried to respond to the new opportunities. But not surprisingly, the level and type of response have been uneven. In 1996–97, twelve African countries established separate telecommunications regulatory bodies. African countries with more liberal telecommunications policies have become continental leaders in the ICT sector. South Africa dominates the scene, with about 95% of the continent's Internet hosts and an information-technology infrastructure comparable to that of many European countries. In South Africa alone, the number of Internet users is estimated at more than 500 000, and the country has a teledensity of 10 lines per 100 people, about 20 times higher than that of the rest of SSA. However, major disparities remain along racial and urban–rural lines. Although almost 90% of white South Africans have telephones in their homes, the same is true of only 12% of blacks (Hall 1998). For Africa as a whole, the ITU estimated that it would cost 28 billion United States dollars (USD) to increase teledensity to 1 line per 100 people (Kobokoane 1998).

Such large-scale investment is beyond the capacity of most African governments, so a growing number of countries are opening up the telecommunications sector to private investors. By mid-1998, 17 African incumbent operators had full or partial private ownership, some of it foreign. Indeed, according to ITU, between 1994 and 1998, telecommunications privatization injected nearly 2 billion USD into African economies. Nonetheless, ITU research suggests that even after a country reaches a teledensity of 1 line per 100 people, it can take 20–50 years to reach a density of 50 lines per 100 people, which reflects high telecommunications development. Jensen (1998) estimated that Africans currently constitute about 1% of global e-mail users. Moreover, it is quite likely that a disproportionate number of African users are foreigners based in Africa or Africans working in donor agencies, embassies, or international nongovernmental organizations (NGOs). Table 1 illustrates the major disparities in Internet use in Africa.

Table 1. Internet hosts in Africa, 1998.

Country	Number of hosts	Country	Number of hosts
South Africa	122 025	Tunisia	69
Egypt	2 013	Mozambique	69
Namibia	640	Nigeria	49
Zimbabwe	599	Burkina Faso	45
Botswana	550	Togo	37
Kenya	458	Uganda	30
Morocco	431	Tanzania	25
Swaziland	330	Algeria	16
Côte d'Ivoire	253	Benin	13
Ghana	252	Angola	4
Zambia	181	Congo	4
Senegal	117	Niger	2

Source: Hall (1998).

Despite these disparities, Internet use is without doubt growing rapidly. Current estimates of the number of users in Africa vary from 800 000 to more than 1 million (Jensen 1998). By mid-1998, it was estimated that in Kenya about 25 000 people had Internet access, and the cost of computers had fallen to about 1 000 USD, owing both to reductions in import duty and to increased competition among suppliers. However, poor telephone connections have continued to be a significant deterrent to new Internet subscribers, as has the high cost of local calls in some countries (Jensen 1998). Moreover, African business has in general been slow to recognize the potential of the Internet. Electronic commerce is only beginning on the continent, despite the obvious potential in industries such as tourism. Finally, although no gender-disaggregated statistics on Internet users in Africa are available, it seems likely that more men than women are users, simply because in Africa men generally have greater access to technology.

Policy

National information-technology policies focused on improving the telecommunications sector and involving industry, management, and local R&D institutes will be essential if African countries want to benefit from the use of the new ICTs. A long-term perspective is needed, focused on achieving clear economic and development goals. Currently, entirely uncoordinated donor efforts are responsible for much of the information technology introduced in African countries (James 1998).

With the notable exception of South Africa, most African countries have given little attention to formulating ICT policies to provide overall structure to the development and growth of the telecommunications sector. Such policies are desirable to establish a well-coordinated development pattern with specific goals, take advantage of opportunities, and optimize investments from governments, donors, and the private sector. However, if women are to participate fully in all aspects of ICT development, then ICT policies must include a gender dimension. Previous African experience in a wide range of sectors from agriculture, to microenterprise, to education, etc., has demonstrated the need to recognize the disparity in men's and women's access to resources and opportunities and make policies to redress it. Most commonly, when policymakers have considered gender issues, it has been only after initial policies have proven ineffective. This new area of policy research therefore provides an opportunity for policymakers to integrate gender concerns into policy-making from the very beginning and "get it right."

Few African countries have articulated policies on the overall development of the ICT sector, although many have elaborated policies specifically to reform the telecommunications sector. Although the countries of Africa are liberalizing their economies, most of the continent's telecommunications networks are still under the control of national governments, with the result that the cost of telephone calls, especially international calls, is kept high and access to telephones is severely restricted. Increased competition, which is starting to occur in countries such as Senegal and Uganda, is leading to a reduction in prices, greater availability of lines, and, in consequence, increased connectivity, not only in urban centres but also in rural districts.

Currently, only 4% of Uganda's population lives in Kampala, but the capital city has 60% of the country's telephone lines. However, in mid-1998, the Ugandan government awarded a second network-operator licence to a consortium of private investors, headed by South African-based Mobile Telecommunication Network (MTN), for a bid of 5.6 million USD. The MTN–Uganda consortium is expected to install 60 000 land lines, in addition to 200 000 cellular lines, thus providing some relief from the current inaccessibility of telephone services outside Kampala. The immediate effect of the entry of the second network operator was a steep reduction in the cost of cellular telephones.

Similarly, Tanzania is currently drafting a new policy to guide the development of the sector into the next century. The policy is expected to reaffirm Tanzania's commitment to competition and private-sector participation and mandate the privatization of the state-owned national operator. The cellular subsector has already been open to competition for some time. In many African countries, the low-income subscriber base and difficult terrain often make land-line networks an unattractive option, and for this reason cellular services are seen as more feasible, often attracting private-sector investment. However, although most of the cellular networks can be used to access the Internet, this often involves a very high cost, which still makes it an unattractive option (Jensen 1998).

Although the telecommunications policies adopted by many African governments are typically intended to promote the spread of ICTs to less advantaged parts of a country, they make no distinctions between the attitudes and needs of male and female users. In fact, it is assumed that such policies will provide equal benefits to all. However, experience has shown that the so-called gender-neutral policies tend to favour men, as men are more likely to have the income needed to purchase telephones or telephone services, and they are more likely to have slightly higher levels of education, which predisposes them to trying new technologies. For this reason, highly targeted efforts are needed to involve women and thereby ensure that their needs are integrated into ICT policies. Women themselves must become involved in ICT policy formulation. The starting point for encouraging women to participate in ICT policy-making is to create awareness in them of the importance of the information revolution and to help them to see the opportunities it holds for women. Women must understand their own information needs and develop sufficient technical knowledge to be credible advocates of their views in policy debates (Hafkin 1998). The new ICTs can marginalize both men and women in Africa. However, women are likely to be slower in adopting the new technologies, unless strategies are developed to deliberately involve women. As will be argued below, these strategies should focus on how to integrate women into ongoing processes while exploring and analyzing the extent to which these processes meet the needs of African women and take account of their perspectives.

Gender and technology

Traditionally, the tendency has been to view new technologies introduced into the global marketplace as gender neutral, having equal potential to be used by either men or women. Engineers in technology development gave no consideration to the symbolic value of technology or, perhaps more important, the symbolic value of the use of technology. As is already well documented, fewer women than men in Africa, as elsewhere, specialize in the sciences or engineering (Rathgeber 1995). Moreover, if women seem to be "fearful" of technology or reluctant to experiment with new technologies, then this is usually interpreted as a "female problem," rather than as a reflection of the inappropriate design of the technologies or the aura of male dominance surrounding their use, or both. Thus, if women have not been active participants in the development and use of new technologies, then it is assumed this has been a result of (1) their own choice or (2) the fact that they have been slow to recognize the importance of a particular new technology. Seldom does anyone consider that women may take less interest in new technologies out of a sense of pragmatism, that is, out of their need to deal with a multitude of tasks, meet a variety of demands, and play diverse roles with limited time. In other words, whether or not some women have a "fear" of technology, they have a pressing need to attend to many diverse duties and have little time to experiment with new technologies simply out of a sense of interest.

To a large extent, this traditional pattern of male and female attitudes toward technologies is replicating itself in the development of the new ICTs. Few if any statistics are available on the involvement of women in this sector, but preliminary observations indicate that women are greatly underrepresented. For Europe and North America, some anecdotal evidence indicates that women who do involve themselves in information technologies tend to bring with them interests and expectations different from those of their male colleagues. For example, early research has shown that women and girls in information technology and engineering tend to be more interested in the social applications of technologies (Keller 1992). Similarly, research in the United States suggested that girls are less likely to be interested in violent computer games, which are often very popular with boys. However, developing software for children has become a substantial industry in North America, with the result that a wide range of computer games are now available, including some designed specifically for girls. Consequently, even preschoolers are achieving a certain degree of computer literacy.

In Africa, too, interest is growing in the potential that ICTs offer women. In the weeks before the 40th anniversary conference of the United Nations Economic Commission for Africa (ECA) in April 1998, ECA joined the World Bank and the Women's Programme of the Association for Progressive Communications in organizing the Afr-fem Internet working group. The group's mandate was to gather field information on the conference themes, which led to numerous lively and lengthy discussions of the potential of ICTs to advance African women's interests. More than half of the group came from South Africa, Kenya, and Uganda. Only one-fifth came from francophone Africa, and half of the francophone group came from Senegal (AWG 1998b). Perhaps not surprisingly, more of the members were Africans living outside Africa, especially in the United States.

The working group focused on the problem of persuading more African women to establish Internet connections. It also noted that the Internet serves as an effective means for Africans living outside the continent to be immediately in touch with those still in Africa. As such, it points the way to the formation of similar working groups to connect African women living in different parts of the continent to discuss issues of common concern, ranging from microenterprise to peace and conflict resolution. However, most of the women with access to e-mail and the World Wide Web still tend to be members of the urban elite.

ICTs as tools of development

Although ICTs evidently can play an important role in African development, it must be emphasized that they are simply tools, means to an end. Provision of telephone services to rural areas is a starting point in making use of these tools and one that has been widely recognized as being of central importance. The benefits of wider telephone service include employment generation and improvements in social services and farming practices. Most importantly, ICTs such as telephones can help to break down the isolation of individuals living in remote rural areas. Perhaps rather optimistically, the United States Agency for International Development (USAID) identified the following outcomes (USAID 1996):

- Reduced migration to urban areas, owing to improved possibilities for small-business and microenterprise development in rural communities;

- Rapid access to assistance during civil emergencies or natural disasters;

- Improved access to health extension services (telemedicine, with remote diagnosis and treatment advice);

- Increased access to market and price information, reducing the opportunity costs for local farmers and traders; and

- Improved educational services, including distance learning.

Although it will take some time for all of these benefits to accrue, it is clear that the provision of telephone access in the rural areas will help to break down some of the rural–urban inequities persisting in much of Africa. It is noteworthy, too, that this list of benefits is very practical in orientation, focusing on improved income opportunities and provision of necessary health and educational information. The services identified by USAID can in most cases be provided by telecentres situated in widely accessible central areas. Telecentres are already established in many African countries. Setting up a telecentre basically involves installing one or more telephone lines in a single location and providing basic assistance for placing calls. Eventually such telecentres may expand their services to include access to fax machines, photocopying, e-mail, the web, and other relevant ICTs. Telecentres can provide services to rural populations, but if private individuals or groups establish them, they can also become sources of income.

In the final analysis, however, ICTs will not have a major impact in rural areas unless they meet people's information needs. This will involve developing appropriate software to provide gender-sensitive, relevant information, sometimes in forms the nonliterate can access. Information for audiences with limited or no educational backgrounds has to be packaged in a meaningful format. But even for literate consumers, especially women, time constraints are important factors. Thus, producers of information would have to ensure that their knowledge packages meet the needs of their consumers, with clear and direct content. The task of producing such packages would provide significant opportunities for both the public and the private sectors.

Finally, it should be pointed out that there is far from universal agreement that ICTs have an immediate role to play in African development. For example, one African communication expert (Obijiofor 1998) argued that more advanced ICTs are inappropriate in Africa at this stage, that they can have little impact in rural communities, and that the telephone itself is the most useful instrument for African communications because it builds on the oral traditions of all indigenous societies. Similarly, many African politicians, senior civil servants, and intellectuals have argued that the continent's primary concern should be to resolve the lingering traditional problems of development, including poverty, illiteracy, and inadequate health services, before diverting scarce resources to the ICT sector. Although such views have merit, they are based on a linear approach of human development, in which advancement is seen as a progressive, step-by-step process. From another perspective, it seems timely to build on the emerging opportunities offered by the new ICTs because once the infrastructure is in place, they would provide the considerable advantage of enabling people to move information and knowledge quickly and cheaply to very remote parts of the continent.

Preparing the ground

If African women are to participate fully in the ICT revolution, then greater efforts must be made to ensure that girls become involved in science and technology (S&T) at an early age. This entails not only improving the science education that girls receive in primary and secondary schools but also including a sensitization process to emphasize that S&T is of lifelong relevance to both girls and boys. To some extent this is already being done. For example, Kenyan newspapers regularly feature articles about girls' participation in science. Moreover, although male scientists still dominate, a few women are starting to be visible in S&T in Africa. However, they are more common in the biological and biophysical sciences, such as medicine and food technology, than in engineering, electronics, or information science.

This situation is not unique to Africa. United Kingdom statistics show that the number of women entering university computer-science courses fell from 24% in 1979 to less than 10% in 1989 (Kirkup 1992). However, with the recognition of the growing importance of information technology during the 1980s, secondary and even primary schools in the industrialized countries have increasingly exposed students to computers, and information technology has become part of the curriculum. In Africa, students' access to computers is confined to only a few elite private schools, usually in or near urban centres. Girls and boys tend to be equally disadvantaged, although awareness of the importance of information-technology and computer skills is growing in many schools and these schools are making efforts to provide some basic equipment for their students. The World Bank has been an active partner in such efforts in Uganda, establishing linkages between a number of Ugandan and US schools through its World Links for Development project. Similarly, the International Development Research Centre (IDRC) has established SchoolNet projects in Uganda and South Africa, creating linkages among schools in each country. These initiatives allow less well-endowed schools to benefit from some of the knowledge resources of the more prosperous schools in the same country.

African educational systems will have to change at all levels to ensure the needed skills base for a broader use of computers and information technologies in all aspects of life. Both men and women will need to acquire various new skills in participatory networking, information-sharing, and facilitating the design, implementation, and maintenance of new communication networks to successfully integrate ICTs into African societies. African users of ICTs will require people with technical skills in computer installation, user training and maintenance, and management of sophisticated communication networks and information services and applications (Crede and Mansell 1998). Acquisition of any of these skills rests on an openness to new ideas and new ways of working. Lifelong learning will be a demand of the ICT age.

The reconceptualization of knowledge

Beyond simple questions of curriculum reform, another more complex set of issues should also be addressed. These issues relate to the conceptualization of knowledge. Feminist philosophers of science have observed that female cognitive structures differ from those of men. This has implications for women's attitudes and approaches to the use of ICTs. For example, Sherry Turkle observed that "the present social construction of programming styles and computer culture encourages one particular style of thinking which is not only repressive for many women, but restricts the potential of computers" (Turkle, quoted in Kirkup 1992, p. 277). As well, Kirkup (1992, p. 279) remarked that

> Turkle demonstrates ... that many women (and some men) are alienated from the computer ... because the computer culture imposes a particular ... "correct" style of interaction, based on a formal, top-down method of working, in which the problem is dissected into separate parts and solved by designing sets of modular solutions.

This suggests that women may deliberately avoid the use of ICTs because the accepted structure of interaction with the technologies goes against their preferred way of dealing with problems and people. If that is the case, then there may be an argument for reconceptualizing the ways we use ICTs or, at the very least, for ensuring that knowledge transferred through ICTs is packaged to conform to female users' preferred learning styles.

In Africa, this may mean combining information transferred through ICTs with more traditional ways of imparting knowledge. For example, an IDRC-supported project undertaken with the International Center for Agroforestry Research, in Nairobi, is developing a system to electronically send information on soil conservation and good farming practices to a community centre equipped with a computer and e-mail facilities in Kabale, Uganda. When the project is fully functional, this technical information will be downloaded and shared with local women's groups, which have already started to "humanize" such scientific information by creating stories and performing dramas to convey not only this information but also commentary on social issues of importance to the community, such as male drunkenness, violence against women, and the importance of keeping children in school. In this way, ICTs are used to disseminate scientific knowledge, but, on arrival at the site, that knowledge is made more interesting and relevant to rural women (and men).

Restructuring of universities and research institutions in Africa

An in-depth discussion of the nature of knowledge and knowledge production is beyond the scope of this chapter, but at least two important factors are relevant to ICTs. The first is that traditional modes of library-based research are fast becoming obsolete and that African institutions must change their approaches to research and knowledge production or risk being completely bypassed in the global marketplace of knowledge and ideas. The second is that the explosion of knowledge generation and the new capacity to immediately move information and ideas around the world have brought on a new world information order. Emerging scientific knowledge and ideas no longer have to go through the traditional channels: being introduced, first, to a small select society of insiders (specialists in the field), being ratified by that group, and then eventually making their way into the mainstream of society. The hegemony of knowledge — tight control by specialists — is being severely challenged. This has both positive and negative connotations. On the one hand, it may lead to a democratization of knowledge and make it possible for ideas and contributions from outsiders to be heard and taken seriously. On the other hand, it has already led to an explosion and surfeit of information, with the resulting "information fatigue."

Perhaps the most difficult task facing knowledge users today is to meaningfully sort out and systematize knowledge and information. ICTs can help individuals and groups gain information on how to improve some aspects of their

lives. However, that information should satisfy the following criteria: it must be
(1) relevant to the needs of the users; (2) comprehensible; and (3) easily available.
These may appear to be self-evident criteria, but in fact they probably pose the
most important obstacles to the wider adoption of ICTs in Africa. The opportunity
costs of the investment in a computer for an individual or even a group are often
too high to make it a worthwhile endeavour if it offers no obvious and immediate
payoff in terms of beneficial information.

The organization and the systematization of useful development-related information for rural Africa are tasks for African universities and research institutions familiar with local conditions and languages. However, African universities
have not readily accepted this challenge. They still tend to operate on the models
of research established in the late colonial and early postcolonial eras, when most
of the universities were founded. Most African universities are not fully computerized. Efforts have been made to introduce computers into university classrooms
and libraries, but the high capital and maintenance costs have made it difficult for
struggling institutions to systematically computerize. Many have depended on donors to provide computers and connectivity.

Unfortunately, most African universities and research institutions still tend
to use computers as sophisticated typewriters and have failed to establish linkages
with colleagues internationally or access wider information bases. The reason for
this may be, in many cases, that users do not have extensive contacts outside their
country or institution to motivate them to use the Internet or e-mail. Nonetheless,
a few institutions were quick to recognize the potential of ICTs. For example, the
medical library at the University of Zimbabwe has been computerized since the
1980s. Consequently, its students have had access to global bibliographic
resources.

Despite the slow move toward computerization and connectivity in African
universities, ICTs probably offer them their best opportunity to minimize and even
overcome the disadvantages they have suffered over the past 20 years as a result
of declining budgets and the consequent inability to develop library collections.
CD-ROMS can provide extensive databases, and they are relatively cheap.

Also, information technologies can enable African universities to develop
outreach services in rural areas, through distance-learning programs. This is done
in Europe and North America. For example, the Open University in the United
Kingdom now offers 14 online courses, and East Tennessee State University is
pioneering an innovative program with the Oak Ridge National Laboratory in the
United States whereby students have remote access to electron microscopes.
Students post samples to the laboratory and then operate the microscopes directly

from a keyboard (Guardian Weekly 1998). Because the cost of computers is still far beyond the means of the average African citizen, various modes of social organization will have to be developed to provide people in rural areas with access to such innovative modes of instruction. Potentially, this might involve a more extensive development of community-based learning centres or telecentres, or both, in rural areas, which is already occurring at a rapid rate in countries like Senegal.

Some specific examples of African activities

Many international organizations actively promote the use of computers and ICTs in Africa. To a considerable extent, their initiatives have tended to focus on the needs of urban users and to view rural women and men as secondary users. This is likely to change in the near future, because of the current expansion of telecommunications infrastructure occurring over most of Africa. As a result of this expansion, women and men in even remote areas will have access to ICTs, and as the market expands more private operators are likely to become active.

Notwithstanding the urban bias, a number of important activities are under way (the following provides a selected overview, rather than an exhaustive listing). Perhaps most significantly, in the late 1990s, ECA began to focus on ICTs. The 1996 ECA Conference of African Ministers responsible for economic and social development and planning adopted a continent-wide ICT strategy, the African Information Society Initiative (AISI). The basic objective of AISI is to end Africa's information and technology gap by bringing the continent into the information age.

The main areas for implementing AISI are policy awareness, national ICT-infrastructure planning, connectivity, training and capacity-building, democratized access to the information society, sector applications, and development-information infrastructure. Of these, the greatest progress has been made in policy awareness: most African countries are aware of the importance of planning a national ICT infrastructure and developing connectivity — some 47 countries now have direct access to the Internet. Ten countries have started to develop national policies. Momentum is also great in the area of democratizing access to the information society, and to respond to this issue the telecentre movement has taken on great momentum. ECA's efforts in democratization of access to ICTs have concentrated on encouraging the full participation of women in the use of these technologies.

IDRC has been promoting information systems in Africa since the early 1970s. Until the mid-1990s, its support was aimed primarily at the establishment of computerized information bases and resources intended primarily for research at African higher-education institutions or government ministries. Since the mid-1990s IDRC's efforts have intensified. The Unganisha project, started in 1997, has focused on providing connectivity for African institutions conducting IDRC-funded research, and now about 35–40% of IDRC's interaction with African researchers is carried out by e-mail.

In 1996, IDRC launched its Acacia Initiative, which has the objective of using ICTs to accelerate economic and social development at the community level. In its first phase, Acacia has targeted four African countries: Mozambique, Senegal, South Africa, and Uganda. Acacia has made efforts to introduce a comprehensive strategy in each country to develop policy, infrastructure, human resources, and content. The initiative takes a special interest in working with women and marginalized members of communities.

Acacia is implemented in Uganda through the National Council of Science and Technology, which has established an overall coordinating secretariat and a number of working groups that focus on the various components of the strategy. The National Acacia Strategy was developed and ratified at a meeting in Kampala in December 1997. This meeting brought together representatives from different strata of society and regions of the country. The strategy was later introduced and discussed in communities in five regions of Uganda. In each case, community members indicated their information needs and priorities. Not surprisingly, these varied somewhat, in accordance with the main income-generating activities of the region. By the end of 1998, two telecentres had been established. Interestingly enough, early evidence, not only in Uganda, but also in other Acacia focus countries, shows that the communities often believe that the telecentres should have female managers.

Many other donors have been active in development-information projects. The United States has undertaken a number of important activities, including the 15 million USD, USAID-funded Leland Initiative, which is designed to strengthen Internet connectivity in 20 African countries, in return for agreements to liberalize the market to third-party Internet service providers (Jensen 1998). The Leland Initiative also aims to enable USAID projects to communicate electronically with one another and share development-related information. USAID is also supporting AfricaLink, which provides connectivity for the agriculture, research, and natural-resources management community in Africa. Moreover, in 1997 the United States government (through Hillary Clinton) pledged 1 million USD to be spent exclusively on women's networking in Africa. This objective of this initiative, known as POWERNET (the "emPOWERment NETwork"), is to form a network of elected female officials in Africa and the United States. POWERNET will enable them to share information and lessons learned in their efforts to increase the participation of women in political processes and economic development. However, to date, USAID has done little to enhance the use of the Internet in rural communities or among the poor in Africa, and these remain areas for further development.

In 1998, in South Africa, SANGONeT, in collaboration with the Commission on Gender Equality, launched a project called Women'sNet, aiming to strengthen South African women's capacity to use the Internet. Women'sNet provides training and capacity-building and has also developed a website (Women'sNet 1999), with content that is useful and relevant to South African women. Its first topics of concentration were the prevention of violence against women in South Africa and the region of the Southern African Development Community and women in small, medium-sized, and microenterprises.

In Uganda, the Forum for Women in Democracy is helping female parliamentarians gain access to the Internet to gather information relevant to performing their roles in the legislative process, with a special focus on legislation affecting women at the community level. Similarly, in Benin and Cameroon, three pilot centres have been set up to provide legal and extension information and education services aimed at improving women's legal and social equality (ECA 1998).

Despite all these activities, much remains to be done to put African women on the information superhighway. In the period just before the 40th anniversary ECA conference, a Ugandan NGO, the Ugandan Women's Organization Network (UWONET), contacted 16 organizations with an interest in the advancement of women in Uganda to solicit their comments and feedback for input into the Afr-fem Working Group. UWONET's initiative received a very limited response, and Afr-fem suggested the following possible reasons for this:

- Organizations may need to be sensitized to the role of the Internet and e-mail discussion groups, especially in quick sharing of ideas, experiences, and solutions to common problems;

- Even those groups connected to the Internet may not be sufficiently trained in the use of the facility;

- Organizations still have limited access to computers with e-mail — most organizations have at most one computer with e-mail–Internet access; and

- None of the participating organizations had e-mail connections at their branches outside Kampala (AWG 1998a).

Despite all the energy going into establishing connectivity and promoting ICTs in Africa, these findings indicate that in reality much remains to be done to sensitize and train women, provide hardware, and develop appropriate content. Nonetheless, as has been shown, ICTs offer new opportunities for African women to improve their daily lives through greater access to useful, practical information on income-generating activities, agricultural-production methods, health, the organization of women's groups, etc. ICTs also give women a chance to share their ideas, insights, and experiences among themselves and with others. As such, if the ICT sector is developed appropriately in Africa, the benefits of the information revolution will help to ease the burden on African women.

References

AWG (Afr-fem Working Group). 1998a. Report on outreach efforts by an African NGO. Global Knowledge Partnership Secretariat, World Bank Institute, Washington, DC, USA. Internet: www.globalknowldge.org:1997/english/archives/mailarchives/afr-fem/afr-fem-jun98/0054.html

———— 1998b. Afr-fem Working Group: summary twelve (6/07–6/13). Global Knowledge Partnership Secretariat, World Bank Institute, Washington, DC, USA. Internet: www.globalknowldge.org:1997/english/archives/mailarchives/afr-fem/afr-fem-jun98/0030.html

Chasia, H. 1998. Developing an African information infrastructure: the need for commitment and vision. Address presented at AFCOM 1998, 9–11 Sep, Arlington, VA, USA. International Telecommunication Union, Geneva, Switzerland. Internet: www.itu.int/officials/chasia/speeches/1998/afcom982.html

Crede, A.; Mansell, R. 1998. Knowledge societies ... in a nutshell. International Development Research Centre, Ottawa, ON, Canada.

ECA (United Nations Economic Commission for Africa). 1998. Summary notes and guide questions for working group discussions: African women and the information age: a rare opportunity. Paper presented at the Conference on African Women and Economic Development, 28 Apr – 1 May 1998, Addis Ababa, Ethiopia. United Nations Economic Commission for Africa, Addis Ababa, Ethiopia. Working Document No. 2.3.

Guardian Weekly. 1998. Digital degrees. Guardian Weekly, 12 Jul 1998.

Hafkin, N. 1998. Making information and communications policies relevant to women. Paper presented at the Conference on African Women and Economic Development, 28 Apr – 1 May 1998, Addis Ababa, Ethiopia. United Nations Economic Commission for Africa, Addis Ababa, Ethiopia. Report on working group 3.1.

Hall, M. 1998. Mixed messages. Paper presented at the International Symposium on Globalization and the Social Sciences in Africa, 14–18 Sep, Johannesburg, South Africa. The Graduate School for the Humanities and Social Sciences, University of Witwatersrand, Johannesburg, South Africa.

James, J. 1998. Information technology, globalization and marginalization. *In* Bhalla, A.S., ed., Globalization, growth and marginalization. International Development Research Centre, Ottawa, ON, Canada. pp. 48–69.

Jensen, M. 1998. An overview of Internet connectivity in Africa. SANGONeT, Johannesburg, South Africa. Internet: demiurge.wn.apc.org/africa/afstat.htm (Cited 20 Sep 1998)

Keller, S.L. 1992. Discovering and doing: science and technology: an introduction. *In* Kirkup, G.; Keller, L.S., ed. Inventing women: science, technology and gender. Polity Press; Open University, Cambridge, UK. pp. 122–132.

Kirkup, G. 1992. The social construction of computers: hammers or harpsichords? *In* Kirkup, G.; Keller, L.S., ed. Inventing women: science, technology and gender. Polity Press; Open University, Cambridge, UK. pp. 267–281.

Kobokoane, T. 1998. Drumbeat of change pulses across African telecom lines. Business Times, Johannesburg, South Africa. Internet: www.btimes.co.za/98/0118/comp/comp5.htm

Obijiofor, L. 1998. Future of communication in Africa's development. Futures, 30 (2–3), 161–174.

Rathgeber, E. 1995. Schooling for what? Education and career opportunities for women in science, technology and engineering. *In* United Nations Commission on Science and Technology for Development Gender Working Group, ed., Missing links: gender equity in science and technology for development. International Development Research Centre, Ottawa, ON, Canada. pp. 181–200.

USAID (United States Agency for International Development). 1996. Southern Africa Regional Telecommunications Restructuring (RTR) program. Providing telecommunications services to rural and underserved areas. Internet: rtr.worldweb.net/1616rural.htm (Cited Jun 1996)

Women'sNet. 1999. Women'sNet. SANGONeT, Johannesburg, South Africa. Internet: www.womensnet.org.za

Chapter 3

GETTING GENDER INTO AFRICAN ICT POLICY: A STRATEGIC VIEW

Gillian M. Marcelle

African policymakers face many economic, social, and political challenges as they seek to improve material living standards and quality of life in Africa and undertake their task of transforming the continent in a complex, rapidly changing, and uncertain environment. Having observed the positive impacts of science and technology (S&T) and in particular the revolution in information and communication technologies (ICTs) in wealthier nations, policymakers in Africa are turning their attention to this area of economic activity. Unfortunately, decision-makers have few directly comparable examples to assist them in developing ICT policies supportive of sustainable development. The challenge of harnessing ICTs for development is difficult and encompasses many issues.

The United Nations Commission on Science and Technology for Development (UNCSTD) captured some of the issues of concern for developing countries seeking to secure the benefits of the so-called ICT revolution:

> ICTs do not offer a panacea for social and economic development. There are risks of unemployment and social and economic dislocation, and these may lead policy makers to give lower priority to the need to create effective national ICT strategies. However, on the basis of the evidence, it is apparent that the risks of failing to participate in the ICT revolution are enormous. Failure to give priority to ICT strategies that enable developing countries and countries in transition both to develop their national infrastructures and to join the GII [global information infrastructure] will exacerbate the gap between rich and poor. There is a growing need to evaluate the social and economic impacts of ICTs and to create opportunities for capacity building that will ensure their beneficial use and absorption within national economies and civil society.
>
> UNCSTD (1997, p. 17, para 62)

In this influential report, UNCSTD also acknowledged that least-developed countries in Africa and other regions will require special treatment if they are to gain access to the financial resources, physical infrastructure, and knowledge base required to successfully harness ICTs for development.

This chapter is concerned with strategies to secure the potential economic benefits of ICTs for all groups in society. As I will show, without a gender perspective the potential benefits of ICTs may bypass girls and women. The economic benefits for girls and women in terms of enhanced income-generation opportunities, employment, and improved quality of life are tremendous, but because technologies are not gender neutral, I will also be concerned with advocating ICT strategies to reduce and manage the potential for ICTs to create economic and social exclusion and reinforce existing social disparities. In other parts of the world this dual character of ICTs — their ability to simultaneously produce economic benefits and social dislocation — is coming under increasing scrutiny from academics and other critical thinkers, and their insights are beginning to influence the policy debate.

Ventura (1997) presented a very clear argument that wealthy countries must act, in partnership with the developing world, to prevent the global information society from causing social dislocations. The United Nations University Institute for New Technologies (UNU–INTECH) has a research program to investigate aspects of this problem. Mitter (1999) presented the findings from that research program. The European Commission mandated the High-level Expert Group (HLEG) to explore issues in using ICTs to foster social embeddedness (HLEG 1997). HLEG's analyses have influenced policy-making at the European, national, and regional levels.

The central purpose of this chapter is to outline strategies to introduce a gender dimension into national ICT policies. This has been a missing element of ICT policy formulation and implementation to date. The analysis will show that, on efficiency and equity grounds, such gender considerations are vitally important. ICT policy-making is no different from other important areas of social and economic development, such as economic justice, human rights, and access to education. It also needs to be considered in its gender dimensions.

As many of the other chapters in this volume confirm, the vast majority of African women live in rural settings, endure dire levels of poverty, and face cultural and legal barriers to exercising and enjoying their human rights. Annex 1 of this chapter is from World Bank (1997). It provides a concise statement of the strategic objectives for gender and development in Africa. Although a small proportion of African women enjoy fairly high levels of income and have access to education, training, and other societal resources, the desired positive impact of ICTs will not be realized for women if access to the transformative role of these technologies is restricted to this small, privileged group. All of Africa's women and men should have the opportunity to benefit from ICTs. Ensuring equitable treatment for men and women will require concerted effort and will exert considerable demands on the institutional capacity of Africa's policymakers. The analysis and recommendations presented here are intended to assist policymakers who are willing and committed to reorienting ICT policy to take account of the needs, aspirations, and constraints of both men and women in African societies.

ICTs as a multilevel phenomenon

The ICT sector is a heterogeneous collection of industry and service activities, including information-technology equipment and services, telecommunications equipment and services, media and broadcast, Internet service providers (ISPs), libraries, commercial information providers, network-based information services, and related specialized professional services. Figure 1 shows the segments making up the composite ICT sector.

As a direct consequence of the sprawling nature of ICTs or perhaps as a result of the difficulty one encounters in defining the ICT sector with any precision, policy-making in this sector is very diffuse. The main policy-making actors include government ministries — which are usually responsible for setting overall policy objectives and direction for other agencies — and independent regulatory bodies, which implement policy directives and are responsible for operational management of the regulatory system. (In wealthy countries, an array of technical and research organizations assist and advise these decision-making and implementation agencies.) In addition to organizations operating at the national level, many regional and international organizations are involved in ICT policy-making. International organizations, such as the International Telecommunication Union (ITU), the World Trade Organization (WTO), and other agencies within the United Nations system formulate policy recommendations and set standards for international best practice.

Policymakers are also influenced by private industry, nongovernmental organizations (NGOs), trade associations, professional bodies, and the intellectual community. The regularity, format, and nature of the consultation between policymakers and these groups of stakeholders vary considerably across countries.

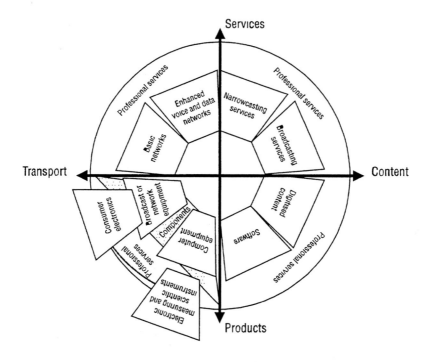

Figure 1. Segments of the ICT (industry and technology) system.
Source: Mansell and Wehn (1998).

This chapter recommends an active interventionist vision for ICT policy-making in Africa. Achieving this objective will not be without problems, but without such a vision there is no hope of realizing the benefits of ICTs. Action is required at various levels of society to ensure that the potential benefits of these technologies are available to African women as well as men and that girls and women do not suffer dislocations as a result of this fundamental shift in organizational and production technologies. The analysis contained in this chapter and in its supporting annexes provides justification and possible direction for policy intervention.

The next section maps out the current state of national ICT policy-making in Africa and provides a brief historical review of the landmarks in this policy-making. It more closely examines the process of ICT policy-making in four countries — Mozambique, Senegal, South Africa, and Uganda — providing details of the policy-making apparatus, assessing the challenges facing policymakers, and reviewing their successes in each of these countries. This is particularly important for making an up-to-date assessment of African policymakers' success in accounting for social variables and, in particular, gender considerations in their ICT policies and programs.

The third section discusses in detail how gender considerations can be taken into account in national ICT policies and sets out clear arguments in support of taking these actions. Finally, the concluding section summarizes the recommendations and actions required for various sets of actors involved in formulating and implementing ICT policies.

Understanding ICT policy

This section sets out a simple framework for understanding ICT policy, reviews the status of national policy formulation and implementation in the ICT sector in an international context, and, finally, presents some empirical findings on how African nations are formulating policy for the ICT sector. At the outset, it is important to note that only fairly recently have efforts been made to define the boundaries of the ICT sector, measure its contribution to national economic output, understand precisely the interaction between this sector and other social and economic activities, and design its policy instruments. Policy intervention in the ICT sector is very much a work in progress. Conceptual frameworks, systems of data collection, policy tools, indicator construction, and evaluation methodologies are all very rudimentary. As a result, in developed and developing countries alike, real change in the structure and functioning of the ICT sector outpaces policy intervention, and therefore the environment for long-term and day-to-day policy decisions is uncertain, rapidly changing, and ever more complex. Some of the basic concepts and terms used in the rest of the analysis are defined in the following subsection.

Definition of ICT policy

A national ICT policy is an integrated set of decisions, guidelines, laws, regulations, and other mechanisms geared to directing and shaping the production, acquisition, and use of ICTs. Because the ICT sector is heterogeneous, extending beyond traditional classifications of industrial or services sectors and because production and diffusion of ICTs are of equal importance, national policies in the ICT sector intersect with a number of other areas of policy-making — technology, media, industrial, and telecommunications policy. Figure 2 shows these areas of intersection among the various policy spheres. Individual countries design their ICT policies according to prevailing objectives, values, and cultural practice. Figure 3 presents a schematic of the various actors involved in ICT policy-making.

Policy-making processes and institutions in the ICT sector

The key elements of policy-making in the ICT sector are the context, or the environmental factors, and policy objectives, tools, and outcomes. As discussed in the introductory section, the lead actors in this system are policy-makers, whose actions directly and indirectly influence other agents in the system — producers and users of ICTs. These elements, working together, constitute the system of policy intervention.

ICT policy-making outside Africa

This subsection reviews the context for ICT policy formulation in the wealthiest countries and describes the policy tools they use. UNCSTD's summary of the best-practice guidelines for formulating ICT policy in developing countries is then considered. The material in this section provides important background for the more detailed discussion of African ICT policy initiatives, not only because this provides a contrast but also because international approaches influence the definition and implementation of policies in Africa.

The context for ICT policy-making in the member countries of the Organisation for Economic Co-operation and Development

The environment for policy decisions is changing dramatically. For example, in the last two decades, the economic structure of the world's wealthiest countries has been significantly restructured. In the member countries of the Organisation for Economic Co-operation and Development (OECD), the services sectors have overtaken the industrial and agricultural sectors as the main source of national income. Major changes have also occurred at the firm level: organizational processes, values, and cultures have all changed fundamentally, which has significantly altered employment conditions, job requirements, management practices, and sources of competitive advantage. In addition to the changes within individual countries and companies, a restructuring has occurred in the international economic system. Some of the features of change in international economic relations

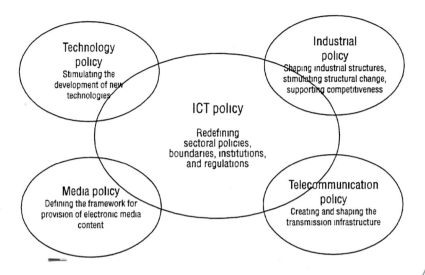

Figure 2. Relationship between ICT policy and other areas development policy.
Source: UNCSTD (1997).

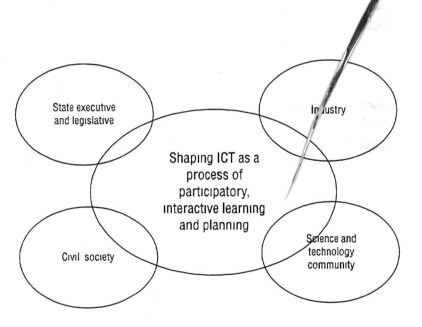

Figure 3. Key agents in policy-making processes. Source: UNCSTD (1997).

include a significant increase in the level of international integration among countries, which has resulted in an ever increasing volume of trade in goods and services, increased internationalization of production processes and multinational ownership of major companies, and globalization of sources of investment capital.

A parallel process of fundamental technological change has accompanied these sectoral shifts, changes in firm organization, and increased internationalization. It is unimportant, for this discussion, to dwell on the direction of causality. It is far more important to emphasize that technological, organizational, structural, and institutional changes have contributed equally to a very complex evolution of the world economic system.

As the processes of economic restructuring, internationalization of production and capital flows, and changes in organizational systems have taken root in the world's wealthiest countries, concomitant changes have occurred in the demand for information-technology-intensive equipment and services. Structural and organizational changes in wealthy economies have led to dramatic increases in the demand for powerful computational devices for office automation, transaction processing, control of production processes, and a host of other applications. Decentralized production systems and increases in internationalization of investment flows and funding sources have stimulated and fueled demand for advanced communication networks with the capacity to deliver vast quantities of information in a variety of formats in real time. The increased disintermediation and growing complexity of the services sectors have resulted in a plethora of information providers and value-added service providers. This, then, is the context for ICT policy decisions in wealthy countries. In this setting, it is assumed that supply constraints are surmountable, and the focus therefore shifts to shaping and directing the production and use of ICTs to maximize the potential benefits of these technologies. Policy intervention is increasingly directed to managing the social consequences of ICTs, in addition to maximizing their benefits, such as the production of wealth, job creation, increased productivity, and the facilitation of technological innovation (OECD 1992, 1996).

Development of policy tools in the OECD countries

Despite the difficulties, OECD countries have made some progress in developing ICT policy tools, and most OECD countries — as well as some exceptional developing countries, such as Singapore — have institutional frameworks, policy instruments, and policy-implementation processes for the ICT sector. In countries that have achieved progress in ICT policy-making, it is possible to identify several types of policy objectives — economic, technological, and sociopolitical. For example, in the economic sphere, OECD policymakers promote production, diffusion, and innovation in the ICT sector through a variety of instruments and processes, including the following:

- Competition policy, which aims to maintain or improve the competitiveness of the producers of ICT equipment and services and to promote competition in network and service provision, on the assumption that increased competition will stimulate increases in the range and quality of ICT goods and services and facilitate improvements in productivity while dampening price increases;

- Trade policy, which aims to increase the size of the accessible market by establishing free trade for ICT equipment and services in international markets; and

- Innovation and diffusion policies, which aim to increase the range of ICT services and to support rapid diffusion of ICT applications.

Similarly, in the technological sphere, OECD policymakers encourage advances in the foundation technologies that underpin the ICT sector. Therefore, they have designed policies to support and direct research and development (R&D) in core ICT technologies (computing, communications, and information management) and to ensure that theoretical and applied research lead to the design, planning, and execution of advanced communications infrastructure. The state's policy-making role in technology has had both push and pull elements. The more traditional and long-standing aspect of state participation is to fund R&D and direct research. However, state agencies are also increasingly taking on the role of the facilitator, which requires systematic and accelerated learning. In this newer role, policymakers encourage the exchange of information between innovators, research producers, and ICT equipment and service providers; set standards for networking and definition of equipment and service; and, through regulatory intervention, encourage deployment of advanced technological solutions.

In the European OECD countries, policymakers have made major advances in articulating sociopolitical objectives for the ICT sector. An influential report of the HLEG recognized that ICTs can have undesirable social consequences and

reinforce existing social inequities (HLEG 1997). In its analysis and recommendations, the report gave guidelines for ameliorating these negative effects.

OECD countries have invested financial and human resources to establish
institutional machinery to achieve the economic, technological, and sociopolitical
policy objectives discussed above. A national innovation system (NIS) is a system
of institutions designed to foster innovation and manage technological change. An
NIS can be specified at the country level, but it is also useful to identify sub-
systems within an NIS. The system for ICT policy formulation and implementation is one such subsystem. Using NIS terminology, one can then say that the
system of innovation in the ICT sector consists of a web of institutions, processes,
and mechanisms to produce, consume, and facilitate or direct the production and
use of ICTs. To support these policy-making activities, OECD countries have
developed institutional capabilities in research, analysis, collection of data,
evaluation, and monitoring.

Best-practice guidelines for integrating ICTs and development

UNCSTD (1997) produced a comprehensive set of best-practice guidelines for ICT
policy-making in developing countries. Topics covered are producing and using
ICTs; developing human resources; managing ICTs for development; facilitating
access to ICT networks; promoting and financing ICTs; creating and accessing
S&T knowledge; monitoring and influencing the rules of the game in the global
information society; and the role of the United Nations system. A full summary
of these is provided in Mansell and When (1998).

UNCSTD concluded that developing countries need to intervene strategically if they are to successfully integrate ICTs and sustainable development.
UNCSTD's (1997) report outlined the scope of ICT policies as follows:

> Effective national ICT strategies should support the introduction of the
> new regulatory frameworks, promote the selective production and use of
> ICTs and harness their diffusion so as to contribute to the development
> of organisational change in line with development goals. ICT strategies
> and policies linked to development objectives need to redefine sectoral
> policies, institutions and regulations, taking into account the need to be
> responsive to the convergence of telecommunication, audio-visual and
> computing technologies.

UNCSTD also emphasized that developing countries need to build organizational
capabilities, such as by creating or strengthening existing institutions, if these

countries are to harness ICTs in support of development goals. Their conclusions included the following specific recommendations:

- Establish a task force or commission to develop a national ICT strategy that identifies priorities, mechanisms for continuous updating, and procedures for implementation.

- Involve as many stakeholders as possible in the formulation of a national ICT strategy, and encourage partnerships for implementing elements of the strategy. An important aspect of these partnerships would be to secure external financing from multinational companies, governments of the OECD countries, bilateral donors, and multilateral and regional financial institutions.

As will be shown later in this section, many of the recommendations would respond to the needs of African ICT policy-making. These guidelines provide a sound foundation for building ICT policy in Africa. UNCSTD's effort is only one of several attempts to delineate best practice in this area. Other important contributions have come from ITU (ITU–BTD 1996, 1998), the United Nations Development Programme's (UNDP's) Sustainable Development Networking Programme (D'Orville 1997), and the World Bank.

What the foregoing shows is that all policymakers, in wealthy and poor countries alike, make policy decisions for the ICT sector in a context of rapid and fundamental change and great uncertainty, and they each attempt to build institutions and mechanisms to assist them in this task. However, the differences in the settings facing the two sets of policymakers are also important. In wealthy nations, policymakers reasonably assume that supply constraints (levels of skills, knowledge, organizational capability, and financial resources) are surmountable and focus their policy interventions on the production and use of ICTs to maximize the benefits of these technologies. Increasingly, even in wealthy countries, policy intervention is also expanding to include management of the social consequences of ICTs, rather than restricting policy objectives to the economic benefits of ICTs. In poor countries, as will be shown for the African case, conditions differ markedly from those of rich countries. Although the international context influences policy-making in Africa, policymakers should take account of their local environments when setting objectives and undertaking interventions.

Development of African ICT policy

Context and objectives

The vast majority of African nations mainly participate in the ICT industry as consumers of equipment and services. A notable exception to this "consumption-only" approach is found in the national telecommunications carriers, which, up until recently, were state-owned companies, with nationals responsible for operation and management of telecommunications networks. In addition, except for Nigeria, South Africa, and possibly some of the North African countries, African nations have had very little R&D capability in ICTs, in either basic or applied research. Furthermore, the level of deployment of ICT equipment and networks in Africa is several orders of magnitude below that of wealthy countries.[1]

Because of these environmental factors and the macroeconomic and social variations between Africa and other countries, the task for policymakers in the ICT sector differs significantly from that of their counterparts in wealthy nations. ICTs are produced and used under very different supply and demand conditions in these two settings. Many African nations have very low levels of per capita income, and this reduces effective demand for ICT services. Africa has not experienced the shifts in economic structure that have elsewhere given rise to the predominance of information-intensive and geographically decentralized services sectors. Thus, the major sources of economic output in the majority of African countries are the agriculture and mineral-production sectors. These sectors are not as information intensive as the services sectors — banking, retail, distribution, tourism, and professional services — which account for a rising share of national output in OECD countries. In addition to gloomy demand conditions, supply responses in the African ICT sector are not automatic, and when they are manifest, they operate at a slower pace than in wealthy economies. Therefore, policymakers in these poor developing countries must take action to stimulate and facilitate supply responses and to support diffusion. These supply responses would include generating skills, knowledge, financial resources, and organizational capabilities. Furthermore, the policy setting is not very conducive, as many governments in Africa operate under fiscal restraint, have a lack of experience in

---

[1] In a comprehensive treatment of sector restructuring in the African telecommunications sector, ITU's Telecommunications Development Bureau concluded that the accelerated pace of change in the African telecom sector is fueled by international investment, liberalization, establishment of regulatory bodies, and, for a few countries, participation in WTO negotiations (ITU–TDB 1998). Its analysis set an optimistic note for the development of networks and the improvement of the quality and range of services in Africa. The African Green Paper and the Communiqué of the African Regional Telecommunications Development Conference (ITU–TDB 1996) represent the best statements of government policy objectives in the telecom sector in Africa.

managing technological innovation in ICTs, have limited access to technological and organizational capabilities required to produce ICTs, and have very limited institutional resources.

Although the context for policy-making in the African ICT sector differs dramatically from that in the rest of the world, three main sets of external agents greatly influence the objectives of the African ICT sector: multilateral agencies, large donors, and international suppliers of ICT equipment and services. This introduces another level of complexity. Although African ICT policymakers lack experience of this sector, they must have sufficient intelligence, integrity, and self-confidence to identify and protect their national interests when negotiating with external agencies.

The case studies presented in the third section of this chapter provide evidence of good practice in national policy-making for the ICT sector, in which efforts are made to identify ICT applications to assist other broad-based development objectives. The following historical review tracks Africa's progress in setting up the institutional mechanisms to undertake these important tasks of formulating and implementing policy.

A historical review of African ICT policy-making

The African Information Society Initiative (AISI) sets out the most important set of policy guidelines for national information policy in the African context. Annex 2 presents a summary of the background and main aims of AISI, as well as reviewing some of the important landmarks in ICT policy-making in Africa.

Empirical findings

EARLY STUDIES OF POLICY-MAKING IN INFORMATICS IN AFRICAN COUNTRIES — Within the ambit of AISI and its forerunners, a number of studies have provided important research and analysis of the readiness of African countries to undertake policy interventions in the ICT sector. One such study reviewed informatics policy in 10 African countries: Cameroon, Congo, Côte d'Ivoire, Ethiopia, Kenya, Madagascar, Nigeria, Senegal, Tanzania, and Zimbabwe. The study defined national informatics policy as a "plan for the development and optimal utilisation of information technology" and reported that limited financial resources, poor institutional capability, and inadequate access to human resources and technological know-how plague Africa's attempts to harness ICTs (Browne 1996).

Interestingly, the study also identified a broad difference between the two language groups. Whereas none of the anglophone countries studied — Ethiopia, Kenya, Nigeria, Tanzania, or Zimbabwe — had elaborated informatics policies, most of the francophone countries had defined them. However, the level of implementation varied considerably across the five francophone countries: Cameroon, Congo, Côte d'Ivoire, Madagascar, and Senegal.

RECENT EVIDENCE: FOUR CASE STUDIES OF NATIONAL ICT POLICY-MAKING — The early studies indicate only very moderate success in formulating and implementing ICT policies. A better understanding of how African countries have progressed toward best practice is presented in the four case studies — of Mozambique, Senegal, South Africa, and Uganda — in Annex 3. In assessing this recent material, I emphasize the extent of gender consideration in the ICT policy efforts already under way.

Data in this section come mainly from four sets of studies commissioned by the International Development Research Centre (IDRC) to provide background and planning material for its Acacia Initiative (Kataman 1997; Mureithi 1997; Musisi 1997; Nyiira 1997) (see also Acacia 1997a, b; IDRC 1997). IDRC has been an important donor for African ICT efforts. As a result, consultants commissioned by IDRC usually have access to key decision-makers and policy-makers. These studies therefore provide a rich source of data. The analysis of these studies was designed to answer six basic questions:

- What are the leading organizations involved in formulating and implementing national ICT policies, and what are the basic documents and instruments used in their policy exercises?

- What are the main policy objectives and priorities for ICT policies in the four countries?

- What progress has been made in the implementation of ICT policy?

- What gaps remain in policy formulation or implementation, or both, and what challenges are still to be met?

- Do the national ICT policy documents identify and treat social objectives, and is gender equity one of the objectives or underlying principles of national ICT policies in these countries?

- What are the recommendations of the Acacia Initiative for ICT policy-making efforts?

Annex 3 provides a summary of the key findings and assessments gained from the review of these case-study materials. Information from other sources, including ITU, the United Nations Conference on Trade and Development (UNCTAD 1995), and my own field experience in South Africa, supplemented the data from the case studies.

The evidence from Africa shows that most countries have made only very modest gains in setting up national ICT policy institutions and that the new ICT policy-making mechanisms still integrate very few social considerations, including very few gender perspectives. However, the pace of change has accelerated dramatically in the last 18 months, and, as the next two sections will show, governments and other key actors can take steps to realize the potential benefits.

Strategies to incorporate gender considerations into ICT policy-making

The best approach to incorporating gender considerations into ICT policy-making would be to undertake two related types of improvement in parallel. The first, discussed in the previous section, would be to make ICT policies more effective; the second would be to develop comprehensive mechanisms to treat gender issues in all ICT policies and programs.

African women's participation in the global information society is hindered by many challenges and barriers, such as infrastructure deficiencies, policy misdiagnoses, and the structural and cultural features of African societies. The analysis in this chapter integrates an assessment of these barriers into a discussion of the positive steps already taken at both the policy level and the microlevel to overcome these barriers. The first step in bringing about the desired changes would be to define an agenda of interventions that African women and their allies can use to make a gender-balanced information society a reality in Africa. In previous work (Marcelle 1999), I presented an agenda for this transformation, organizing key actions as follows:

- Focus public-policy intervention;

- Allocate ICT development resources to women;

- Provide and improve telecommunications infrastructure;

- Build technological capability (the human-resource component);

- Facilitate and encourage the involvement of women in technological innovation;

- Create culturally resonant content;

- Design and deliver appropriate training mechanisms; and

- Increase effective demand for ICT products and services.

This section of the chapter draws extensively on the conceptual analysis done to define a framework for building an information society conducive to African women's active participation (Marcelle 1999). This treatment extends and updates that earlier work by taking account of the data provided in the Acacia country-strategy reports and reviewing progress made in policy implementation.

Focus public-policy intervention

Empirical research has confirmed that policy-making in technological fields often ignores the needs, requirements, and aspirations of women, unless gender analysis is included. Even when gender is introduced at a conceptual level, policymakers often rely on very poor, outdated, incomplete, and inaccurate data. Furthermore, women from developing countries are poorly represented in the national and international decision-making bodies that determine S&T policy, and this under-representation can lead to ineffective and gender-blind policy-making. To argue that gender analysis and awareness are important principles in ICT policy-making, African policymakers can draw on the recommendations of international initiatives, such as the UNCSTD Gender Working Group; the WomenWatch Expert Group (WomenWatch 1996); the United Nations Educational, Scientific and Cultural Organization – Society for International Development's Women on the Net project (WON 1997); the Beijing Platform for Action; and the Commission for the Status of Women. As AISI and the Acacia Initiative make further progress, important policy guidelines specific to the African context are likely to emerge.

One of the first tasks of policy intervention must be to launch an awareness-raising campaign and training to sensitize ICT policymakers to gender-equity issues. It would also be important to concurrently sensitize gender and development policymakers to ICT issues. Opportunities for learning can be found in both these fields, but few programs meet the needs of both groups of important actors. In fact, often the units for ICT and development planning and promotion and those for gender-related programs operate separately, even within a single bureaucracy, and have little or no coordination.

The United Nations Economic Commission for Africa (ECA) has demonstrated its willingness to bridge these institutional boundaries within its own organization and may well emerge as a source of expertise for African countries seeking to introduce similar initiatives. For its 40th Anniversary Conference — African Women and Economic Development: Investing in Our Future — in April and May 1998, it brought together the region's senior economic-development planners and decision-makers to consider ways to integrate gender issues into all its policies and programs, and this chapter was one of several papers commissioned for this important ECA conference.

To produce results from policy intervention, guidelines must be formulated to ensure the introduction and implementation of gender concerns at the project- or program-delivery level. Policies should also incorporate rigorous evaluation and monitoring procedures. Although many countries have ratified international treaties and conventions to secure gender equity, records on implementation have been poor. Further, as the international community has been unable to enforce these undertakings or impose sanctions or penalties on recalcitrant governments, civil-society organizations should play a critical monitoring role.

In Africa, planning efforts have little integration between ICT policy and national social, economic, or S&T development. Each of these mandates is undertaken with little coordination. Governments and other stakeholders should make a concerted effort to improve integration across the various policy-making organizations, as separation and poor coordination produce many significant negative results — duplication of effort, reduced opportunities for organizational learning, limited cross-fertilization of ideas, and fragmentation.

These more general improvements in ICT policy-making would improve the climate for successful integration of gender considerations, as an integrated policy-formulation process is more likely than one split along disciplinary boundaries to be alive to the importance of social considerations. An interdisciplinary approach to ICT policy-making is more likely to be capable of handling complex societal issues, such as those encountered in introducing Western technologies in Africa, and make the process beneficial to African women.

Recent developments in national S&T policy-making emphasize the importance of accounting for social and cultural conditions in strategies for technological development. Gender imbalances and gendered access to employment, income, training, property rights, control over the use of time, etc., are important

features of social organization that have the potential to retard the rate of technological development. By acknowledging that gender is a critical element in social
systems and by addressing gender inequality early in the formulation of ICT
policies, African leaders would improve their countries' chances of entering the
information age on beneficial terms.

Even with a greater level of coordination in national and sectoral policy-
making, integration of gender considerations will have to be pursued at many
levels. As shown in the national case studies in Annex 3, various policy-making
agents operate in the ICT field, itself already comprising very diverse elements
(infrastructure, applications, tools, and technologies). This is not unique to ICT
policy-making. Feminist scholars and advocates working in diverse aspects of
women's empowerment have studied and mastered the art of designing and
implementing policy interventions in complex arenas. The international feminist
movement has fine-tuned its ability to intervene in policy-making arenas by
undertaking multiple points of entry and increasing the focus of advocacy efforts.
These strategies proved themselves during previous United Nations world
conferences — in Beijing, Cairo, Copenhagen, and Istanbul — but have yet to be
extended to the debates on building the information society. Women's efforts in
health, education, and human rights are in many ways similar. The priorities are
to reduce the increasing disparity in access and control, improve women's access
to decision-making, and improve education and training systems. The lessons from
these successes need to be brought to bear, with increased intensity, on the
procedures involved in planning and shaping of the so-called information society.

Many African nations are presently restructuring their telecommunications
sectors, using technical analysis, advice, and support from agencies such as the
World Bank, ITU, and other multilateral agencies. The state of the art in telecommunications policy and information-society planning recognizes and actively
promotes deregulation, institutional reform, consideration of rural-development
objectives, redefinition of universal service, tariff reform, and convergence of
policies for basic telecommunications and other telematics services. Policymakers
are increasingly aware of the need to consider the different requirements of
various segments: rural versus urban, residential versus business, small business
versus large companies, etc.

Until very recently, no consideration was given to the gender-differentiated
impacts in this policy formulation. The landscape has changed: because of an
intervention led by UNU–INTECH and the United Nations Development Fund for
Women, ITU considered gender issues at the World Telecommunications Development Conference in March 1998. Because of this policy advocacy, ITU also

established a Task Force on Gender Issues, mainstreaming gender in ITU's work. The program of work commits ITU to assisting member states with the implementation of gender analysis in their national telecommunications-policy planning, introduction of gender disaggregation into its statistical series, and integration of gender considerations into programs, such as the Universal Right to Communicate, telemedicine, tele-education, and telecommunications and the environment. (For information on the ITU Task Force on Gender Issues, see ITU [1998, 1999].) African governments have shown a keen interest, but they reiterate a critical need for technical assistance to achieve these ambitious objectives.

Clearly, some African countries share the goals of the Task Force on Gender Issues. For example, South Africa's *Telecommunications Act* of 1996 sets goals for the extension of a modern information and telecommunications infrastructure to disadvantaged groups, including women. However, in practice very little governmental action or clear thinking on how this policy will be implemented has emerged. The answers are unlikely to emerge from within the mainstream telecom policy and regulatory bodies. Broader consultation is required.

Many important initiatives have come from the NGO community, such as South Africa's Women'sNet, a project jointly managed by the South African Commission for Gender Equality (CGE) and SANGONeT (an ISP specializing in NGO networking). Women'sNet has the potential to provide a focus for a coordinated and specialized intervention in the policy process in South Africa and thus provide a model for other countries. It will be important to evaluate the success of tha attempt by Women'sNet to combine advocacy at the highest levels with service delivery and training. The South African Council for Scientific and Industrial Research (CSIR) has also supported the formation of a pan-African gender working group to undertake high-level policy advocacy backed up by research and policy analysis. This organization, the African Information Society Gender Working Group, is now operational as a registered NGO in South Africa.

In August 1998 the Gender Unit of the South African Department of Communications convened a national workshop to identify strategies to introduce gender considerations into national communications policy. The regional body of regulators (the Telecommunication Regulators Association of Southern Africa) adopted a resolution at its annual general meeting in November 1998 to include gender issues in its work. What these examples show is that (at least at the level of rhetoric) policymakers in Africa are prepared to address gender issues and that the NGO sector is moving further into policy advocacy.

Allocate ICT development resources to women

Projects and programs for women's empowerment in Africa often suffer from inadequate resources and uncertainty in project funding. The vulnerability of ICT projects related to gender equity is largely due to the fact that they are, in the main, NGO-led projects. One certainly hopes that the many connectivity projects springing up in Africa will include requirements to target a fair share of financial and other technical resources specifically to the task of reducing gender inequality in electronic-communications networking. The many Multiple Purpose Community Centres (pilot schemes) may provide a vehicle for this targeting. Although many of these community-level programs included no gender considerations when they were conceived, this is beginning to change. The development of a strategic gender framework that applies to all existing and pipeline projects in the Acacia framework may provide good insights on ways to achieve gender-equity objectives at the project level. Because the Acacia Initiative includes a monitoring and evaluation component, it should be expected to yield very valuable data on the problems that such initiatives are facing and the methods needed to solve them.

As part of the effort to ensure that resources are directed to women, a set of gender-disaggregated statistics on the proposed beneficiaries of some of the major connectivity projects in Africa may be useful. Some very valuable work has already been done to catalogue ICT initiatives currently under way or planned in Africa, but the data are not disaggregated by gender of proposed beneficiaries.

Provide and improve telecommunications infrastructure

Telecommunications networks, which provide the backbone for ICT services and applications, are poorly developed in Africa. Although Africa has 12% of the world's population, it has only 2% of its telephone lines, and more than half of these are in the largest cities. Sub-Saharan Africa provides only 1 line per 235 people. The costs of installing and maintaining lines is higher in Africa than in other countries, even other developing countries, and the service is quite unreliable. Despite this limited access and poor quality, the demand for telecommunications service is remarkably high, according to the standard measures (numbers on waiting lists, etc.). What is more, when African men and women have access to telecommunications facilities, the levels of use are much higher than in other developing countries, as measured in minutes of outgoing traffic. Network configuration in Africa still largely mirrors colonial patterns of trade and communication flows. International telecommunications traffic is routed via Europe, and traffic between former colonizers and African nations still accounts for the lion's share of total volume. For many countries in Africa, interregional traffic is only a small percentage of the total volume of outgoing and incoming traffic.

Data on computer use and availability in Africa are not as widely available. But the available fragmentary evidence is sufficient to suggest that, except for South Africa, the region is plagued with many problems in this field. Personal computers are not manufactured within Africa, so they attract high duties and import tariffs. This, according to TitahMboh (1994), can multiply the cost of basic computer equipment and consumables in Africa by as much as 10 times over that in the country of manufacture. Africa also has limited access to training, technical information, computer spare parts, and repair services; unreliable supplies of electricity; and increasingly obsolete technology. The importation of computer equipment adds to the foreign-exchange debt burden of many African nations.

Although many initiatives in Africa aim to ameliorate the problems of inadequate infrastructure, few if any specifically address women's unique needs and requirements. Gender-specific issues related to the development of Africa's telecommunications and ICT infrastructure arise because the vast majority of African women are poor and live in rural settings. Network modernization and development must take these two characteristics of African women into account to provide them with an affordable communications infrastructure.

Gender justice must be included in the criteria used to make network architecture and equipment choices to ensure that equipment and service providers offer cost-effective and appropriate solutions. Unless decision-making processes change dramatically, Africa's ICT networks and services will remain accessible to only a small minority. ECA has recognized that it can play the role of the honest broker in supporting African governments as they choose network equipment. Thus, ECA will be sponsoring a conference with the aim of evaluating technological options for connectivity in Africa. Some of the Acacia country strategies also tackle this issue by identifying the need to carefully evaluate cost-effective technologies for expanding ICT networks, such as wireless in the local loop (WLL) solutions (Musisi 1997).

Choosing the most appropriate technological solution for the transmission network is of course only one element of the network-planning process. It is equally important to select customer-premises equipment that is rugged, has low maintenance costs, and will survive the vagaries of the African power supply. Network-management software, routing, and controlling devices are also important elements of the overall network solution. One must also select these with care and attention to the local conditions (Boakye 1995).

To motivate (or mandate) private companies to provide network infrastructure affordable to poor rural women unable to pay commercial rates, policymakers will have to use creative regulatory instruments. Universal-service principles define conditions for telecommunications network providers to ensure that basic services are affordable to the majority of the national population. In Africa, it is recognized to some extent that these principles must take account of the realities of the region and borrow regulatory mechanisms from industrialized countries only if they make sense in the local environment. The major difficulty with making universal access a reality in Africa is the prohibitive cost of network expansion, particularly with private investment. Private-sector entities cannot be coerced into financing network expansion in rural Africa, but regulatory policy can ensure that universal-access obligations accompany access to profitable markets in urban centres. For example, the South African Telecommunications Regulatory Authority is investigating ways to use the Universal Service Fund to contribute to meeting the universal-service targets of the *Telecommunications Act* and the Telkom licence. Although this chapter cannot treat this matter in detail, suffice it to say that the policymakers and new regulators in Africa will require nerves of steel and considerable skill to achieve their legitimate public-policy objectives when negotiating with international private investors, who for the most part define their interests very narrowly.

An alliance is needed between organizations involved in gender and development and the civil-society organizations and government bodies that promote rural development. Such an alliance can strengthen the voice of the disadvantaged groups that in Africa have tended to be marginalized from policy debates.

Build technological capability

Africa needs to build a technological capability in ICTs, with an explicit human skills and know-how component. Technological capability is unfortunately also in short supply in Africa. The number of graduates in S&T fields, at both secondary and tertiary levels, is woefully inadequate. This is not surprising, given the high rate of illiteracy, but it is made even worse by the brain drain, which is leading many of Africa's highly skilled professionals to leave the region. This overall skills shortage is much greater in the case of female technologists.

The *World Science Report* (UNESCO 1996) provides valuable information on the level of scientific human resources in Africa; it also provides gender-disaggregated data for a selection of countries. Given the acute shortage of S&T specialists, African governments should be encouraged to establish programs to develop the relevant skilled personnel in ICT-related disciplines. However, such programs will require financial resources that many cash-strapped African governments do not have. The local and international private sectors can each play an important role in filling this gap. If funding is available, a first step in building human skills and knowledge in ICTs would be to undertake national audits of ICT expertise, ensuring that all such studies collect gender-disaggregated data. Accompanying the audits should be strategic programs to encourage and support the entry of a greater number of women and men into these fields. This will require a concerted effort.

Lydia Makubu, President of the Third World Organisation of Women in Science, summarized the current status of women's involvement in science in Africa as follows:

> At the present time, women are grossly under represented in science at all levels of the educational system and in particular at university level. The reasons for this are many and complex and include socio-cultural attitudes towards girls enrolled in scientific disciplines and the attitudes of girls and women themselves towards the study of science, which is generally regarded as a male domain.
>
> Makubu (1996, p. 330)

Once women have entered ICT-related fields, employers should encourage and facilitate their active participation through employment policies and women-friendly work practices. The forms these supportive policies take are likely to vary, depending on the specific age, class, and educational background of the women in the workplace and the nature of their paid and unpaid work in ICTs. Employers should directly encourage women to participate in all levels of the technology-creation and technology-commercialization process. Although little statistical evidence is available, it is well known that few women are among the managers, policymakers, and technologists who lead the development of ICT strategies in the majority of African countries.

Women can also collectively make the S&T world a more tolerable environment for themselves through networking and other development programs. Women are helped to enter and remain in these professions through the work of the OFAN consortium (a collaboration of organizations concerned with women in S&T, set up to coordinate activities for the Beijing World Conference on Women); national women-in-science organizations; and other professional bodies, such as the Third World Organization of Women in Science. Many organizations have developed mentoring and other outreach programs. These organizations deserve the support of the national and international community. Some NGOs already active in ICT projects recognize the need to include internal training and support for female technologists. Two good examples are Abantu for Development train-the-trainers workshops and SANGONeT's technical training within the ambit of the South African Women'sNet.

Facilitate and encourage the involvement of women in technological innovation

The three main sites of production of ICT products and services are private-sector companies, academic institutions and public-sector research bodies, and not-for-profit organizations. All these must be targeted for policy intervention if Africa's women are to be brought more fully into the process of designing, testing, producing, and improving technological tools and applications. The private-sector companies selling equipment and services in Africa should be encouraged to fund more R&D on technological adaptation. University–private-sector collaboration should be improved, and the NGO sector's technological capability should be strengthened.

One of the most important areas of technological investigation for Africa's women is research on human–computer interaction to improve human manipulation of ICT devices using speech, visual icons, and non-keyboard devices. Some effort has been made in this direction at CSIR in South Africa. These projects should be expanded and strengthened to enable Africa to produce basic and applied research on non-English-language computer processing and control systems and applications. Such research might be of immense benefit to African women, the majority of whom are nonliterate and do not have English as their mother tongue.

A second factor to be taken into account in designing ICT equipment for African women's use is that the physical settings in which these devices will be used are very different from those in industrialized countries. African settings differ not only in natural conditions, such as humidity and dust, but also in the fact that the women are more likely to be caring for a child or children and managing income generation and other domestic responsibilities while using a computer. Health and safety features that accommodate this multitasking would be beneficial to Africa's women.

Create culturally resonant content

One of the most significant barriers to the use of ICT products and services in Africa is the predominant use of English in the information products of electronic-communication technologies. Africa has several thousand languages and dialects, and very few ICT products contain material in these languages.

Another important factor is that little of the information found on ICT networks is produced in Africa. Although African women are likely to benefit from, and to be interested in using, ICT networks to access international information, their enthusiasm will be much greater if they can use these networks for a two-way flow of information. Support for African women's content-creation and networking efforts therefore must be a priority of any national ICT strategy with gender-equality objectives. The many projects aiming to support African women as information providers include the Gender in Africa Information Network; Women'sNet (South Africa); the ECA African Centre for Women (the organizers of the 40th anniversary conference); and Environment, Development, Action. These initiatives should be well integrated with efforts to set up telecentres and library extension programs, as they may have potential for cross-sharing of technical and human resources.

Also important is ensuring that women have their say in determining which applications and information products are made available in their communities. The relevance of any information product may vary according to the preferences, lived realities, and aspirations of its consumers. The Gender Working Group of the Acacia Initiative emphasized that women should participate in assessing applications and tools and went on to suggest that the assessment methodology should take into account the general and specific needs of diverse groups of women (GWG–Acacia 1997). A needs assessment may reduce the chances of a community's receiving ICT applications that are irrelevant to the women's values and priorities. Unless women's participation in technology selection is made a prerequisite, they are likely to continue seeing ICTs as distant and meaningless. With women's full participation, ICTs are more likely to serve their interests.

Inadequate information management also diminishes the cultural relevance of ICTs. Growing evidence points to significant gender differences in the use of ICT devices and services. Women are likely to be more interested in tools that enable them to find relevant information in databases and web pages quickly. However, as browsing and search tools on the Internet are not particularly efficient, searching is very time-consuming; for women, whose time is in short supply, this is a serious disadvantage.

Design and deliver appropriate training programs

Women should have access to well-designed training programs that develop hands-on skills and provide motivational training materials, user-friendly manuals, and local user support. Under these conditions, the overall learning experience of African women encountering ICTs will be more rewarding.

Training for women should include technical training, trouble-shooting, and problem-solving skills. The design of the programs should take into account the experiences of academics and NGO trainers. Self-education and other open-learning methodologies are useful pedagogic methods for introducing women to ICTs and can be used to stimulate debate on ICT-related social and political issues. As noted earlier, the training programs for women include SANGONeT-run training through Women'sNet and training from Abantu for Development. These training programs should have a closer linkage to Acacia pipeline projects (Mozambique and South Africa) to maximize their impact.

Increase effective demand for ICT products and services

Poverty continues to be very real problem in Africa and presents an effective barrier to the diffusion of ICTs. However, to make progress, the region need not adopt the Western model of one or more ICT device per household. There are alternative models that would take into account the relative paucity of effective demand and in so doing lead to an alternative model of ICT–society interaction that would better integrate ICTs into the fabric of African societies.

Many recommendations have been made for improving access to ICTs for women in poor countries. For example, the WomenWatch expert-group meeting suggested that women be given access to existing United Nations resources, for example, through the network of national United Nations documentation centres and the Sustainable Development Networking Programme. In addition, it is important to facilitate distribution of equipment to developing countries through subsidized bulk procurement and distribution programs.

Several NGOs are already undertaking pilot projects to establish tele-centres. As this approach focuses on providing community-level access, it is by definition more in line with Africa's level of effective demand. Ernberg (1997) argued that telecentres can change the business model for delivery of telecom services. His analysis demonstrated how telecentres can generate traffic (and revenues) for common carrier providers, which strengthens the business case for rapid deployment of telecentres to form a rural transmission and switching network.

Conclusions

From the above analysis and arguments, it should be clear that the inclusion of a gender perspective in national ICT policy-making in Africa would be both feasible and desirable. The second section provided background information on the status of national ICT policy formulation. The third presented an eight-point agenda for organizing such interventions. It is critically important that the interventions undertaken to integrate gender perspectives into ICT policy-making proceed from a well-informed and thorough understanding of the African system of ICT policy and planning.

This chapter has argued that the outcomes of any policy decision are determined by the institutional and social contexts, by the objectives, and by the processes and tools used for implementation. The recommendations that follow take these issues seriously and recognize that the existing character of national ICT policy-making systems determines the points at which gender issues can be inserted into the policy debate. These recommendations pertain to general-level improvements in ICT policy-making, as well as strategies to have gender perspectives included. This concluding section is organized as a set of recommendations for the key actors involved in the process of policy formulation and implementation and includes some remarks on how countries may operationalize such a gender strategy. The recommendations are supported by empirical and conceptual analysis, and, wherever possible, references are made to the sources of supporting evidence.

Recommendations for key actors in ICT policy formulation and implementation

The key actors in ICT policy formulation and implementation are national governments, multilateral agencies (including bodies in the United Nations system), donor agencies, and private-sector and civil-society organizations.

National governments

Integrating gender considerations into national ICT policy formulation and implementation will require strong, effective leadership from the state. African governments should play a leadership role in articulating a clear vision and strategy for ICT development. This should take account of local contexts and legitimate demands for gender justice. Relevant organizations in the public sector, such as line ministries and regulatory bodies, should develop the vision, design the strategy, and undertake the tasks, working in partnership with other key agents. It is very important that the state be proactive in ensuring that the development of the ICT sector and the application of ICTs proceed in the national interest. Improving the socioeconomic environment for girls and women to enable them to harness these technologies is an important and pressing challenge. The process is not automatic, and the state must therefore play a crucial role in setting the direction for production and use of ICTs.

African governments should take five key steps:

1.   Define and specify measurable goals and objectives for the ICT sector and
      applications. These goals should include improving the contribution of
      ICTs to poverty alleviation, health care, food security, environmental
      security, technological advance, and human-resource development. The
      potential beneficiaries of these policies should be clearly identified and
      should include "girls and women" as an explicitly defined category. Gov-
      ernments should also recognize that this category is not homogeneous and
      ensure that policies are in place to benefit girls and women of diverse
      social backgrounds, levels of education, ethnic origin, and racial back-
      ground. In Africa, it is particularly important to take into account rural
      women as potential beneficiaries of ICTs and their needs.

      • The evidence considered in this chapter has shown that African gov-
         ernments have made inadequate progress in defining clear goals and
         objectives for ICTs and development. Although some countries have
         expressed interest in ensuring that ICTs are used for social development
         and that they are made accessible to rural communities, measurable
         goals and strategies are needed to further develop this vision.

      • The relative lack of progress can be partially explained by the fact that
         leadership for developing ICTs has been in the hands of the line
         ministries (most often transport and communications or telecommunica-
         tions), which define their mandates very narrowly. Success in using
         ICTs for development requires an impetus larger than sectoral concerns.
         Countries where more than one ministry sets and implements the
         agenda make faster progress. Senegal is one such African country. In
         addition, as UNCSTD's guidelines and the experience of OECD coun-
         tries show, a multidisciplinary approach that cuts across traditional
         departmental boundaries is needed to formulate strategies to ensure
         women's entry and survival in the emerging information society.

2.   Create the necessary institutional structure to develop and steer a vision of
      ICTs and development and to achieve the goals set out in that vision. A
      variety of organizations are needed to undertake the analysis; define the
      goals; negotiate with other stakeholders; plan, evaluate, and monitor the
      project; and manage all the elements of the national ICT strategy. These
      organizations need the right staff teams and adequate resources, empower-
      ing authority, and decision-making structures. As stated earlier, the internal

dynamic of ICTs imposes a pressing need to strengthen the technology sensing and assessment capability of African ICT policy-making bodies. Accessing this technological expertise does not mean that the line ministries need to employ these individuals in permanent positions, which is not often done even in OECD countries. But it does mean improving the mechanisms for policymakers to support and interface with experts in other locations, such as academia, research organizations, and the private sector. The task facing African ICT policymakers is to create a system of organizational capabilities, rather than a single institution.

The UNCSTD guidelines and the AISI framework suggest that national commissions are suitable for playing this leadership role. Each African government would need to establish a commission with the most appropriate bodies and individuals. The third section presented the detailed arguments for including representatives of women's organizations and experts in gender and development issues in those policy-formulation processes. Although no African country has so far done this systematically, this is also true in many other parts of the world. This is mainly due to the fact that the primary agents in ICT policy-making do not have the in-house expertise to undertake these tasks, as will be discussed later.

3. Secure advice and strengthen technical expertise in ICT-related fields. Policymakers should use research findings and insights drawn from rigorous analysis to develop policy tools that will help them realize their policy objectives. For example, African ICT policymakers need to develop new tools to enable them to incorporate socioeconomic objectives in their decisions concerning network modernization, industry structure, tariff policy, licencing decisions, incentives for R&D and innovation, and systems for training and learning.

  • ITU's Telecommunications Development Bureau has provided technical assistance to African countries seeking to reform their telecommunications sectors and has restructured its work program to provide timely, effective assistance. ITU recognizes that capability-building is an essential requirement in Africa. Although it has worked most closely with telecommunications companies, ITU is finding ways to improve its relations with other important stakeholders. For the technical analysis and development of policy tools, it remains an important source of expertise. ITU has made progress in taking account of the telecom-development needs of rural communities and in analyzing the impacts that changes in industry structure have had on developing countries. ITU is committed to ensuring that its technical-assistance mandate extends to helping policymakers incorporate gender considerations into their telecom development. The AISI framework includes a gender component, and recent efforts have been made to apply a gender framework in the Acacia Initiative. As these programs produce deliverables they will also provide actual data on attempts to integrate gender into ICT policies and plans in Africa.

4.   Develop consultative mechanisms to ensure that the process of policy formulation, implementation, and review involves all key actors. National governments and some key actors, such as multilateral development agencies and ITU, have well-developed, regular communications, although, as noted previously, their communications tend to occur along traditional lines. For example, in many countries, the ministry of communications interacts regularly with ITU, but not with the World Bank or UNCTAD. In addition, there are few organizational structures at the national level that permit negotiation or debate among various line ministries.

The AISI framework and the Acacia Initiative are particularly strong in arguing for and demonstrating the potential benefits of this approach to ICT policy planning and implementation. Evidence from South Africa, Senegal, and Uganda clearly shows that the greater participation of a wide range of interest groups improves the policy-making process. It is still too early to assess the impact on particular groups of intended beneficiaries, but the approach of the Acacia Initiative clearly provides an entry point for marginalized and disadvantaged groups. Given the influence of the AISI framework, it is important for the action program to call for an open, participatory policy process.

These consultative processes must have the participation of women's organizations and gender and development specialists. It would not be an intractable undertaking to identify the women and men with the skills and experience needed to represent the interests of girls and women in these forums and to develop the necessary policy instruments. More creative approaches to identifying these resources are needed; there are women with experience in ICTs in universities and the private sector, and there are female gender and development experts who can be trained in ICT policy issues. This challenge for human-resource development must be squarely faced. South Africa and Uganda are making great strides in incorporating gender considerations into a variety of social-development programs, and the lessons learned from the South African CGE and the Ugandan Ministry of Gender can be brought to bear on the issue of incorporating gender considerations into ICT policy in Africa.

5.   Develop improved capacities to review policy objectives, monitor and evaluate programs, and respond to changes in the technological and socioeconomic environment. ICTs are a fast-changing set of technologies. The impacts of the production and use of ICTs change very rapidly and take unexpected forms in local environments. ICT policy needs to be adaptive and responsive if it is to be effective. As noted in the early sections of this chapter, this is a challenge to policymakers in both developed and developing countries. Individual African countries are unlikely to be well-placed to establish all the elements of a complete institutional system for ICTs. Subregional cooperation is therefore needed to develop systems (and institutions) to formulate ICT policy and manage the sector. Subregional institutions can assist national governments by providing technology-evaluation and technology-monitoring capabilities and by strengthening national technology-assessment capabilities. A reform of the system of technical cooperation with bilateral donors and multilateral bodies is also needed. Unequal partnerships with external agents lead national governments to neglect their responsibilities to set and review objectives and to develop adaptive capabilities. Reform of technical cooperation such that the roles of national governments and lenders are mutually recognized and respected would improve the likelihood of African governments' taking charge of national ICT policies and strategies.

Multilateral donors and agencies

The review of ICT policy-making in the second section established that all the major multilateral development-finance agencies, some specialized agencies in the United Nations system, and large donor agencies have a presence in Africa. The AISI framework coordinates many of these efforts and is becoming the preferred point of entry for external actors supporting development of ICTs in Africa.

One of the problems facing Africa is that some countries have become very popular sites for pilot studies and policy experimentation by donors and multilateral agencies, but other countries are left out. This pattern of duplication of effort in a few countries is counterproductive and should be reduced.

The previous subsection raised another important issue concerning multilateral agencies and donors: the reform of technical cooperation to require external agents' acceptance of a leading role for African governments in articulating and implementing national ICT strategies. Owing particularly to the underdevelopment of institutional systems for ICT policies in Africa, the balance of power in these relationships does not always reflect this more appropriate division of labour between national governments and external agents. The evidence presented in the earlier sections confirms that multilateral agencies, United Nations bodies, and donors have made very valuable contributions to the development and implementation of ICT policies in Africa, and it is hoped that as national governments make more progress, the balance of power will shift between these two sets of key actors.

The AISI framework, spearheaded by the ECA, identifies gender issues as important elements of national ICT strategy, and this framework is compatible with the recommendation that national governments take the lead in developing and implementing ICT policies, with external agents providing support. Multilateral bodies, including the United Nations system and its specialized agencies, should assist national governments with a variety of supporting resources, including, but not limited to, technical expertise for design of policy tools, financial support, and other assistance with institutional capability-building. Africa has thoroughly identified and well-documented requirements and needs in the ICT sector. External agents should continue to support the AISI as a mechanism for coordinating their efforts in Africa.

Private-sector organizations

International suppliers of ICT equipment and services, as well as domestic firms in the ICT sector, have important roles to play in integrating ICTs and development goals. The private sector is an important and powerful interest group, whose demands exert considerable influence on the direction of ICT policy in Africa. Unfortunately, both local and foreign private-sector companies have tended to emphasize short-term profitability in their strategies for entering and competing in the African ICT sector. This short-term orientation explains the woefully inadequate levels of reinvested profit, R&D, training and human-resource expenditure in the African ICT sector. As the private-sector lobby is very powerful and often has more experience with ICTs than central-government agencies, short-term commercial objectives have considerable weight in the overall definition of ICT policy objectives.

Undue emphasis is placed on profitability because companies operating in the African telecommunications market have been highly profitable. However, the levels of network coverage have been among the lowest in the world. The challenge for the international and domestic private sectors will be to expand the ICT sector in Africa while maintaining its profitability. A number of models of market expansion in other developing countries can be adapted to the African context. Fast growth of ICT networks, an increasing range of services, and the development of applications suitable for the local context are possible futures for the African ICT sector. Encouraging signs are already apparent in the growth rate of mobile networks in Africa and the expansion of WLL-infrastructure systems.

The major challenge for private-sector organizations in Africa will be to develop enough confidence and long-term orientation to invest in market development. In the African context, this would require technological investment in applications and tools that are better suited to the local environment. Africa has large underserved potential markets for ICT equipment and services. The strategies used to expand markets in wealthy countries will not succeed in Africa. In Africa, private-sector companies should lend their support and resources to the efforts to develop and expand networks through telecentres and other community-owned facilities. Firms operating in the continent should also invest more in R&D geared to producing tools and applications to meet the needs of potential local consumers.

The third section outlined the specific requirements of Africa's women as a group of potential consumers of ICTs. Private-sector organizations should make an effort to respond more effectively to these requirements. Companies that succeed at doing this will achieve their commercial objectives and make a contribution to Africa's development.

To play an active role in integrating gender concerns into ICT development, private-sector organizations can also adopt proactive employment policies that encourage and facilitate the participation of women in a wide spectrum of fields related to ICTs. Private-sector organizations in the African ICT sector include large companies, such as the national telecommunications carriers and the branches of international suppliers of ICT equipment and services; and smaller companies, such as ISPs, computer-service companies, and community-owned telecentres. Women should have job opportunities with various levels of responsibility in any of these settings. Given the serious shortage of female technologists, private-sector organizations should also demonstrate their commitment to achieving the goals of gender equity in the ICT sector by providing and supporting training programs specifically designed for girls and women.

Civil-society organizations

A number of civil-society organizations are involved in the production and use of ICTs in Africa. The companion papers on the Acacia national strategy, agriculture, education, universal access, democratization, and health (Chapters 2, 4, 5, 6, 7, and 8, respectively, of this volume) provide up-to-date information on the importance of civil-society organizations in promoting the production and use of ICTs. Marcelle (1999) claimed that civil-society organizations, particularly women's organizations, have been at the forefront in advocating the integration of ICTs and sustainable-development goals and programs. The electronic-communication programs for women have emphasized that ICTs can be of tremendous service in human-rights campaigns, environmental management, and improved information exchange between Africa and the rest of the world.

Women's ICT programs in Africa face many problems, including inadequate funding. Very recent evidence has shown that civil-society projects are cooperating more effectively with governmental bodies, and these partnerships may reduce some of this financial uncertainty. However, civil-society organizations should be making efforts to improve the income-generating capacities of their projects to enable them to maintain some independence from other key agents in the ICT policy process. This is particularly important because civil-society organizations often play a critical monitoring role and force governments to be more accountable to a wider range of constituencies. If you are not financially independent, it is unlikely you will be effective as a critic for very long.

Whenever possible, civil-society organizations should participate fully in consultative processes involved with ICT policy-making. Women's ICT programs in Africa have tended to focus on service delivery, rather than on policy-making and advocacy. However, this is changing slowly, and projects such as Abantu for Development, Women'sNet, the African Gender Institute's Communications Links, and the African Information Society's Gender Working Group are all good examples of this trend. It should be encouraged and supported. Multilateral agencies, national governments, and the private sector can support this trend by including civil-society organizations in their capability-building exercises. For example, if ITU or other United Nations agencies start training programs to improve the capacity of national governments to take gender into account in ICT policy-making, civil-society organizations should be given the opportunity to participate in these programs. Achieving this will require special attention, as the lines of communication between multilateral agencies and civil-society organizations in ICTs are not always open.

Operationalizing the gender strategy

The recommendations made here are based on a number of simplifying assumptions about the political and institutional contexts. Theoretical and empirical evidence, such as that presented in Goetz (1997), cautions against naive optimism. The authors in that book argued that despite improvements in the rhetoric, the outcomes of many programs in gender and development have failed to "alter the asymmetrical distribution of resources and social values which contribute to the social construction of gender inequality and differences." Goetz suggested that "the project for gender-sensitive institutional change is therefore to routinize gender-equitable forms of social interaction and to challenge the legitimacy of forms of social organisation which discriminate against women." She also argued that such a project must go beyond the type of gender training used in development programs that have emphasized attitudinal change as the key change agent. Gender-redistributive policies, such as those recommended in this chapter, tend to create opposition and resistance because they challenge existing norms, values, and cultural practices and promote the reallocation of material resources. However, such policies are needed to successfully operationalize a gender strategy.

A successful gender strategy for ICTs in Africa must also recognize that the definitions of *gender* and *gender equity* vary according to local context; it would be simpler from a purely technical standpoint if there were a universal definition and accepted understanding of the desirable outcomes of a gender strategy for ICTs, but this is not the reality. Strategies for ICTs in Africa must therefore define goals and objectives in dialogue with all the key actors and potential beneficiaries. Change agents must make realistic assumptions about the required resources and must assess the venues of likely resistance. When opportunities for transformation appear, strong leadership is needed to bring about the desired outcomes. Individually and collectively, the key actors operate in gendered social and political environments, in which the social value and interests of men and women are continuously negotiated. This makes the project of bringing gender justice into the ICT sphere more complicated because there is no unifying understanding of this project, its desired outcomes, or the consequences of achieving these outcomes.

Despite these very valid and important qualifications, developing strategies to include a gender perspective in ICT policy is a valuable development project. This analysis has shown that it can improve the material conditions and quality of life in Africa. Taking no action is not an option, and this chapter has outlined a way to design and sustain a program of action.

References

Acacia. 1997a. Acacia National Strategy for Mozambique. International Development Research Centre, Ottawa, ON, Canada. Mimeo.

———— 1997b. Acacia national strategy for South Africa. International Development Research Centre, Ottawa, ON, Canada. Mimeo.

Boakye, K. 1995. Telecommunications technologies: Opportunities for developing countries. *In* United Nations Conference on Trade and Development, ed., Information technology for development. UNCTAD, New York, NY, USA. pp. 184–199.

Browne, P. 1996. Study of the effectiveness of informatics policy instruments in Africa. ECA, Addis Ababa, Ethiopia. Internet: www.belanet.org/partners/aisi/policy/infopol/sumbrown.htm

D'Orville, H. 1997. Communications and knowledge-based technologies for sustainable human development. United Nations Development Programme, New York, NY, USA. Internet: undp.org/undp/comm/index.html

ECA (United Nations Economic Commission for Africa). 1996. The African Information Society Initiative (AISI): a framework to build Africa's information and communication infrastructure. ECA, Addis Ababa, Ethiopia. Internet: bellanet.org/partners/aisi/more/aisi

Ernberg, J. 1997. Universal access through multipurpose community telecentres — a business case? Paper presented at the Global Knowledge Conference, Jun, Toronto, ON, Canada. World Bank, Washington, DC, USA; Government of Canada, Ottawa, ON, Canada.

Goetz, A.M., ed. 1997. Getting institutions right for women in development. Zed Books, London, UK.

GWG (Gender Working Group) – Acacia. 1997. Minutes of meeting held on 6th–7th November 1997. Mimeo.

HLEG (High-level Expert Group). 1997. Building the European information society for us all — final policy report of the High-level Expert Group. European Commission, Luxembourg.

IDRC (International Development Research Centre). 1997. Stratégie Acacia au Sénégal. IDRC, Ottawa, ON, Canada. Mimeo.

ITU (International Telecommunication Union). 1998. World Telecommunications Development Conference. WTDC-98, 23 Mar – 1 Apr 1998, Valletta, Malta. ITU, Geneva, Switzerland. Final report. Internet: www.itu.int/wtdc-98/

———— 1999. Gender issues. ITU, Geneva, Switzerland. Internet: www.itu.int/ITU-D-Gender/index.htm

ITU–TDB (International Telecommunication Union's Telecommunications Development Bureau). 1996. Telecommunications policies for Africa. ITU, Geneva, Switzerland. Africa Green Paper.

———— 1998. General trends in telecommunication restructuring. ITU, Geneva, Switzerland.

Kataman, A. 1997. Effective use of ICTs by communities for national development: a discussion of content determinants. Report prepared for International Development Research Centre, Ottawa, ON, Canada.

Makubu, L. 1996. Women in science: the case of Africa. *In* United Nations Educational, Scientific and Cultural Organization, ed., World science report. UNESCO, Paris, France. pp. 329–333.

Mansell, R.; Wehn, U. 1998. Knowledge societies: information technology for sustainable development. United Nations Commission on Science and Technology for Development; Oxford University Press, New York, NY, USA.

Marcelle, G.M. 1999. Creating an African women's cyberspace. *In* Mitter, S., ed., Social exclusion in the information society. Routledge, London, UK. (In press.)

Mitter, S., ed. 1999. Social exclusion in the information society. Routledge, London, UK. (In press.)

Mureithi, M. 1997. Policy options for ICT use in rural communities in Uganda. Mimeo.

Musisi, C. 1997. Technology and infrastructure options for ICT use in rural communities in Uganda. Report produced for International Development Research Centre, Ottawa, ON, Canada. Mimeo.

Nyiira, Z.M. 1997. The ACACIA national strategy for Uganda: background vision and implementation strategy. Mimeo.

OECD (Organisation for Economic Co-operation and Development). 1992. New technologies: opportunities and policy implications for the 1990s. OECD, Paris, France.

———— 1996. Employment and growth in the knowledge-based economy. OECD, Paris, France.

TitahMboh, C. 1994. Information technology networking in Africa: ARCT experience, May 1994. Paper presented at the LSE Conference on Globalization and IT Networking, 16–17 May 1994, London, UK. London School of Economics, London, UK.

UNCSTD (United Nations Commission on Science and Technology for Development). 1997. Report of the Working Group on Information and Communication Technologies for Development. Prepared for the 3rd Session, 12 May, Geneva, Switzerland. UNCSTD, E/CN.16/1997/4, 7 Mar.

UNCSTD–GWG (United Nations Commission on Science and Technology for Development Gender Working Group), ed. 1995. Missing links: gender equity in science and technology for development. International Development Research Centre, Ottawa, ON, Canada.

UNCTAD (United Nations Conference on Trade and Development), ed. 1995. Information technology for development. UNCTAD, New York, NY, USA.

UNESCO (Nations Educational, Scientific and Cultural Organization), ed. 1996. World science report. UNESCO, Paris, France.

Ventura, A. 1997. An information technology agenda to benefit the underdeveloped countries. Presentation of the Science Advisor to the Prime Minister of Jamaica at the Research Partnerships for Sustainable Development Meeting, Dutch Ministry of Foreign Affairs, Leiden, Netherlands. Mimeo.

WomenWatch. 1996. Report of the Expert Workshop on WomenWatch: Global information through computer networking technology in the follow-up to the Fourth World Conference on Women, 26–28 Jun 1996, New York, NY, USA. United Nations Development Fund for Women, New York, NY, USA.

WON (Women on the Net). 1997. Project publication: UNESCO–SID international annotated multicultural guide to women working on the net. Expert Group workshop report. United Nations Educational, Scientific and Cultural Organization, Paris, France.

World Bank. 1997. Gender strategies for sub-Saharan Africa: an overview. Knowledge, Information and Technology Center, Washington, DC, USA. Findings No. 85. Internet: worldbank.org/aftdr/findings/english/find85.htm

Annex 1: Key issues

The World Bank has increasingly recognized that development in sub-Saharan Africa (SSA) requires the full participation of both men and women and has articulated four interconnected priority issues and related strategic objectives:

Key issue 1: Women's central economic role, especially in agriculture and the informal sector

Women are a key economic resource in Africa, comprising about 60% of the informal sector and providing about 70% of total agricultural labor. Women's central position in economic production in SSA contrasts with the systematic discrimination they face in accessing the basic technologies and resources needed for their economic role. This gender-based discrimination limits economic growth. It markedly affects macro-economic policy and performance (supply response), and has important repercussions for economic efficiency and equity.

Key issue 2: Gender bias in access to education, health, and other basic social services

Gender differentials persist at all levels of education and the gap widens at the higher levels. Low levels of education and training, poor health and nutritional status, and limited access to resources depress women's quality of life and hinder economic efficiency and growth. Female education is the investment with the highest social returns. It is the catalyst that increases the impact of other investments in health, nutrition, family planning, agriculture, industry, and infrastructure. Design of health interventions must take into account women's specific health needs, with a particular focus on reproductive health, AIDS, and gender violence, [women's] multiple responsibilities, and the demands on their time.

Key issue 3: Time poverty — a critical gender dimension of poverty in Africa

Poverty in Africa is pervasive and growing. Regional analysis recognizes that growth is necessary but that the pattern of growth is crucial for sustainable poverty reduction. Poverty in Africa has an important, if difficult to quantify, gender dimension. A key component of female poverty in Africa is "time poverty," as there are significant time allocation differentials between men and women. Women work longer hours than men ... and their workload, derived from simultaneously carrying out multiple roles, imposes severe time burdens and harsh trade-offs, with important economic and welfare costs. Balancing competing time uses in a framework of almost total inelasticity of time allocation presents a particular challenge to reducing poverty in Africa.

Poverty in Africa is compounded by the complexity of household structures and relations in Africa. Evidence suggests great diversity in the structure and composition of households, where men and women have largely separate sources and uses of income and resources. This often leads to marked inequality in intra-household resource allocation.

Key issue 4: Raising women's participation

Women in Africa are systematically under-represented in institutions at the local and national level and have very little say in decision-making ... . Gender barriers limit women's participation and reinforce power gaps. As civil society emerges, women's organizations constitute an important social capital resource for strengthening the social institutions necessary for a market economy. Women constitute an important source of opinion (and opposition) on the subject of economic adjustment in Africa, and hearing their voices and listening to their needs is essential for endorsement of successful economic reform in Africa.

Synergy and complementarity among strategic gender objectives

Each of these strategic objectives has an important contribution to make to achieving the goal of sustainable poverty reduction. There are important interconnections and trade-offs among economic production, child bearing and rearing, and household/community management responsibilities that assume particular importance given the simultaneous competing claims on women's labor time. From a gender perspective, inter-sectoral linkages, as between girls' education and domestic tasks (especially water provision), rural development and transport, and the population/ agriculture/environment "nexus", are critical. The contribution of these strategic objectives to development and poverty reduction in Africa can be greatly amplified through concurrent actions in each of these areas, so that multiple and mutually reinforcing benefits can be achieved.

World Bank (1997, executive summary)

Annex 2: The African Information Society Initiative[2]

Background

In May 1995, the 21st meeting of the ECA Conference of Ministers, comprising the 53 African ministers responsible for economic and social development and planning, adopted Resolution 795, "Building Africa's Information Highway." In response to this resolution, ECA appointed its HLEG on Information and Communications Technologies in Africa to draft an action framework to use ICTs to accelerate the socioeconomic development of Africa and its people. The HLEG comprised 11 experts on information technology in Africa. They met in Addis Ababa, Cairo, and Dakar and communicated further by e-mail. The result of their work was the document *The African Information Society Initiative (AISI): A Framework to Build Africa's Information and Communication Infrastructure* (ECA 1996). The document was submitted to the 22nd meeting of the ECA Conference of Ministers in May 1996 and adopted through Resolution 812, "Implementation of the African Information Society Initiative."

Linking information technology and development

The action framework calls for, among other things, the elaboration and implementation of plans for a national information and communication infrastructure, involving development of institutional frameworks and human, information, and technological resources in all African countries and the pursuit of priority strategies, programs, and projects to assist in the sustainable buildup of an information society in African countries.

AISI aims to ensure that building Africa's information society will help Africa accelerate its development plans; stimulate growth; and provide new opportunities in education, trade, health care, job creation, and food security. It should also help African countries to leapfrog stages of development and raise their standards of living.

---

[2] This annex is adapted from ECA (1996).

Partnership

AISI was put in place through the collaborative actions of a network of partners sharing the aim of promoting connectivity and information-technology development in Africa. Included among the original list of ECA partners were ITU, UNESCO, IDRC, and the Bellanet International Secretariat. After the 1995 meeting of the ECA Conference of Ministers, the World Bank joined these organizations, and the Global Information Infrastructure Commission has supported the initiative on behalf of the private sector. With the launch, in March 1996, of the Special Initiative on Africa, with, among others, the program Harnessing Information Technology for Development (HITD), the United Nations Industrial Development Organization and UNCTAD have joined the group of collaborating agencies, sharing objectives on ICTs for development and working together for their implementation. In the area of training, the United Nations Institute for Training and Research has also associated itself closely with these activities.

AISI is a guiding framework for ICT policy in Africa. Resolution 812 of the May 1996 ECA Conference of Ministers called on the partners in the HITD initiative to use AISI as a guiding framework. AISI was also endorsed at ITU's African Regional Telecommunication Development Conference in Abidjan, in May 1996, and the Organization of African Unity's July 1996 summit in Yaounde. AISI has had the participation of other organizations, such as the Agence universitaire pour la Francophonie (university office for francophone people), Commonwealth Network of Information Technology for Development, Food and Agriculture Organization of the United Nations, Telecommunications Foundation of Africa, UNDP, and the World Health Organization.

Annex 3. Case studies of national ICT policy-making.

Lead organizations involved in national ICT policy-making and basic policy instruments	ICT policy objectives and priorities	Progress in implementation	Challenges for policy-making and gaps in existing policy framework	Treatment of social objectives, particularly gender issues	Recommendations from Acacia country-strategy reports
Mozambique					
National Telecommunications Institute of Mozambique, responsible for sector policy, regulation, and supervision of state-owned carrier	Restructure the telecommunications sector and improve operational efficiency of national operator	TDM established in 1992 as an independent commercial entity and has been accelerating network expansion	There is no overall framework for national ICT policy-making, but the government is enthusiastic and keen to build on the research and training capability of CIUEM and to use ICTs for poverty alleviation	Existing policies do not include any treatment of social issues, including gender	Support development of national informatics policy and assist the formation of a broad-based forum to debate ICT priorities and design strategies for the sector
Telecommunications Act (in 1992)		Licencing phone shops for resale of voice capacity	Several donors and multilateral agencies are present in the country; this raises the issue of ensuring that national priorities continue to determine and define the evolution of ICT policy and also requires that care be taken to avoid duplication, set clear priorities, and co-ordinate efforts	CIUEM's senior staff includes one woman who is active in gender and development work and led the Mozambican delegation at the Fourth World Conference on Women in Beijing	Demonstrate technology applications and support content and applications development, especially in education and health
					Set up telecentres in rural communities

Assist in program management, monitoring, evaluation, and reporting by applying community-surveillance methodology

Facilitate strengthening of TDM's technology assessment and CIUEM's training capabilities

Senegal

Post and Telecommunication Research and Regulation Department in the Ministry of Communications, responsible for applying policy directives and formulating regulatory proposals	Transfer ownership of SONATEL (telecom network operator) to the private sector through strategic equity sale	Good progress on establishing a reliable, modern digital network	Extending policy scope to social objectives while building on the progress already made in improving operation of the telecom sector	Telecom-policy formulation has focused almost exclusively on performance of the operator and sector structure; an opportunity exists to expand policy scope	Formalize a framework for coordinating inputs of stakeholders and donors; support the policy-formulation process and encourage a widening of the scope of those policies to take account of the interests of the disadvantaged

(continued)

Annex 3. Continued.

Lead organizations involved in national ICT policy-making and basic policy instruments	ICT policy objectives and priorities	Progress in implementation	Challenges for policy-making and gaps in existing policy framework	Treatment of social objectives, particularly gender issues	Recommendations from Acacia country-strategy reports
		Senegal (continued)			
NTCC is an arbitration authority and a consultative body that reports to the Office of the President; NTCC is a powerful body that sets the vision for telecom policy in the country; NTCC has mandated a national commission to investigate and assess key aspects of telecom development	Undertake major tariff reform and adopt cost-oriented tariffing; targets for tariff reduction set at 5% per annum	Good complement of skilled staff, including at technical and managerial levels; senior staff in SONATEL are well organized, and the management association provides professional development and skills upgrading; productivity in SONATEL has improved steadily	Given the profitability of telecoms in urban Senegal, sector reform should tie franchises in cities to universal-service obligations for rural network development	Women's NGOs and other stakeholders concerned about gender issues are active in Senegal but have not been able to influence the development of national ICT policy	Carry out needs-assessment studies; launch an awareness campaign
Telecommunications Act (in 1996)	Facilitate international competitiveness of Senegal's services sector by reducing cost and improving quality of telecom inputs	Small private operators have been permitted to set up public phone booths (telecentres) and resell voice, telex, and fax services; by 1995, there were 1 500 private operators	Telecommunications is regarded as a strategic industry in Senegal; NTCC's mandate should be extended to include a wider range of telematics services and take account of the interests of users		Evaluate telecentres to identify mechanisms to encourage young people to use these services

The success of telecentres has provided access and employment; these facilities can be upgraded and improved and used as a basis for development of other capabilities, such as electronic-publishing skills

Senegal can play a leadership role in West Africa; policymakers should take up the challenge of sharing their experiences with neighbouring countries and provide technical assistance, when possible

Launch a multilevel program for human-resources development, involving formal and informal institutions and taking steps to encourage and support participation of women and young people

Establish a software-engineering centre

(continued)

Annex 3. Continued.

South Africa

Lead organizations involved in national ICT policy-making and basic policy instruments	ICT policy objectives and priorities	Progress in implementation	Challenges for policy-making and gaps in existing policy framework	Treatment of social objectives, particularly gender issues	Recommendations from Acacia country-strategy reports
Department of Communications, leading in policy formulation	Expand telecommunications network to previously disadvantaged communities	Network roll-out program is proceeding through monopoly operator, TELKOM	Reconciling the sectoral restructuring objectives and the social objectives: black empowerment and participation of women in telecommunications	*Telecommunications Act* includes provisions to redress gender imbalance and other areas of disadvantage	Facilitate an Information Society Policy process, led by the Department of Communications but involving all relevant government departments, including Education, Health, Arts, Culture and Science and Technology, Industry and Trade, Finance, and Environment, and provisional governments and civil-society organizations
Independent regulatory body, SATRA, which includes oversight for the broadcasting industry, which was previously under the jurisdiction of the Independent Broadcasting Authority	Encourage and support participation of black South Africans in the telecommunications industry	Experimentation with telecentres as mechanism for rapid decentralization of communications infrastructure	Leveraging the installed network base to build a world-class capability in ICTs	Consultative process involved in drafting of the *Telecommunications Act* did not explicitly deal with gender issues; however, these are likely to be raised in the consultation process for the new *Broadcasting Act*	Expand telecentres as training centres and support other training initiatives

Department of Trade and Industry and Department of Arts, Culture and Sciences	Expand the range of ICT services and maintain quality of service delivery	Regulatory body established and working well with implementing agencies, such as the Universal Service Agency, and the Department of Communications (central government)	Increase capacities of users at community level, including development of high-level engineering and software-engineering skills
		Harnessing ICTs for development of the majority of South Africans, rather than an elite	
Telecommunications Act (in 1996)	Establish a first-class regulatory structure in the telecommunications industry		Pilot applications of ICTs in malaria prevention and treatment and education
Broadcasting Act (currently under review)	Facilitate use of new technologies in the development of a national broad-band communications network		Stimulate development of tools and technologies to facilitate use of ICTs by people with limited literacy skills and whose mother tongue is not English
			Develop evaluation methods to strengthen the voice of the disadvantaged in policy processes

(continued)

Annex 3. Concluded.

Lead organizations involved in national ICT policy-making and basic policy instruments	ICT policy objectives and priorities	Progress in implementation	Challenges for policy-making and gaps in existing policy framework	Treatment of social objectives, particularly gender issues	Recommendations from Acacia country-strategy reports
Uganda					
Ministry of Works, Transportation and Communications	Upgrade and expand the telecommunications network infrastructure to more effectively deliver new services, increase geographical distribution and coverage of the network, increase telephone density, and serve unmet customer demand, including that in rural communities	Restructuring of the telecommunications industry, including privatization and licencing of multiple operators, has made good progress; new regulator, the Uganda Communications Commission, has been established	Lack of coordination across decision-making bodies	TSPA does not explicitly identify any groups for special treatment within rural communities	Facilitate multistakeholder national forum
Ministry of Information	Provide for stable, orderly regulation of the telecommunications sector to attract private investment and facilitate government withdrawal from ownership of telecom operators	Pilot projects for telecentres have been set up in rural communities	Emphasis on the network component of ICTs		Support the establishment of a fund for rural communication development
Uganda Communications Commission			Insufficient consultation with a broad range of stakeholders		Support the establishment of a policy framework for introduction of telecentres as a way to extend ICTs to rural areas

TSPA (in 1997)	Existing urban bias in network coverage requires very large investment and policy intervention	Pilot new technologies and support content creation and applications to use ICTs for trade, commerce, and education
Uganda Communications Act (in 1997)	Does not address some of the contradictions in present restructuring plan	

Source: Based on primary and secondary data, Acacia country studies, and interviews with ITU and UNCTAD officials.

Note: CIUEM Computing Centre of Eduardo Mondiane University; ICT, information and communication technology; ITU, International Telecommunications Union; NGO, nongovernmental organization; NTCC, National Telecommunications Co-ordinating Committee; SATRA, South African Telecommunications Regulatory Authority; TDM, Telecommunications Department of Mozambique; TSPA, Telecommunication Sector Policy Announcement; UNCTAD, United Nations Conference on Trade and Development.

Chapter 4

APPLICATION OF ICTS IN AFRICA'S AGRICULTURAL SECTOR: A GENDER PERSPECTIVE

Hilda Munyua

This chapter analyzes some of the key problems facing women in the agricultural sector and the efforts made to address communication issues and other problems. Various needs assessments have been conducted for women in the agricultural sector. This chapter also identifies some needs and reports on how these are being met. In most African countries, investment in information and communication technologies (ICTs) has focused mainly on the urban areas, although ICTs have a great potential to help meet the needs of rural female farmers and to benefit rural communities. This chapter presents a few examples of activities already undertaken and looks at some policy implications of the broader use of ICTs.

For the purposes of this chapter, *gender* does not refer to women; rather, it refers to the socially or culturally established roles of women, men, and children, which means they can share roles and complement one another. Understanding the roles of both men and women gives a complete picture of the agricultural production system.

Background

Agriculture is the mainstay of most African economies and occupies a pivotal position in the development of the continent. Despite the importance of agriculture, improvements in this sector have been uneven and on the whole disappointing, with a current development growth rate of 1.7% (Diom 1996). This slow rate of development has been compounded in the recent past by recurrent crop failures, a high human population (expected to reach 300 million by 2000 [Diom 1996]) economic recession, and escalating external debt. These factors — coupled with agricultural mismanagement, escalating costs of production, and difficulties with the structural-adjustment programs of the World Bank and the International Monetary Fund — have led to food scarcity and insecurity. All this implies an urgent need to address the issues retarding agricultural production in Africa, especially in sub-Saharan Africa (SSA). This requires an understanding of how the farming systems work in practice.

In any farming system, it is important to recognize the various roles of men, women, youth, and children. In Africa, women constitute 70% of the agricultural workforce and produce 80% of the region's food (Gellen 1994a; Blumberg 1994). Their important contribution to local and national economies is not, however, reflected in the resources allocated to the peri-urban and rural female food producers.

Female and male farmers in Africa face similar problems, but they affect the female farmer more adversely. The major problems include weak extension services; nonadoption of technologies; low status (and therefore noninvolvement) in decision- and policy-making; varied and heavy workloads; poor access to credit; and lack of access to education, training, agricultural inputs, supportive policies, or (as emphasized in this chapter) information to improve farming.

Information is essential for facilitating agricultural and rural development and bringing about social and economic change. Unfortunately, most African countries have not devoted adequate attention to providing their citizens with access to information, especially in rural areas, where 70–80% of the African population lives (Youdeowei et al. 1996). Information initiatives should, therefore, be geared to strengthening the grass roots, with special emphasis on women, and be developed in places without public libraries or other information resources. This may be achieved by setting up functional, integrated information systems in rural and peri-urban communities, which would bring in new and diverse resources to enable women to access information.

Traditional and modern ICTs can be used concurrently to speed up the circulation of information. In many African countries, ICTs are used to greater and lesser degrees in drama, dance, folklore, group discussions, meetings, exhibitions, demonstrations, visits, farmers' field schools, agricultural shows, radio, television, video, and print. Solar, satellite, and fibre-optic technologies are now in use for computers, telephones, and facsimile. Telecentres have been established in villages. Where appropriate, rural female farmers can tap these resources and access information using the new ICTs, such as e-mail, the World Wide Web, electronic networks, teleconferencing, and distance-learning tools. Information can empower rural female farmers to participate in decision-making, exchange ideas with others in developed and developing countries, and improve the quality of life of the people of Africa.

ICTs have changed education, training, service delivery, and people's lives in the more wealthy nations and in the research sectors of some developing nations, which pioneered the use of ICTs in less wealthy nations. In South Africa, ICTs have also been used in rural communities. In South Africa, Senegal, Uganda, and other countries, ICTs have created employment, helped to develop telecommunication and networking opportunities in rural areas, and acted as delivery vehicles for distance training and education.

Key problems facing women in the agricultural sector and possible solutions

Africa's food producers, who are mainly rural women, have been "invisible" and resource starved for a long time. They have been described as "the lifeline of society" and have employed a number of strategies to ensure household food security (Oniang'o 1996). Most of these women, especially in SSA, face such problems as lack of supportive policies, weak extension services, constraints in land tenure and ownership, limited access to credit, restricted access to training and education, heavy workloads, and nonadoption of new agricultural technologies.

Lack of supportive policies

The rural woman farmer is often depicted as an exploitable "tool" or "instrument" and as "weak" and "ignorant." Traditions, customs, cultures, and religions in Africa have also rendered women second-class citizens. Ruth Meena, as quoted by Matsebula (1997, p. 5), pointed out that

> although the statutory laws of Swaziland as in most African countries *prima facie* permit women to hold public office, their impact can be, and frequently is, reduced by customary and religious practices which continue to define the role and place of women in society.

Women's lack of involvement in decision-making and policy formulation has impeded development in the agricultural sector and has resulted in decision-makers and policymakers neglecting most of the key issues affecting women. Policymakers, planners, and donors should learn from Julius Nyerere, former President of Tanzania, who remarked in 1987 that

A person does not walk very far or very fast on one leg. How can we expect half the people to be able to develop a nation? Yet the reality is that women are usually left aside when development needs are discussed.

IFAD (1989, p. 3)

As a result, the following have occurred:

- Women in many African countries are organizing themselves into groups and movements to press for their causes at all levels.

- Governments are beginning to appreciate the plight of marginalized women and to consider gender issues. Emphasis is now on women's issues, which are deliberately included in development plans.

- The Advocates for African Food Security (a coalition of nongovernmental organizations [NGOs], United Nations agencies, and governments) is empowering women to participate in policy-making and policy implementation (Engo-Tjega 1994).

- The World Bank has pressed for more women to work in high-profile and decision-making positions (World Bank 1996). These women, along with other women in decision-making positions at all levels in the agricultural and development sectors, are expected to influence policies and incorporate gender considerations into agricultural policies. When women gain more autonomy and take responsibility, they will be more critical of the structures that discriminate against them and suppress development. They will begin to ask questions. Sustainable agricultural production requires the full participation of rural female farmers. Women therefore need the enabling processes to allow them to access the relevant information.

- African Women Leaders in Agriculture and the Environment is addressing the lack of women's representation in policy arenas and playing a catalytic role by training professional women and supporting professional women's efforts to reach female farmers (Blumberg 1992; Winrock International 1997).

Weak extension services

In most African countries, agricultural extension services, which are central to economic-development programs, are nonexistent, weak, or unsatisfactory. Unfortunately, even where extension services are available, the content and mode of service delivery are often insensitive to the needs of female farmers (Dunn 1995). As pointed out at the 1985 Women's Conference in Nairobi, new technologies are usually introduced to help men (IFAD 1989). The basic assumption is that women carry out only menial tasks, such as weeding, thinning, and transplanting, and that the traditional tools they use, such as hoes, are sufficient to enable them to step up and sustain productivity. Such generalizations are, however, ill-conceived. Men and women have different perspectives and experiences, and they must work together to realize the maximum benefit.

Blumberg (1994) observed that only 7% of extension time and resources is devoted to African female farmers and that only 7% of extension agents are female. This gender inequity, coupled with poor extension packages, inadequate delivery approaches, and cultural and religious barriers, is further compounded by transportation and communication problems. Female extensionists work more effectively with female farmers (Dunn 1995). This is particularly true in Muslim communities. Hence, extension services need to train and recruit more women. Consequently,

- Some countries, such as Nigeria, have adopted affirmative-action initiatives — hiring more female extension agents to work with rural female farmers and retraining male extension agents to work with women (Pena et al. 1996); and

- The International Fund for Agricultural Development (IFAD) has worked to increase the number of female extension workers and female trainers and trainees throughout the projects it finances in Africa (IFAD 1989).

Constraints in land tenure and ownership

Although a generalization would be unwarranted, in most East and southern African countries, men own or control the land. In Kenya, a girl can use her father's land, but she cannot own it. In Zimbabwe, women cannot own land in community or resettlement areas. In Swaziland, Tanzania, and Uganda, women have the right to use national land but cannot own it (Martin 1993). Thus, in most land-tenure systems, a woman has no right to introduce appropriate, affordable agricultural technologies without her husband's or family's approval. The men, who are often employed in the nonagricultural sector, may not be aware of new or improved farming methods or crop diversification and be in no position to offer advice. As a result of this situation, unsustainable farming methods persist, despite declining production and increasing postharvest losses.

Obsolete customary marriage and inheritance laws, traditions, and cultures need to be reviewed to redress this problem and moderate the current discrimination against women. Whereas African traditionalists may view the act of changing traditional practices as a failure to adhere to cultural norms, women need equal rights to land and support and an opportunity to manage farms (Harrison 1996).

Women's ownership of land may not be in itself the panacea for the low agricultural productivity observed in central and most of southern Malawi, where a matrilineal family system operates. In that society, women have more rights over the land, and they work and distribute it at their discretion. But the same problems prevail in Malawi as elsewhere — in agricultural production, postharvest storage, and marketing. Most of the men migrate from the land to find employment in other sectors, as this system does not encourage them to invest in agriculture (Phiri, personal communication, 1997[1]). Examples of what some countries have done are summarized below:

- The Kenya government has attempted to redress the inequitable situation by advocating joint family decision-making on land use and disposal through the state-controlled land boards. To ensure that women are consulted during decision-making, the government insists that wives participate in deliberations to decide which local community leaders or elders will be seconded to the land boards.

- In Mozambique, the movement to redress the imbalance was spearheaded by the new National Farmers Union (NFU). This is an association of about 430 local cooperatives and farmers' groups, led by a woman grass-roots leader. NFU lobbies for farmers and provides them with training in leadership, management, and marketing. The main objective of NFU, however, is to press the government to issue land-ownership deeds to rural women. Despite the expected resistance from the male-dominated bureaucracy, the union has assisted about 95% of its members to secure deeds of ownership (Lima 1994).

---

[1] G. Phiri, Malawian scientist, CAB International, Nairobi, Kenya, personal communication, Dec 1997.

From these examples, it should be apparent that female farmers in rural Africa need information on land rights, which should be communicated using appropriate technologies so that women will know their rights and know where to go for help. Women need to share success stories and functional models so that they can learn from one another, particularly where governments have not done enough.

Limited access to credit

As a result of the land-tenure laws in place in various African countries, deeds of ownership are often issued to men, which leaves women without the most common collateral — land. Therefore, credit facilities for women are needed, not only to foster their independence, improve their lives, and give them a sense of ownership (Creevey 1996), but also to enable them to buy basic agricultural inputs, such as fertilizers and seeds and introduce new agricultural technologies.

The situation is changing in a number of African countries. Women are organizing themselves in groups to obtain credit from institutions such as IFAD, the United Nations Development Fund for Women (UNIFEM), self-help women's groups, and credit cooperatives. For example,

- In the Gambia, the Women in Service Development Organisation Management was founded by some 30 female leaders and now has 60 000 active members, who are eligible for training, in addition to being able to obtain loans from a revolving fund (Senghore and Bojang-Sissoho 1994).

- The Kenya Women's Finance Trust, founded in 1981, has been giving credit to rural women. To date, it "has not had a single defaulter" (Gellen 1994a, p. 6). Experience has also shown that measures to increase women's income enhance the welfare and status of entire families. In addition, enabling women to contribute directly to the upkeep of the family instils in them a sense of independence and enhances their confidence and self-esteem.

- In South Africa, the recently restructured Land Bank provides new financial services to the agricultural community. According to GCIS (1998), rural women can borrow as little as 250 ZAR (in 1999, 6.105 South African rand [ZAR] = 1 United States dollar [USD]).

Restricted access to training and education

Most rural women, who are often poor, lack both the means and the opportunity to obtain a formal education. When training opportunities for rural agricultural producers arise, they mostly go to the men, who usually already have some formal education, although it is more important to expand and enhance the production knowledge of the principal workers — the women. Some women also opt out of training programs because of cultural, religious, or family pressures (Blumberg 1992). It is critical that African countries create a pool of female trainers of trainers, well versed in participatory training methods. These women would then be able to prepare training packages and programs appropriate and accessible to rural women. Such trainers would, of necessity, consolidate their knowledge and skills to share their experiences with other female farmers.

Girls at primary and secondary schools and colleges need career guidance to sensitize them to the crucial role of women in agricultural development and thereby encourage them to enrol in agricultural programs. This would ensure a steady rise in the number of women managing the various agricultural sectors. Schools, colleges, and universities must therefore offer gender training.

The following are some of the many groups offering agricultural and literacy training in Africa:

- Winrock International trains African women in leadership, with programs aimed to equip rural women to understand and cope with the changes wrought by economic liberalization and the new technologies (Winrock International 1997).

- The All-African Council of Churches has launched projects similar to those of Winrock International in several countries, including Kenya and Zimbabwe. These are projects to teach rural women about economic issues and agricultural policies and equip them with practical skills in management and accounting (Gellen 1994b).

- Some African governments have also participated in projects to empower women. The Nigerian government, for example, initiated a program to offer gender-issues retraining for home economists, who are themselves farmers. This program started in Imo state but has since spread to all the other states of Nigeria (Blumberg 1994).

These projects have been very successful in empowering women to explore and participate actively in debates on farming issues in their areas. A more significant impact is expected to follow when a "critical number" have been trained. Training programs and educational materials successfully used elsewhere can be made accessible to other stakeholders within and outside the country to train more women and harness a greater multiplier effect. Electronic technologies, such as those used in the World Bank's African Virtual University pilot project, may be adapted for use among rural farmers — an African "virtual farmers' field school."

Heavy workloads

Apart from being agricultural producers, women are also responsible for domestic chores; the family's education, nutrition, and health; parenting; and meeting the household requirements for fuelwood and water. UNIFEM has worked to reducing this workload, recommending labour-saving devices such as water tanks, which would reduce the time women spend fetching water and free up some time to become involved in development initiatives or engage in recreational activities. In the Gambia, for example, women have received credit to buy small, diesel-powered grinding mills. These reduce the time the women spend processing food from 4 hours to 5 minutes (Gellen 1994a). Where tradition and culture allow, women and men should share household and community chores to give women more time for agricultural issues.

The questions that beg to be addressed are the following: How many rural women know about these time-saving technologies? Are such technologies appropriate, affordable, sustainable, and useful to other rural African women? Can such information be made available to a wider audience in the peri-urban or rural African environment? If these conditions are met, then ICTs can play a major role in creating awareness, enhancing information exchange, and ultimately enabling women to adopt technologies with the potential to bring positive change.

Nonadoption of new agricultural technologies

As already mentioned, the general picture of growth in African agriculture is grim. Despite the technological advances in irrigation, crop varieties, agroforestry, and fertilizers, most technologies do not reach female farmers, as they receive no information about them. Most rural farmers are illiterate and poor and do not adopt new technologies because they lack knowledge and cash. Future growth must come from yield increases, achieved through the use of improved seeds and other planting materials and better agronomic practices and harvesting and processing techniques. Although there is no general rule about it, in some situations where a man leads the household, the wife can say little about the decision to adopt a new agricultural technology, and men make most such decisions.

These men have higher levels of education and more time, and they control the income generated by the farm. Female farmers will have to be empowered to take more control and manage the farm. Women will need access to credit and training on new and appropriate technologies. Also, agricultural researchers should do more adaptive research to ensure that the new technologies are suitable for the female farmers' agroecological zones and management constraints.

Information needs of women

Women in rural areas have very little access to information. They are mostly poor, illiterate, and unable to afford even the very most basic forms of ICTs, such as radios and telephones. Nevertheless, rural women actively seek and disseminate information. So ICTs must be appropriate to enable women to gain access to information efficiently and cost-effectively. Gender considerations have, however, not received the attention they deserve in the design and use of information services or in the application of ICTs. We must identify the types of information required to meet the needs women express, to determine the information gaps, and to select the ICTs and services to best close these gaps.

Meeting the information needs of rural female farmers

The lack of reliable and comprehensive information for rural female farmers is a major hindrance to agricultural development. They require information on agricultural inputs; market prices; transportation systems; product potential; new environmentally sound production techniques and practices; new agricultural technologies; new markets; food processing and preservation; decision-making processes; the resource base; trade laws; and trends in food production, demand, and processing. Women also need to exchange indigenous knowledge. However, most available local information is packaged in a raw form and therefore difficult to access or use (Paquot and Berque 1996). The situation is compounded because women do not know where to find this information. Moreover, current mass media and communication systems have not been used to maximum effect in development. Information should be accessible to female farmers at selected sites, with various ICTs to facilitate easy access to relevant information and information exchange.

Available data on women's contribution to agriculture are unreliable and out of date. We need to systematically identify the information needs of the rural and peri-urban women in various communities, countries, and regions, as their needs are varied and diverse. Very few studies have assessed the information needs of women in agriculture, but most of these studies show that a great demand for information remains unmet. The following are some of the few needs-assessment surveys conducted in this area:

- In Nigeria, a study was conducted (using questionnaires) in Oyo state to determine the information needs of women in agriculture. The response rate of the study was 80% (Oladokun 1994). The study showed that women were eager to express their views and that their information needs were similar to those of the male farmers. The study further revealed that the female farmers were more likely to employ modern farming methods and that their information needs were far from satisfied. The respondents wanted information on all farming activities, including loan schemes, local market prices, export prices, price of raw materials, credit, cooperation, and the technical, social, and commercial aspects of farming. According to this study, the prominent communication channels used to disseminate this information were informal. The major sources of information were personal contacts and cooperative society. Documentary sources were mostly unavailable, and Oladokun consulted personal correspondence, followed by technical reports from the extension unit and newspaper articles.

- The Environmental Liaison Centre International (ELCI) held a workshop in 1997 to assess the information and communication needs of Kenyan NGOs and community-based organizations (CBOs) (ELCI 1997). ELCI invited the coordinators of the information and communication exchange network from Tanzania and Uganda to share the experiences of these countries, which had already held similar workshops. Other such workshops were organized in Zambia and Zimbabwe. A good number of these organizations work with rural women.

To avoid duplication of effort and to optimize the use of scarce resources, stakeholders should work together to ensure that women's information needs are met. The stakeholders include governments, donors, development organizations, NGOs, CBOs, and the private sector. Information products developed for farmers or women's groups in other developing countries can be adapted to suit the needs of these groups and then disseminated to other rural communities.

Some African countries, such as Ghana, Mozambique, and Uganda, have to a certain extent come to recognize the importance of a reliable telecommunications infrastructure and its role in empowering rural communities to participation in social and economic growth. It is therefore necessary to identify suitable ICTs to best serve their needs.

The target communities and beneficiaries

The main beneficiaries of better access to information in the agricultural sector would include the following:

- *Rural female farmers* — Women are the ultimate targets and need information to empower them to be more productive and to escape marginalization.

- *Women's groups and their leaders* — Women's groups have helped one another in cultivation, thatching, and other activities. Their leaders need training and information to be better representatives. Once empowered with information, they can determine how best to "sow the seed" among female farmers.

- *Farmers' organizations and unions* — Farmers' organizations and unions (including trade unions) work closely with people at the grass roots and need information to more effectively represent farmers.

- *School girls and youth groups* — Young men and women, who will be the future leaders, decision-makers, and farmers, need to learn about ICTs early in life to be aware of their potential to enhance development and improve job prospects in the future.

- *Media women* — Women working in the media should be aware of the agricultural-information needs of women generally so that the media can repackage and target the relevant information. Media women themselves need ICTs to tap into other media networks, such as Womenet: this is a fax network for media women that disseminates news around the world.

- *Extension and research services* — We need to bridge the researcher–extensionist–farmer gap to ensure that feedback from farmers goes to researchers and that new technologies are appropriate and meet the most important needs of farmers.

- *Religious, national, and international organizations with agricultural-development programs* — NGOs and CBOs play a valuable role supplementing government development efforts by working directly with rural communities and must have comprehensive, up-to-date information to enable them to capture, document, and disseminate indigenous knowledge in simple terms.

- *Government and national, regional, and international institutions* — Governments and institutions need to be aware of the activities of the other players and the needs and priorities of each other's countries and regions to know what types of collective action to take for the benefit of all. Knowledge can help them to develop more pragmatic programs and projects.

The potential of ICTs to meet the information needs of women

The number of ICT workshops and conferences taking place all over Africa and the world indicates how important these technologies are to development. They have transformed information processes everywhere, and technological advances have reduced the world to a "global village," unbounded by language, distance, or culture. The emerging electronic-communication networks will no doubt offer several new channels for the exchange of information and numerous opportunities for the rural woman farmer. The value of information is increasing, and many African countries, such as Mozambique, South Africa, and Uganda, are gaining a much greater appreciation of the "information culture."

Information is of limited use, however, unless we package and communicate it appropriately. Appropriate, fast, diverse, comprehensive, and low-cost ICTs can accelerate food production in the continent and bring the "invisible African woman" into the limelight. Zijp (1994) presented a table with an overview of information technologies and their representative applications, requirements, advantages, disadvantages, and costs. The choice of technology and communication medium largely depends, however, on telecommunications infrastructure available and the user's background.

The choice of ICTs should be driven by needs, not technology, and feedback should be obtained on an ongoing basis to assess the users' satisfaction or dissatisfaction and the technology's impacts. Female farmers need to become sensitive to differences in ICTs to appreciate their potential to increase agricultural productivity. As Giovanetti and Bellamy (1996) pointed out, illiterate farmers also require repackaged and audiovisual information products. An information officer may have to guide users to the appropriate sources and medium of information. The essential features of various ICTs are examined below.

Traditional and modern ICTs

Radio

In Africa, the radio plays a major role in delivering agricultural messages. Along with the newspaper, radio is one of the main sources of information for rural women. The media can do more to circulate information to rural female farmers and should include time for debate and feedback. The findings of a study on rural radio listening in the Meru, Nithi, and Tharaka districts of Kenya indicated a penetration of 69% among rural households. But men owned 80% of the radios. Listenership patterns indicated that women preferred programs containing easily understood, interesting, and relevant information (Morgan 1993). The following are examples of organizations involved in the production of radio and audiovisual programs for farmers in Africa:

- The Technical Centre for Agricultural and Rural Co-operation (CTA) has a program to support rural radio and development of audiovisual aids. CTA works with many individuals and institutions circulating information to farmers in Africa, Asia, and the Pacific.

- The Farm Radio Network (FRN), based in Harare, Zimbabwe, and its partner, the Developing Countries Farm Radio Network, in Toronto, Canada, have had great success in Africa. This service broadcasts programs developed by ministries of agriculture and agricultural institutions for women, youth, and extension agents on training and education in health, nutrition, and agriculture. FRN pays particular attention to the needs of rural farmers in East and southern Africa and provides up-to-date practical information on agriculture and health. The network also relies on "rural communicators," who translate current research findings into local languages and disseminate and broadcast them in response to the listeners' expressed needs.

- The Union of National Radio and Television Broadcasting of Africa, a continental organization, is dedicated to developing all aspects of broadcasting and plans to pool together relevant programs for female farmers and redistribute them to local radio and television stations (Youdeowei et al. 1996).

Television

Television would be a good communication medium for African female farmers. Owing to language barriers, shortage of electricity, and the high costs of television, however, it has had little success in disseminating information to these farmers. According to Alfaro (personal communication, 1997[2]), who is the coordinator of the Sustainable Development Networking Programme (SDNP) in Mozambique, television in that country is broadcast mostly in Portuguese. But not all Mozambicans, especially not those in the rural areas, understand Portuguese. Scheduling is also very important if television and radio programs targeted to female farmers are to have an impact. Listenership patterns of the target group must be considered in establishing an appropriate schedule of transmission.

Audiovisual media

Audiovisual media are popular with illiterate rural women, and these media give rural farmers an opportunity to see and discuss complex agricultural techniques before using them. Audiovisual technology also improves mental retention, and for this reason educators are making increasing use of videos, television programs, films, slides, and pictures, particularly in training sessions.

Print technology

The print medium holds great potential for the women who can read. Urban and rural newspapers, posters, pamphlets, and booklets have all been used successfully in the past. The United Nations Educational, Scientific and Cultural Organization (UNESCO) supports a very successful rural-newspaper program in Kenya. In many African countries where there are national agricultural information centres, including Ethiopia, Ghana, Uganda, and Zambia, relevant information has been appropriately repackaged in pamphlets, posters, booklets, handbooks, videos, films, cassettes, and radio programs. Such packages have proven very popular in rural farming communities. They are in some cases translated into appropriate local

---

[2] T. Alfaro, National Coordinator, SDNP, Maputo, Mozambique, personal communication, Dec 1997.

languages, based on user demand. However, most countries need to strengthen these centres and run them sustainably. Some of these centres, such as the Agricultural Information Centre in Kenya, used to be run using project funds, and these centres collapsed after their projects wound up. Some of their equipment needs replacement or repair, and their government budgets fall far short of their requirements.

Facsimile technology

Communicating agricultural information will remain a problem in geographically isolated rural areas or low-population rural areas without the "critical numbers" to warrant heavy investment in electronic communications such as e-mail and the Internet. In some of these situations, fax technology can help. Telecentres can carry relevant information and repackage it to meet the information needs of specific women's groups. Women need, for example, market information or information on how to grow a specific crop or control particular pests. This information can be further distributed by fax, postal service, or other ICT.

E-mail

Most rural areas have no information resources. An e-mail system would enable many women and intermediary agencies working with rural farmers to exchange ideas, transmit data, access information, and communicate it to a wider audience. E-mail would ensure the rapid transfer of farming technologies from research station to farming community and feedback from farming community to research station. As well, e-mail would make mail delivery faster and help to contact farmers in remote rural areas. In addition, it would make responses to queries more spontaneous and timely and provide cost-effective dissemination of new information and multiple copies of reports or other documents. Information about daily market prices might be transmitted to farmers through e-mail, provided at a central location, and perhaps disseminated more widely by NGOs, CBOs, extension workers, etc., with the radio or other media. However, e-mail technology requires a good power supply, a reliable and affordable telecommunications system, and a well-trained staff to assist end-users and maintain equipment.

Discussion lists (listservs)

African female farmers' groups and other individual farmers and youth groups in developing or developed countries should have discussion lists, or listservs, for discussion of the female farmers' common interests. With this technology, messages arrive at a mail server, which distributes them to all members on the list.

Listservs can function to disseminate information on commodity market prices, new agricultural technologies, and the means to control new disease outbreaks. This technology can benefit both buyers and sellers — whether individuals, groups, or cooperatives — and indicate what products are available, where they can be found, and their costs. This would provide farmers with a competitive edge over brokers or dealers. Discussion lists can facilitate feedback from farmers. Female farmers visiting another country or farm can discuss their experiences, opinions, problems, or progress in putting what they have learned into practice. This can stimulate regular discussion and debate and provide a forum for rural female farmers to express their views. Listservs can also help decision- and policymakers to better appreciate the needs of rural female farmers. A listserv can act as a question-and-answer service for farmers or enable them to inject their own point of view.

Local field staff and farmers harbour a lot of useful information, which can be tapped and disseminated using e-mail or a listserv. Diverse stakeholders who have otherwise worked independently on similar issues can work as a multidisciplinary team and build on their complementary strengths.

Newsgroups

Subscribers to e-mail newsgroups can select types of news to meet their interests. This service, offered free of charge by news servers, can give farmers a forum for discussing a wide range of subjects. Nyirenda (personal communication[3]) noted that Malawi currently has many loan schemes but that some borrowers have no information on feasible investments. Newsgroups can also provide a forum for disseminating ideas on constructive small-business projects, and rural telecentres can also act as information source points. This service can help to disseminate information on specific topics of interest to female farmers, such as new technologies, agronomic practices, soil-conservation techniques, pest outbreaks and methods for combatting them, and market prices. A newsgroup might be designed to work in the same way as the "Try It Yourself" section in the Kenya Institute of Organic Farming's *Foes of Famine Newsletter*. In this section, farmers describe their indigenous agricultural techniques. Other farmers from all over Africa are then encouraged to try out the technique and give their feedback through the newsletter. Researchers eventually visit the farms to validate the technique, carry out on-station trials, and disseminate their findings through the same newsletter. With a

---

[3] P. Nyirenda, Head, Department of Physics and Electronics, Chancellor College, University of Malawi, and National Coordinator, SDNP, Malawi, personal communication, Dec 1997.

newsgroup, such information might also be disseminated to many more farmers and feedback might be conveyed from farmers, not only in Africa, but also in Asia and Latin America.

File-transfer protocol

File-transfer protocol is a service designed to send and receive data files and programs across a network. Using this service, intermediary centres in the rural areas would be able to access and transmit text files, images, documents, and pictures relevant to agricultural-development programs.

The Internet

The Internet has grown to be the world's most important communication medium. It is a reasonably inexpensive, fast, two-way medium and a powerful tool for storage, retrieval, and dissemination of information. It is also good for publishing. The Internet can introduce new information resources and open new communication channels for rural farmers (Richardson 1996).

The Internet can increase literacy and agricultural productivity. We might develop products such as an African virtual farmers' field school and make it accessible to female farmers with no formal training in agriculture. A traditional farmers' field school requires a group of farmers to assemble on a farm and meet with their facilitators, but a virtual farmers' field school would permit meetings on the Internet, in "cyberspace." Farmers would receive their training at telecentres or wherever the facilities were made available, with materials and tutoring supplied through the World Wide Web.

Admittedly, not all learning can take place at a distance; however, this technology would permit highly qualified facilitators to simultaneously meet farmers from various developing countries. Courses would be transmitted by satellite from the developing regions of Africa, Asia, and Latin America or from the developed regions, using a programed timetable. This service might also link community telecentres in Africa and provide for South–South dissemination of indigenous knowledge, resources, ideas, experiences, and success stories. Web pages of agricultural stakeholders might be published to help avoid duplication of effort and to enhance cooperation.

According to Jensen (1998a), an Internet consultant, 16 countries in Africa had full access to the Internet in 1996, but in only 5 of these countries was this service available outside the capital city. Today, most African capitals (about 49) are connected, and more than 11 African countries have Internet service in rural areas. Almost all the remaining African capitals plan to have full Internet facilities before the end of the year. Communities need the Internet. Internet strategies should be "developed in conjunction with intended beneficiaries and stakeholders" (Richardson 1996, p. i). NGOs, CBOs, extension departments, associations, and unions serving rural farmers can take advantage of the technology, even where the farmers are unable to directly harness it. These organizations can carry out "web mining" and repackage and disseminate critical information for their rural stake-holders, using other appropriate technologies.

Electronic conferencing or teleconferencing

Teleconferencing can enable rural and peri-urban women's groups and leaders to participate in conferences and have virtual discussions with experts, without having to travel to cities or go abroad. This technology can also enable women's representatives to express their informed opinions and participate in decision-making and policy formulation.

Networking

Networking is an informal system. It enables people with common interests or concerns to exchange information with one another or develop professional contacts. It involves establishing contacts and encouraging reciprocal exchange of information and voluntary collaboration (Starkey 1997).

Networking has the potential to improve the quality of life and has become crucial to enhancing access to information. Networking enables pooling and sharing of resources and has the potential to disseminate information around the community, country, region, or abroad. Local networks, such as the Farm Information Network – East and Southern Africa (FINESA), have been successfully established to access vital information, and more such networks would be desirable. Some members of FINESA in Zimbabwe have requested scripts in local languages to ensure a wider readership (Vogtle 1997). Much more has been done in networking in the research sector in Africa. Abegaz and Levey (1996) described a research network that links five universities. Rural female farmers or their intermediaries can tap into such networks and have access to critical agricultural information to enhance agricultural development.

CD-ROM technology

CD-ROM technology has a high storage capacity, and it is fast, robust, and user friendly. Hence, it is an excellent medium for storing and disseminating full-text documents and training materials for rural areas without telecommunications infrastructure.

Several agricultural databases are available on CD-ROM. The main ones are CAB Abstracts from CAB International (CABI), Agris from the Food and Agriculture Organization of the United Nations (FAO), Agricola from the National Agricultural Library in the United States, Sesame from the Centre de coopération internationale en recherche agronomique pour le développement (centre for international cooperation on agronomic research for development), and Tropag and Rural from the Royal Tropical Institute. Case studies at universities in Tanzania, Zambia, and Zimbabwe have demonstrated widespread recognition of CD-ROM technology as a cost-effective, locally feasible medium for accessing databases (Levey 1994).

The American Association for the Advancement of Science has undertaken a 3-year program to promote access to information in SSA, with a special focus on CD-ROM technology. The pilot project has been successful, and it is clear that

> bibliographic databases on compact disc, coupled with reliable document delivery services, can satisfy the needs of many users. Although it took longer than anyone envisaged to build up demand, utilisation went up almost everywhere, and the project is considered to be a success story.
>
> Abegaz and Levey (1996, p. 3)

CABI recently launched its Crop Protection Compendium CD-ROM, a multimedia, user-friendly, PC-based product. It has text, maps, and illustrations on pests, crops, natural enemies of pests, and pest-control methods. This product allows the user to search, browse, or link to other databases.

Another example is The Essential Electronic Agricultural Library (TEEAL), which the Albert R. Mann Library (Cornell University), in association with the Rockefeller Foundation and cooperating publishers, launched in February 1999. This product contains, on 100 compact disks, the full-text images of 130 important scholarly journals (1993–96). TEEAL also includes the FAO's monograph series. Annual updates of the journals are to be released 1 year after publication (Cornell University 1998).

Products like these can be accessed anywhere and can be excellent tools for extension workers and farmers. Farmers can access CD-ROMs to find information on rearing animals, growing crops, or identifying pests or to look up prices of inputs and farm products.

Telecentres — a way forward

Telecentres, with ICTs and telecommunications facilities, were introduced in Scandinavia in the 1980s to address some of the problems of smaller and isolated communities. Users receive technical support and training, and community committees manage the centres. The concept has now spread to rural areas in Australia, Brazil, Canada, some European countries, South Africa, and the United States. Many of these centres are now self-sustaining (see Annex 8).

In Africa, rural telecentres are growing rapidly. They could provide all the above services, as well as collecting information from farmers and cooperatives on available products, local market prices, new crops, new technologies, and indigenous knowledge. This information could then be repackaged and disseminated more widely, using other communication technologies. Government information could be accessed at these centres via ICTs, such as e-mail and the Internet. This would promptly update farmers on prevailing government policies and new skills, techniques, and services. Via e-mail or other media, the farmers could then send their own views or requests for details or clarification to the appropriate department.

ICTs can provide farmers with guidance on where and when to sow, harvest, process, and market their produce to avoid having to off-load their goods at throw-away prices in the local markets, and buyers can use ICTs to determine prevailing market prices. ICTs will pave the way for dialogue among researchers, extensionists, and farmers in rural communities, enable female farmers to contribute to decision-making and policy formulation, and forge bridges between people in urban and rural communities. Other communication methods, such as meetings, conferences, and social gatherings, can be expected to complement the new services offered at telecentres, which may also become centres of business and community activity.

Planned and ongoing activities

In Africa, numerous current or planned initiatives rely on modern ICTs in social, economic, health, agricultural, and cultural development. Some of the organizations and countries involved in these initiatives and their activities are briefly described below.

United Nations Economic Commission for Africa

The United Nations Economic Commission for Africa (ECA) has taken the lead in helping African countries overcome their information and technological problems and launched the African Information Society Initiative (AISI) for this purpose. AISI is an action framework to build Africa's ICT infrastructure. It outlines the development of Internet nodes and services in Africa. Annexes 1 and 9 contain details of ECA's activities.

International Development Research Centre

The International Development Research Centre (IDRC) launched the Acacia Initiative (see Annex 2) in 1997, with the aim of empowering communities in SSA through the use of ICTs to facilitate access to information and thereby unblock economic and social development. The program covers policies, issues, ICTs, their application, and telecommunications infrastructure. Acacia has pilot projects in Mozambique, Senegal, South Africa, and Uganda. In Uganda, the initiative has set up three telecentres in rural areas. These pilot projects focus on the community and ensures a process of continuous learning. IDRC has also funded several other activities on electronic communications in Africa.

United Nations Development Programme

The SDNP of the United Nations Development Programme (UNDP) (see Annex 3) is an intersectoral network for exchanging vital information on and expertise in sustainable human development (SHD). The program has linked government organizations, NGOs, the private sector, universities, and individuals in about 40 developing countries (with 10 operational in Africa) through electronic and other networking links. SDNP is using ICTs (such as e-mail, electronic bulletin boards, fax, and phones) and posters and supports decision-makers and other stakeholders on SHD issues. It lays heavy emphasis on national capacity-building. At the joint regional workshop of SDNP and the Internet Initiative for Africa (IIA), in Maputo, Mozambique, in December 1997, these two organizations were challenged to pay greater attention to grass-roots communities and find ways to make their projects more sustainable after their project funding is complete.

IIA (see Annex 4) is a participatory initiative operating in 12 countries in SSA: Angola, Burkina Faso, Cape Verde, Chad, the Gambia, Mauritania, Namibia, Nigeria, São Tomé and Principe, Swaziland, Togo, and Zaire. It is working to improve access to reliable and up-to-date information for sound decision-making. The initiative aims to establish information and decision-support systems to enhance policy formulation throughout the SHD policy process, with use of the Internet to provide efficient and reliable service.

Food and Agriculture Organization of the United Nations

FAO has developed partnerships with other organizations and local people, and through these partnerships it has helped local people develop indigenous communication processes through the use of traditional ICTs, such as radio and video. The organization is in the process of developing an Internet approach for rural agricultural communities. In collaboration with the Department of Rural

Extension Studies at the University of Guelph, in Canada, it supported the Electronic Communication and Information Systems fact-finding mission (see Annex 5 for details) (Richardson 1996).

World Bank

The World Bank has launched its global Information for Development Programme (InfoDev). InfoDev has given rural dwellers a chance to access "tailor-made new technology." In rural Kenya, for example, InfoDev funds low-cost wireless telephone systems. In South Africa, it funds a computer network, giving the country's poorest townships access to basic information. As a result of InfoDev, cocoa and coffee growers in Côte d'Ivoire can dial London for commodity prices, and, in Cameroon, small businesses can use the Internet to sell their products abroad. InfoDev is funded by international financial institutions, governments, NGOs, and the private sector. Illiterate adults access the system with the help of their literate children (Lanfranco, personal communication, 1997[4]).

United Nations Educational, Scientific and Cultural Organization

UNESCO has established pilot multipurpose community telecentres in some countries, including Benin, Mali, Mozambique, Tanzania, and Uganda. The goal of these centres is to take the Internet beyond the capital cities. Centres of excellence have also been established in Gabon, Kenya, Senegal, Tunisia, and Zimbabwe, with the aim of providing a network for cooperative development, training programs, and support for building national centres of excellence. UNESCO started experimental rural centres in some Central and West African countries to advance knowledge, fight illiteracy, and ensure the circulation of ideas at all levels in rural areas. In addition, UNESCO established the Regional Informatics Network for Africa (see Annex 6).

United States Agency for International Development

The Leland Initiative of the United States Agency for International Development (USAID) targets 21 African countries, and its primary purpose is to disseminate the benefits of the Internet. In Uganda, USAID supports a project called Investment in Developing Export Agriculture, with the goal of improving rural people's income by expanding the production and marketing of selected crops and products

---

[4] S. Lanfranco, IDRC, Ottawa, ON, Canada, personal communication, 1997.

(Cochrane 1997[5]). The project established the Agribusiness Development Centre, a resource centre providing information to agribusiness firms and associations. It offers information on current market conditions, supply and demand, new product developments, future markets, and political events. The staff repackage information, tailor it to the needs of Uganda's agricultural export and investment sector, and disseminate it to subscribers by courier, fax, and postal service.

Environmental Liaison Centre International

ELCI's network is working to create a more sustainable world through a global process of sharing ideas, information, and experience with development in the environmental sector. The centre is planning electronic post offices to enable CBOs to use electronic communications (see Annex 7).

African agencies

In 1998, the Ministry of Food and Agriculture in Ghana was considering the development of electronic-commerce applications for small and medium-sized producers and exporters, in collaboration with national associations for nontraditional exports (handcrafts, peanuts, bananas, pineapples, etc.). A website would be developed to enable exporter–producers to publish information on their companies, production capacities, products, and prices. The website would allow exporters to promote their businesses and enhance their competitiveness (IICD 1998).

In Tanzania, Telecom Systems Ltd and the Computer Centre of the University of Dar es Salaam are planning a community telecentre project to use appropriate ICTs to develop networks for education, agriculture, health, and other development activities in remote urban and rural areas, where 85% of the population live. Five community telecentres were to be established in phase 1 of the project (IICD 1998).

Participating and implementing agencies

The many potential leaders and players among participating and implementing agencies range from donors, to regional and national organizations, to grass-roots organizations and leaders:

- The female leaders of the rapidly expanding number of women's groups, associations, unions, donor and development agencies, NGOs,

---

[5] Cochrane, J.A. 1997. Case study for the Integrated Pest Management Information Communications Workshop. AfricaLink, Arlington, VA, USA. Draft. 2 pp.

and CBOs could accelerate women's and girls' use of ICTs in agriculture. Female leaders could receive training or employment at telecentres and then serve as role models for other women and girls in their communities. These leaders could act as cost-effective vehicles for the dissemination of relevant information to many more rural female farmers.

- Donor and development organizations can participate in policy dialogue, provide skills in their areas of competence, and sponsor information-exchange forums for women, such as field days, workshops, exhibitions, and publications. Organizations such as CARE, which have been working with rural communities to improve their productivity and welfare, would also be good partners. Such organizations could share their experiences and the lessons learned. Similarly, organizations that have been working closely with female farmers or others in the agricultural sector would provide good links because of their experiences with their own projects. IFAD, for example, has supported many rural women's economic activities in Africa and has given full recognition to female farmers. The British Council is also actively involved in building information communities in Africa (see Annex 10).

- International bodies could complement the work of ongoing and planned initiatives, as these bodies have been involved in various activities that need to be systematically implemented for greater impact. These bodies include the FAO, which supports the improvement of agriculture and the betterment of the lives of rural people and has a historical and major role to play in helping rural communities realize the benefits of ICTs. The Consultative Group on International Agricultural Research and its agricultural research centres should participate, as they were pioneers in the adoption of modern ICTs in Africa and have useful lessons to impart. The Special Programme on African Agricultural Research collaborates with regional and national organizations to develop regional frameworks for action and would be useful in the role of a participating agency. The Technical Centre for Agricultural and Rural Co-operation (CTA), whose mission is to provide African, Caribbean, and Pacific countries with better access to information for their agricultural and rural development, initiated the Committees for Regional Agricultural Information Programmes and Strategies. These could contribute their wealth of information and experience in delivering information to rural communities, to avoid repeating past mistakes.

- Some of the regional bodies capable of playing a major role are the following:

    - Intergovernmental Authority on Development;

    - Institut du Sahel (institute of Sahel);

    - Association for Strengthening Agricultural Research in East and Central Africa (ASARECA);

    - Indian Ocean Commission (IOC), which developed a proposal for an integrated information program for agricultural and rural development in eastern Africa, with the support of CTA;

    - Southern African Centre for Cooperation in Agricultural and Natural Resources Research and Training (SACCAR), which developed a proposal for the Integrated Agricultural Information Programme for Southern Africa, with support from CTA; and

    - Conférence des responsables de recherche agricole en Afrique de l'Ouest et du Centre (conference of agricultural researchers in West and Central Africa), which has been working on a proposal like those of SACCAR, ASARECA, and IOC.

- Professional associations with potential in this area include the following:

    - International Association of Agricultural Information Specialists;

    - Association for Farming Systems Research Extension, which held its 1998 international symposium in South Africa; and

    - Other international, regional, and national associations.

Professional associations like these can bring together the various players, including those engaged in the production and dissemination of agricultural information.

- National agricultural research and extension systems and the private sector will also be key players in ensuring increased agricultural productivity.

Implications of policy for the broader use of ICTs

In a paper on policy constraints, Jensen (1997, p. 13) noted that the poor level of telecommunications facilities in Africa is due largely to policy factors and is "the most critical inhibiting element" in agricultural development. The prerequisites for female farmers to have access to, and benefit from, available information are the formulation of appropriate supportive policies and regulations to empower women, adequate resource allocations, telecommunications infrastructures, and the awareness of the potentials of ICTs. However, change cannot happen without political will and good governance.

African governments need to understand the importance of a communication infrastructure that reaches remote parts of every country. Progress is being made, and African leaders are committed to journeying into the information age. African ministers of communications met in Cape Town in February 1998 and mapped out programs to develop a rural telecommunications policy, a regulatory framework, and human resources (Naidoo 1998). However, women should have greater representation in policy-making bodies so they can press for the use of gender-inclusive language in agricultural, information, and telecommunications policies.

Governments will have to formulate appropriate policies and be committed to bringing policy discussions to the forefront, with the participation of all the stakeholders. At present, the regulations are rigid; telecommunication tariffs and import duties on information-technology equipment are high; and the economic planners fail to fully appreciate the role of information in transforming the economy. Also lacking in most African countries is a competitive environment to stimulate the provision of affordable services using modern ICTs. The need to liberalize markets to encourage competition cannot be overemphasized.

Technology standards also need to be harmonized to ensure compatibility and cooperation all over Africa and beyond. Policies must be formulated to

- Encourage adoption of ICTs;

- Reduce telecommunications costs;

- Ensure an adequately qualified and skilled workforce (including women) to operate and maintain the new technologies; and

- Give priority to the relevance and added value of the content.

Discussion, conclusion, and recommendations

Africa needs to use every available method to maximize the use of technologies to step up food production. In addition, governments in Africa need to agree on a general ICT strategy and help to implement it. Modern ICTs can promote agricultural development on a much greater scale than traditional ICTs can. E-mail and CD-ROMs have brought many benefits to urban communities in Africa, and recipients of services, including female farmers, cannot help but enter the information age. Telecentres in urban communities may serve as one-stop shops, where the rural population can use telephone, fax, and e-mail services and have access to resources from other locations, such as libraries and centres for distance learning, telemedicine, and agricultural and government information. However, conducive policies and the harmonious development of a reliable telecommunications infrastructure in rural areas are crucial to the realization of positive effects. The implementing agencies' approach to introducing telecentres must stimulate local participation, build awareness of the potential benefits of ICTs, support needs assessments, and help build a user base. To ensure that ICTs address women's needs and constraints, women must participate in the decision-making process used to set up the system.

Women carry out most of the work in rural areas. They therefore need to learn more technical and organizational skills and be at the centre of decision-making. This is why it is so important to keep rural women informed and provide avenues for them to reach consensus. Sustainable agricultural production requires the full participation of rural female farmers, and therefore mechanisms need to be in place to facilitate the communication process and allow the voices of rural female farmers to be heard. The challenges in rural areas will be to improve the accessibility of information and to increase the quality and quantity of information to be exchanged.

To ensure the relevance of African extension research, information on new agricultural technologies and market information should be repackaged in a format and language appropriate for rural women. Information must also be affordable. Undertaking this could create a number of jobs, reduce rural–urban migration, and reverse the brain drain in some African countries. Building skills to identify, write, and produce such repackaged information should be a priority for every African country.

Institution-strengthening and capacity-building are also important. Information officers who staff the community telecentres (preferably women) should have the skills to handle the available technologies. They should therefore receive adequate and relevant training to assist people visiting the telecentres. It is also important to note that a critical mass of staff is needed to make an impact and that the telecentres will require aggressive promotion.

The rural population, particularly women, will need exposure to new ICTs and training, if these technologies are to be used to enhance development. The elite rural women and some female leaders will require training in computers, information technology, and communication and management skills. It may initially take time to build up demand for modern ICTs, but this can be speeded up by creating awareness and instituting promotion campaigns, along with training. The retention of trained personnel needs to be addressed, and a monitoring and evaluation system is also needed.

To be sustainable, the use of modern ICTs as development tools must be introduced in response to the needs of rural female farmers and under the guidance of an ICT policy. All stakeholders will have to support this process and collaborate in it. All stakeholders should bear the operating and maintenance costs to ensure that the projects do not end up as "white elephants" when donor funding ceases.

Changing the land-tenure systems, adopting ICTs, providing training facilities, feasible financial services, information sources, and supportive policies, and allocating resources cannot individually solve all the problems of the rural female farmer. All the various approaches of the stakeholders must be integrated. This should be directed not only to empowering the agricultural producer but also to ensuring that increased productivity is sustainable. Rural female farmers need to be determined to solve their own problems, proactive in seeking solutions, and keen to adopt appropriate ICTs, rather than shying away from them.

The challenge to heads of state and government leaders will be to establish the political will and good governance to formulate policies to make ICTs more accessible. H. Norton, FAO Representative in Kenya, said that "only heads of state and government leaders are in a position to set policy for all sectors of their national economies. Only they have the clout" (Were 1996, p. 7). Fraser and Villet

(1994, p. 7) stated that "the use of communication no longer depends on the availability of technology: it depends on the will and decisions of policy makers to exploit its potential."

Development agencies, governments, and the private sector therefore need to work harmoniously to design projects for ICTs or incorporate ICT components into agricultural-development programs and projects in the rural areas. When deciding which communication medium or ICT to use, the program or project planner needs to consider the specific requirements of a given community.

References

Abegaz, B.M.; Levey, L.A. 1996. What price information? Priority setting in African universities. American Association for the Advancement of Science, Washington, DC, USA. 40 pp.

Blumberg, R.L. 1992. African women in agriculture: farmers, students, extension agents, chiefs. Winrock International Institute for Agricultural Development, Morrilton, AR, USA. Development Studies Paper. 43 pp.

——— 1994. Reaching Africa's "invisible" farmers. African Farmer, 11, 14–15.

Cornell University. 1998. The Essential Electronic Agricultural Library. Cornell University, Ithaca, NY, USA. 18 pp. Internet: teeal.cornell.edu

Creevey, L. 1996. Changing women's lives and work: an analysis of the impacts of eight microenterprise projects. Intermediate Technology Publications Ltd, London, UK. 228 pp.

CSIR (Council for Scientific and Industrial Research). CSIR: your technology partner for scientific and technological solutions. CSIR, Pretoria, South Africa. Internet: www.csir.co.za

Diom, B. 1996. The rural development challenges faced by ACP countries. In The role of information for rural development in ACP countries: review and perspectives. Proceedings of an international seminar, 12–16 Jun 1995, Montpellier, France. Technical Centre for Agricultural and Rural Cooperation, Wageningen, Netherlands.

Dunn, K. 1995. The busiest people in the world. Ceres, 27(4), 48–50.

ELCI (Environmental Liaison Centre International). 1997. The Kenya NGO/CBO information and communication needs assessment workshop (draft report), held 21–24 September, Nakuru, Kenya. ELCI, Nairobi, Kenya. 49 pp.

Engo-Tjega, R.B. 1994. Give women a place at the policy table. African Farmer, 11, 12–13.

Fraser, C.; Villet, J. 1994. Communication: a key to human development. Food and Agriculture Organization of the United Nations, Rome, Italy. 36 pp.

GCIS (Government Communication and Information System). 1998. The building has begun! Government's report to the nation. GCIS, Pretoria, South Africa. 47 pp.

Gellen, K. 1994a. Unleashing the power of women farmers. African Farmer, 11, 2–6, 42.

———— 1994b. Expanding women's economic knowledge. African Farmer, 11, 10-11.

Giovanetti, J-F.; Bellamy, M. 1996. New information technologies: which products, which technologies, which professions? *In* The role of information for rural development in ACP countries: review and perspectives. Proceedings of an international seminar, 12–16 Jun 1995, Montpellier, France. Technical Centre for Agricultural and Rural Cooperation, Wageningen, Netherlands. pp 157–179.

Harrison, P. 1996. The greening of Africa: breaking through in the battle for land and food. Academy Science Publishers, Nairobi, Kenya. 380 pp.

IDRC (International Development Research Centre). 1999. Acacia: studies and reports by categories. IDRC, Ottawa, ON, Canada. Internet: www.idrc.ca/acacia/stcat.htm

IFAD (International Fund for Agricultural Development). 1989. Women: the roots of rural development. IFAD, Rome, Italy. 22 pp.

IICD (International Institute for Communication and Development). 1998. E-journal research. IICD, The Hague, Netherlands. Internet: www.iicd.org/ejournal/

Jensen, M. 1997. Policy constraints to electronic information sharing in developing countries. The Internet (Nov–Dec), 13–15, 41.

———— 1998a. An overview of Internet connectivity in Africa. Association for Progressive Communications, San Francisco, CA, USA. Internet: www3.sn.apc.org/Africa/

———— 1998b. An overview of Internet connectivity in southern Africa. Paper presented at the Carl Duisberg Gesellschaft Workshop on HRD Needs in ICT Driven Economic Development, 26–29 Oct 1998, Pretoria, South Africa. Carl Duisberg Gesellschaft, Koln, Germany.

Levey, L.A., ed. 1994. CD-ROM for African research needs: some basic guidelines. American Association for the Advancement of Science, Sub-Saharan Africa Program, Washington, DC, USA. 76 pp.

Lima, T. 1994. Women's co-ops spur Mozambican farmers' union. African Farmer, 11, 16–17.

Martin, D.M. 1993. Laws and the impoverishment of women. World Bank, Washington, DC, USA. World Bank Information Sheet No. 1.

Matsebula, T. 1997. Constitution and right of women in society. The Swazi Observer: Yebo Weekend Observer Magazine, 20–21 Dec, p. 5.

Morgan, K.L. 1993. Research findings on rural radio listenership in Meru and Tharaka Nithi districts (Kenya). Agricultural Information Centre, Nairobi, Kenya. 42 pp.

Naidoo, J. 1998. The African connection: report of the African ministers of communications. Africa Telecom, Cape Town, South Africa. 15 pp.

Oladokun, S.O. 1994. An empirical study of information needs of women in agriculture (WIA) in Oyo State, Nigeria. IAALD Quarterly Bulletin, 39(4), 319–323.

Oniang'o, R.K. 1996. African women's strategies to advance household food security. *In* Turpin, J.; Lorentzen, L.A., ed., The gendered new world order: militarism, development and the environment. Routledge, New York, NY, USA. pp. 163–176.

Paquot, E. 1996. The role of information in rural development issues in ACP countries. *In* The role of information for rural development in ACP countries: review and perspectives. Proceedings of an international seminar, 12–16 Jun 1995, Montpellier, France. Technical Centre for Agricultural and Rural Cooperation, Wageningen, Netherlands. pp. 85–111.

Paquot, E.; Berque, P. 1996. Summary of the achievements of the CTA since the seminar "Montpellier, 1" 1984. *In* The role of information for rural development in ACP countries: review and perspectives. Proceedings of an international seminar, 12–16 Jun 1995, Montpellier, France. Technical Centre for Agricultural and Rural Cooperation, Wageningen, Netherlands. pp. 61–83.

Pena, C.; Webb, P.; Haddad, L. 1996. Women's economic advancement through agricultural change: a review of donor experience. Food Consumption and Nutrition Division, International Food Policy Research Institute, Washington, DC, USA. FCND Discussion Paper No. 10. 47 pp.

Richardson, D. 1996. The Internet and rural development: recommendations for strategy and activity. Food and Agriculture Organization of the United Nations, Rome, Italy. Final report. 42 pp.

Senghore, I.; Bojang-Sissoho, A. 1994. Women's "wisdom": banking on themselves. African Farmer, 11, 7.

Starkey, P. 1997. Networking for development. International Forum for Rural Transport and Development, London, UK. 104 pp.

Vogtle, J. 1997. Zimbabweans want scripts in local language. FINESA News, 2(4), 3.

Were, E. 1996. Talks aim to end world hunger. Gender Review, 3(3), 7–10.

Winrock International. 1997. Sustaining women's leadership in Africa: a proposal submitted to the Ford Foundation for the African Women Leaders in Agriculture and the Environment Program. Winrock International, Nairobi, Kenya. 22 pp.

World Bank. 1996. Implementing the World Bank's gender policies. World Bank, Washington, DC, USA. Progress Report No. 1. 24 pp.

Youdeowei, A.; Diallo, A.; Spiff, E.D. 1996. Synthesis of regional studies of agricultural information needs of African countries. *In* The role of information for rural development in ACP countries: review and perspectives. Proceedings of an international seminar, 12–16

Jun 1995, Montpellier, France. Technical Centre for Agricultural and Rural Cooperation, Wageningen, Netherlands. pp. 113–138.

Zijp, W. 1994. Improving the transfer and use of agricultural information: a guide to information technology. World Bank, Washington, DC, USA. World Bank Discussion Paper No. 247. 105 pp.

Annex 1: United Nations Economic Commission for Africa

ECA has taken the lead in assisting African countries to overcome the information and technology gap and launched AISI to this end. This is an action framework to build Africa's information and communication infrastructure. The framework outlines the development of Internet nodes and services in Africa. The ECA Conference of African Ministers responsible for economic and social development and planning adopted this initiative in 1996. ECA is also working closely with UNESCO, IDRC, the World Bank, the International Telecommunication Union, and other agencies and partners. AISI helps African countries develop action plans to establish information systems and services and national ICT infrastructure plans and projects.

ECA is also trying to coordinate donor groups and give them guidance to avoid duplication of effort. IDRC, USAID, and the Government of the Netherlands have supported ECA's efforts to promote connectivity in Africa since 1989. With Dutch funding, the commission has been setting up low-cost nodes in eight African countries, and with funding from IDRC, it has been supporting connectivity work in the greater Horn of Africa.

Annex 2: International Development Research Centre

IDRC launched the Acacia Initiative in 1997 to empower communities in SSA through the use od ICTs to facilitate access to information and thereby enhance economic and social development. The program was piloted in Mozambique, Senegal, South Africa, and Uganda, and its issues include policies, ICTs and their application, and telecommunications infrastructure. Acacia focuses on the community and ensures a process of continuous learning.

Acacia will also look at the content issue and use appropriate ICTs to assist in building and disseminating critical and relevant information for African communities. Acacia has been setting up multipurpose telecentres in rural and disadvantaged communities in Mozambique, Senegal, South Africa, and Uganda and is particularly interested in involving women and youth groups. It has been working with the Telecommunications Foundation for Africa, other partners, such as

ECA and CABI, donor and technical agencies, international organizations, NGOs, CBOs, public and private bodies, and institutional groups in local communities. Its aims are to connect rural communities, establish telecentres, and explore the capability of telecentre models to meet the needs of the users and generate income.

The Acacia Initiative also supports research on the introduction of ICTs in SSA. Research topics include youth, gender, and technology research and development; social and political impacts; and human-resource development. IDRC continuously monitors and evaluates the initiative for feedback and correction. The reports of the various studies commissioned by Acacia have focused on rural development, agriculture, education, health, youth, and gender (IDRC 1999).

The IDRC-funded Capacity Building for Electronic Communication in Africa project has established the first public-access nodes and strengthened others in more than 30 countries in SSA.

Annex 3: UNDP's Sustainable Development Networking Programme

SDNP focuses on creating SHD. SDNP resulted from the 1992 Rio Earth Summit. Environmental and economic leaders at the summit agreed that a key component of a sustainable future would be early access to and deliberate sharing of information and expertise among all nations. SDNP is an intersectoral network and has linked government organizations, NGOs, the private sector, universities, and individuals in about 40 developing countries (10 of these in Africa). SDNP enables the exchange of vital information and expertise through electronic and other networking links.

SDNP uses ICTs (such as e-mail, electronic bulletin boards, fax, phone) and posters and supports decision-makers and other stakeholders on SHD issues. SDNP has built up awareness of the Internet in several African countries and has been instrumental in developing the demand and market for the Internet. The program has also identified national and global sources of information, created national directories, and provided access to reliable information on a regular basis through electronic networks.

SDNP lays heavy emphasis on national capacity-building, particularly training of trainers, and has helped create the African Internet Forum (AIF). This forum aims to ensure the strategic collaboration of independent donors in the development of sustainable Internet communication infrastructures. This is to be achieved through sharing of information, focused project implementation, and support to existing efforts of indigenous Internet service providers (ISPs). AIF works on Internet-policy issues through national and regional meetings, encouraging grass-roots support for access to the Internet. It works with the private and public sectors to increase the demand for and supply of Internet services. AIF also facilitates Internetworking in Africa.

Each member country has a node, and SDNP provides seed money for 2 or 3 years to enable the node to build its user community and to shift from external to local financing. Each SDNP is country owned and has a national coordinator and steering committee. The country office of UNDP provides guidance in the formation of the steering committee. At the Joint Sustainable Development Networking Programme and Internet Initiative for Africa Regional Workshop, held on 15–19 December 1997, in Maputo, Mozambique, SDNP and IIA were challenged to pay more attention to grass-roots communities and find ways for the projects to sustain themselves after the project period.

Annex 4: UNDP's Internet Initiative for Africa

IIA is a UNDP participatory initiative operating in Angola, Burkina Faso, Cape Verde, Chad, the Gambia, Mauritania, Namibia, Nigeria, São Tomé and Principe, Swaziland, Togo, and Zaire — 12 countries in SSA. The implementing agencies are mostly private-sector and national institutions that have established Internet services and enhanced current Internet services to strengthen economic and social development. IIA is working to ensure access to reliable and up-to-date information for sound decision-making and aims to establish information and decision-support systems to enhance SHD-policy formulation, using the Internet. IIA has established links with African governments, ECA's AISI, SDNP, the United Nation's Special Initiative on Africa (a program to harness information technology for development by building the infrastructure needed to construct the Africa information society), and UNDP country offices. The hope is that these organizations and programs will become full partners in building and facilitating the capacity of the present and future generations of Africans to use ICTs.

IIA is using UNDP country offices as focal points for activities; communicating with and coordinating governments, NGOs, academics, and private-sector organizations to establish Internet services; and using SDNP coordinators wherever they can help and complement each other's efforts. The project will run for 3 years from 1997, and half of the funds are expected to come from governments and UNDP country offices.

Annex 5: Food and Agriculture Organization
of the United Nations

FAO has pilot projects using communication-for-development methodologies in Chile and Mexico. It has developed partnerships with other organizations and local people, and together they have used traditional ICTs like radio and video to assist local people in developing indigenous communication processes.

FAO is developing a rural Internet approach for rural agricultural communities. It has worked in collaboration with the Department of Rural Extension Studies, University of Guelph, Canada, to support an Electronic Communication and Information Systems fact-finding mission. The mission interviewed many Internet supporters and pioneers. FAO is collaborating with partners to implement Internet pilot projects for rural development. The strategy is to promote policies for rural development and establish Internet pilot projects to develop indigenous applications for youth and women. The pilot projects also support the rural and agricultural education sector, local ISPs, and local Internet entrepreneurs; help develop Internet capability; create Internet awareness in the rural agricultural community; and build local capacity.

Annex 6: United Nations Educational, Scientific and
Cultural Organization

The Regional Informatics Network for Africa is a UNESCO initiative funded by Italy and North Korea. It was launched in 1992. The network is active in 30 UNESCO member countries, with focal points in universities and research centres. The participating countries obtain support in the form of equipment, training, and building connectivity.

UNESCO has established pilot multipurpose community telecentres in various countries, including Benin, Mali, Mozambique, Tanzania, and Uganda, with the goal of taking Internet connectivity beyond their capital cities. The project came to an end in 1997, but some countries, such as Angola, Eritrea, Ethiopia, and Nigeria, received extensions. The network links with SDNP, Leland, and other similar initiatives in Africa.

UNESCO has established centres of excellence in Gabon, Kenya, Senegal, Tunisia, and Zimbabwe to create a network for cooperative development of training programs and support the creation of national centres of excellence. UNESCO also runs the Intergovernmental Informatics Programme, a global informatics program with regional and continental programs for Africa.

In 1994, UNESCO, in cooperation with African specialists, started experimental rural centres in some Central and West African countries to advance knowledge, reduce illiteracy, and ensure the circulation of ideas among people in rural areas, no matter what their level of education. These centres have blended into local networks and use both traditional and modern ICTs. The program covers all sectors and gives particular attention to self-sufficiency, reliability of food supplies, health, education, democracy, and women in society.

Annex 7: Environmental Liaison Centre International

ELCI is a network of more than 900 NGOs and CBOs in more than 100 countries. ELCI is working for a more sustainable world through a global process of sharing ideas, information, and experience with development in the environmental sector. Many of ELCI's NGOs and CBOs are in Africa, where ELCI has been operating a node at its headquarters, using Fido software, which is designed to work where phone lines are not very reliable. This technology is good for the rural areas; unfortunately, it does not provide access to the Internet. The centre is planning to establish electronic post offices to assist CBOs in using electronic communications, with some 10–20 CBOs sharing one post office. One organization in Loitoktok, Kenya, has been identified to serve as an electronic post office, and ELCI is currently looking for appropriate software.

Annex 8: Telecentres

Telecentres were introduced in Scandinavia in the 1980s to use information technology and telecommunications facilities to address some of the problems experienced in small, isolated communities. Users receive technical support and training, and community committees manage the centres. The concept has spread to rural areas in Australia, Brazil, Canada, some European countries, South Africa, and the United States. Many of these centres are now self-sustaining.

In Australia, the government established its telecentres program in 1992. The community manages the telecentres, and various organizations work together and build on what is available through self-help, with a view to developing various sectors of the community through access to information. The focus is on improving farm and business management and increasing local employment. These centres provide information on efficient marketing, improved production, sustainably increased yields, health, and other relevant and appropriate topics, and the centres are linked to many other information services and telecentres. They have helped to curb illiteracy and have proven very popular as learning centres. Many rural people with little education have started to study again at these centres.

In South Africa, multipurpose community centres have appeared in rural, isolated, and remote areas to serve as shared information and communication facilities. In addition to information technology and telecommunications facilities, these centres also provide user support and training for community members who cannot afford to install their own facilities and for individuals who lack the skills to use the tools. Specialized personnel who operate the centres also work as facilitators for distance-learning programs, as managers and operators of the services, and as technicians who maintain the equipment. These centres have been widely accepted. Their numbers are increasing at all levels of the public and private sectors.

In the rest of Africa, rural telecentres might also collect from farmers and cooperatives information on available products, local market prices, new crops and technologies, and indigenous knowledge. This information could then be repackaged and disseminated more widely. Governments could use ICTs such as e-mail and the Internet to promptly update farmers on prevailing government policies and services and new skills and techniques, and farmers could then use e-mail or other ICTs to send queries to government departments for details or clarification. Farmers could obtain advice on sowing, harvesting, processing, and marketing their produce, rather than off-loading their goods at throw-away prices in the local markets. Buyers could also use ICTs for prices information.

ICTs will pave the way for dialogue between researchers and rural communities; for teleconferences to enable female farmers to participate in decision-making and policy formulation; and for bridges between urban and rural dwellers. Other communication methods, such as meetings, conferences, and social gatherings, can still be expected to complement the new services offered at telecentres, and the telecentres themselves might become centres of business and community activity.

Annex 9: Council for Scientific and Industrial Research

The Council for Scientific and Industrial Research (CSIR) in Pretoria hosts a project to facilitate information exchange in support of AISI. The Centre for Information Society Development in Africa established CSIR in 1997. It serves as the Secretariat for the Global Collaboratory for Information Society Development in Africa. Its objectives include assisting with the implementation of AISI, Internet connectivity, and democratization of access to information. In conjunction with the University of Witwatersrand, CSIR is developing the Building a Telecentre Network for Africa to facilitate information exchange between various African telecentre projects (CSIR 1999).

Annex 10: British Council

The British Council held a 3-day conference on Building the Information Community in Africa in Pretoria, on 22–25 February 1999. Supported by IDRC, the
British Council, and other development agencies, the conference focused on the
use of ICTs at the community level in Africa. The event was to provide a forum
for African ICT practitioners to exchange information with each other and with
the development community (Jensen 1998b).

Chapter 5

RETHINKING EDUCATION FOR THE PRODUCTION, USE, AND MANAGEMENT OF ICTS

Cathy-Mae Karelse and Fatimata Seye Sylla

Part 1: Anglophone Africa[1]

The information age has dramatically increased the potential for sharing information across the globe. However, the promise of the global information society (GIS) is tainted with problems of power, monopoly, and control, so issues of access to information, quality of content, and knowledge-production capacity abound. In terms of information infrastructure, gross inequalities are evident on the African continent. For example, South Africa has more than 90% of the connectivity of the entire continent, but the teledensity in sub-Saharan Africa (SSA) is still less than 1 line per 200 inhabitants, with a poor-quality network still in place (Jensen 1996). To expand on this point, it is worth noting, with Marcelle (1997, p. 2), that

> Africa has 12% of the world's population and only 2% of its telephone lines. Over half of all these lines are in the largest cities. There is only one telephone line for every 235 persons in sub-Saharan Africa. The costs of installing and maintaining lines are higher in Africa than in other countries, even when compared to other developing countries, and reliability of services [is] quite poor.

Women are further removed from the information infrastructure than men within this already impoverished context. Questions pertaining to the beneficiaries and proponents of the GIS thus remain pertinent. It has been stated, for instance, that

---

[1] The author of part 1 is Cathy-Mae Karelse.

in developing countries, "technical change aimed at benefiting people in rural areas ... tended to benefit men more than women" (UNCSTD–GWG 1995, p. 8).

This is particularly problematic on the African continent, where more than 80% of the population lives in rural areas (Kularatne 1997). It appears then that information and the new information and communication technologies (ICTs) have to be carefully used to combat existing inequalities in our societies. In the words of Burch (1997, p. 1), "Information technology obviously will not solve the world's problems. But wisely deployed and developed, it has proven to be a powerful tool for promoting social causes." The emphasis on the development of information infrastructure in Africa is quickly shifting from an exclusive concern with technical connectivity to issues of content and the capacity to shape and exploit the new networks.

At a recent AFCOM conference, Derrick Cogburn, Director of the African Regional Programme of the Global Information Infrastructure Commission, confidently stated that Africa's connectivity challenges would be resolved in the next 3–5 years (WTC 1997). This bold statement is to a great extent borne out by various initiatives undertaken by donor agencies and foreign companies, such as the Acacia Initiative of the International Development Research Centre (IDRC), the African Information Society Initiative (AISI) of the United Nations Economic Commission for Africa (ECA), and the AfricaLink initiative of the United States Agency for International Development. To a greater or lesser extent, these initiatives underscore the need to focus efforts on the development of capacity to fully participate in shaping and using "infostructures" for socioeconomic and political development. Implicit in this assertion is the need for Africans to develop both a consciousness and a self-consciousness about the role and value of information in shaping our lives and our continent. Initiatives such as AISI (which was presented to the ECA Conference of Ministers in May 1996 and adopted through Resolution 812) have embraced the need to participate in creating the GIS. Although AISI identifies the importance of improving the quality of life for every African, along with other similar ventures, it still has to shift from policy to practice and realize the opportunities presented by ICTs.

In this part of this chapter, with a focus on anglophone Africa, I discuss the kinds of skills that citizens require to fully participate in the information society and to shape society to improve the quality of life of people as a whole. Special attention is paid to the education of women as a means to ensure that they have equal access to the information society and benefit from it. This chapter considers women's distance from ICTs, as well as the critical role ICTs could play in further subordinating women. Cognizance is also taken of women's general distance from decision-making positions and technical-type positions of employment, both of which are crucial in the formation of the information society. A review is made of the kinds of skills and education women require to bridge these gaps, and recommendations are made on ways to redress the gender imbalances.

At the outset, it should be noted that because the ICT environment is undergoing constant and rapid innovation, discussions of these issues are also permanently shifting and changing. As Braman (1997, p. 16) explained at a recent conference convened to explore issues of ICT education,

> The subject of study — effects of the use of information technologies — is constantly changing because the technological environment itself is continuing to change ever-more rapidly and in a qualitative manner. Social, political, economic and cultural effects of the use of new information technologies themselves feed back in to the ways in which technologies are used. Thus some of the effects understood in the past simply no longer work in the same way in today's environment.

Globalization, information infrastructure, and ICTs

Globalization, which includes economic, cultural, and communication shifts, presents the paradox of new forms of imperialism coexisting with the potential for the developing world to use the new ICTs to advance more rapidly and participate fully in shaping development. In the context of global competition, information can be used either to promote development or to perpetuate inequality and subordination. The global information infrastructure, including ICTs, has become the primary means of mediating and attaining information and, it can be argued, power. Information, irrespective of the channels through which it is communicated, is a fundamental resource for development (Kularatne 1997). It is the basis on which people make decisions. It allows people to communicate with others about their lives and to assert their experiences as valid. Indigenous information, usually transmitted through traditional information structures, is highly relevant to people living in indigenous areas. As IDRC's Gender and Information Working Group (GIWG) stated,

> Acquiring knowledge is the first step toward change, whether this change be technological, social, economic, cultural, legal, or political. Information is the catalyst, fuel, and product of this process of transformation. Inevitably, information systems — both formal and informal — play a central role in our lives.
>
> IDRC–GIWG (1995, p. 267)

ICTs can make a significant contribution to processes of transformation and people-centred development, but they have to be innovatively used to promote new approaches to development, rather than merely automating traditional social methods and systems. In other words, the new ICTs may quite simply reinforce traditional social relations encapsulating gender subordination, or they may be used to transform these social relations by improving opportunities for women to participate fully in shaping the ongoing development of the information society. A good example of the use of ICTs to advance the position of women is women's use of ICTS in the run-up to the United Nations World Conference on Women in Beijing. But ICTs can, as is argued later, also introduce new types of subordination and help to strip women of power they may have held previously. Appleton et al. (1995), for example, reported that ICTs have been introduced in contexts in which their use has resulted in the subordination of women. This underlines the point that ICTs are manipulated and used by people — these technologies have no will to act on their own.

One of the features of the global economy is the perpetuation of inequalities between societies. Social inequality is mirrored within societies, reflecting not only gender disparities vis-à-vis continued oppression of women, but also class disparities among women. With regard to societal discrepancies, much has been said about how the GIS is marking new forms of imperialism, with information continuing to flow from the developed to the developing world but flowing only minimally in the other direction. Thus, despite the rhetoric of partnership and collaboration, it has become evident that if Africa does not claim its contribution to the GIS, it will not achieve the shift from information consumption to knowledge production.

It is now generally accepted that the information infrastructure as a medium is not an end in itself; rather, the messages transmitted through this medium are extremely politically and ideologically loaded. Content has thus become an ever important issue. Within this context, it can be assumed that those who generate knowledge and have the competencies to articulate and spread this knowledge improve their capacity to influence decision-making. An appropriate example of this is Synergie, Genre et Développement (SYNFEV, Synergy, Gender and Development), which promotes sustainable development from a gender perspective. It operates in francophone Africa (Huyer 1997). SYNFEV has set up networks to promote communication for women and is distributing information, including new content developed in women's areas, to interested organizations in Senegal. SYNFEV's experience shows that developing capacity for participation in the information society must include requisite skills to work with information and produce new knowledge.

Many people in Africa are as yet unaffected by ICTs and uninvolved in shaping their use, notwithstanding their lack of access to these technologies. This is why mass programs to prepare people to use ICTs to ensure sustainable development have not, as yet, been implemented. Telecentres and multipurpose community centres are models for bringing the information infrastructure to increasing numbers of people. Telecentres have been described as

> a location which facilitates and encourages the provision of a wide variety of public and private information-based goods and services, and which supports local economic or social development.
>
> IDRC (1997, p. 1)

The Multipurpose Community Telecentre Pilot Projects are a joint initiative of the International Telecommunication Union, the United Nations Scientific and Cultural Organization (UNESCO), IDRC, and their national and local partners in Africa (IDRC 1997). These pilot projects will have to assess their contribution to advancing the position of women.

The issue of human-resource development for women is complex. Women are traditionally disadvantaged educationally, and they have historically been in even shorter supply in technically oriented work or study. The problem is further compounded by the fact that women appear to be alienated by ICTs, which are considered part of the male domain. A recent assessment of information literacy among higher-education students found that the female students were less competent in the use of information technologies than the male students (Sayed and Karelse 1997).

It has been argued that environmental literacy, alongside information literacy,

> is a pre-condition for sustainable development in all countries. Environmental literacy involves three necessary elements: a strong foundation in relevant local knowledge and experience, including indigenous environmental knowledge; access to appropriate and relevant S&T [scientific and technological] knowledge through informal and formal education; and open communication and access to information with regard to all potential environmental risks and benefits of particular S&T interventions. Women's central role in environmental use and management in developing countries, and their disproportionate lack of access to formal education and to Western S&T expertise, make improving their access to environmental knowledge and information especially important.
>
> Kettel (1995, p. 45)

This serves to expand the understanding of the various kinds of literacies men and, more especially, women need to become fully involved in the information society.

The importance of information literacy for development

There is much talk these days of learning societies and multiskilled workers. The emphasis is on lifelong learning to feed the ongoing development of our societies. Human capital is the most valuable asset in the GIS, owing to the rapidly advancing shift to knowledge economies, in which resources created through *"brain power* are increasingly more valuable in wealth creation than natural resources" and in which value is created with information (Lipani 1996, p. 4, my italics). The emphasis on learning and information is enforced by the fact that information and knowledge are dynamic entities in constant states of flux and growth. According to Lenox and Walker (1993, p. 312), "there is more information in a single edition of the *New York Times* than a man or woman in the sixteenth century had to process in the whole of his or her life."

The volume of information people need to process is overwhelming, and this often leads to information overload. To learn for life, therefore, people need the ability to navigate a range of information systems, vehicles, and highways, and they need the skills to work with information critically. As a result, information skills have become key survival and competitive weapons in the global marketplace; for the purposes of this chapter, skills should be seen to include knowledge and values (Babb and Skinner 1997). In a highly technological society in which businesses are more information focused, smart workers will be required to navigate their way through a vast array of information resources and to use information critically to be productive and to make informed decisions.

It is this condition — a much greater appreciation of the economic significance of knowledge and learning and of the value of a skilled workforce and smart workers — that has focused attention on learning cultures. The demand to have smart workers is, however, precisely the kind of requirement that the GIS imposes with little regard for its contribution to development.

One of the implications of the demand for a skilled workforce is the need to develop flexible learning cultures. Legacies of authoritarianism and rote learning have severely undermined and depressed citizens, so the challenge to provide high-quality education in a framework of lifelong learning seems great. In keeping with this challenge, information literacy features prominently on agendas for educational transformation. This prominence arises not only from a desire to develop the capacity for lifelong learning but also from a commitment to develop an information society to improve the quality of life for our people and enable them to participate in shaping the GIS. It is believed that information literacy both delivers the kinds of skills needed for the GIS and helps learners develop the consciousness and self-consciousness needed to

- Take cognizance of their experience as an information resource; and

- Exercise their critical faculties in deciding how to articulate this experience with the world at large so that they influence globalization.

The latter will ensure that local knowledge systems are not simply engulfed by larger and, in some respects, more aggressive ones. African experiences and women's experiences in particular have to be brought into the GIS to make it truly global.

Information literacy teaches people how to learn, thus enabling lifelong learning. As Lenox and Walker (1993, p. 322) argued, "in the decades ahead, those who cannot read, write and think as well as analyse, evaluate and use information resources effectively, will be an endangered species." However, this begs the question, What kinds of information and knowledge are being produced And what distinguishes one from another?

Types of knowledge systems

Various types of knowledge have been identified, including disciplinary, or formal knowledge, which is derived through investigations in particular disciplines (often at institutions of higher learning); and tacit knowledge, which is embodied in people, accumulated through personal experience and acquisition, and influenced, obviously, by a range of sociocultural factors.

Knowledge produced at institutions of higher learning, especially scientific knowledge, has been highly gendered and has presented itself as being the "truth." As this type of knowledge increasingly faces charges of inappropriateness and unaccountability,

> institutions will in particular also need to be able critically to evaluate whether, as is often claimed in transformation debates, certain bodies of knowledge in a discipline are global (usually referring to aspects of a discipline that relate to Western society and values) while others are local and therefore presumably of lower intellectual status.
>
> Ekong and Cloete (1997, p. 5)

Indigenous and local knowledge systems have to be regarded as part of the GIS, not through its appropriation of them, but through their assertion of their place and voice in it. The perspectives of local knowledge systems must be brought to globalization if we are to use the ICTs for sharing, exploring differences, and expanding the "whole." One of the greatest difficulties of globalization is that it places much greater emphasis on "difference," with more developed groups constantly striving to quantitatively engulf less powerful information systems.

In explaining the difference between knowledge and information, the Office of International Assessment of the National Research Council suggested that

> the National Knowledge System of a country comprises those institutions that control and regulate the flow and use of knowledge in the economy and society, together with linkages among them and with the outside world. Information may be thought of as a transmissible form of knowledge, having a similar relation to knowledge as currency has to wealth: a medium of trade. Information and experience both contribute to knowledge. Knowledge itself goes beyond transmissible information to embrace codified knowledge, embodied knowledge and tacit knowledge and skills.
>
> NRC (1996)

It can be argued that what communities embrace, beyond knowledge itself, is wisdom, which enables them not only to learn from their collective experience but also to formulate new directions for innovation that advance their discoveries and knowledge bases. Indigenous knowledge systems respect the wisdom of those elders who have transcended personal interest and work for the group as a whole. Wisdom ensures that growth is not an end in itself but serves the interests of the entire community and beyond. It brings into play an element of consciousness not bent simply on efficiency but on issues of quality and sustainability.

Despite these commentaries on knowledge and the oft-cited slogan "information [or knowledge] is power," knowledge bearers do not necessarily have automatic access to power. Although women are prominent producers of knowledge in the developing world (a fact to which many authors have attested), this has not automatically improved their sociopolitical or economic standing (Rathgeber 1995; UNCSTD–GWG 1995; Huyer 1997). Thus, although women hold significant power vis-à-vis their acquisition of knowledge and their generation of technology based on this experience, significant numbers of women are not in classical positions of power, decision-making positions of political structures, or advisory positions in companies. This challenges the notion that knowledge is power. The notion of power is itself admittedly relative. The power these women do have derives from their knowledge, which enables them to use resources and live. When new technologies or commerce dislocates this knowledge, these women depend increasingly on others for their survival.

Indigenous knowledge systems usually embody complex systems of planning and understanding that differ from systems in Western industrialized nations. According to Appleton et al. (1995, p. 57), whereas

> the generation of science and technology is directly linked to centralised control over the distribution of information, information in local knowledge systems is the common property of integrated social groups.

The authors, drawing on the work of earlier researchers (Shiva and Dunkelman) went on to argue that although

> women's knowledge systems tend to be holistic and multidimensional, the introduction of agricultural technologies usually results in "resource fragmentation undermining the position of women ... the woman's role becomes more and more that of a labourer as she loses her control over production and access to resources.
>
> Appleton et al. (1995, p. 59)

Introducing systems or ICTs into local knowledge systems without due regard for these social relations could, in fact, introduce new disparities. In contexts of gender differentiation, for instance, incorporating ICTs can disadvantage women and reinforce their subordination. What seems to be called for is an articulation between local knowledge systems and the new ICTs so that the latter simply build on the efficiency, effectiveness, flexibility, and sustainability increasingly apparent in the former. The interface must be directed by local groups, though, to avoid the dangers of appropriation, imposition, and general ignorance.

Before considering ways to use ICTs to advance the position of women, I examine, in the following section, women's educational experience in Africa. African women's lack of educational opportunities is a fundamental obstacle to their participation in the information society and their use of ICTs.

Barriers to schooling and social participation for women

The gendered nature of society means that women and men perform distinct roles and functions, which leads them, at some level, to have different experiences, generate different knowledge, and articulate different information needs. This kind of gender differentiation has often led to women's subordination such that the practical interests of women

> are congruent with deeply held beliefs about women's roles in various aspects of their lives. These beliefs, or ideologies, are embedded in cultural practices, religious beliefs and practices, and other aspects of our society.
>
> Wolpe et al. (1997, p. 23)

In the context of globalization, gender disparities in student enrollments and literacy levels that reflect the social subordination of women are well acknowledged. Despite attempts to address these imbalances in developing countries, where the gaps are significantly larger than within developed countries, the literature still records gross inequalities in women's and men's levels of literacy and participation in formal education. A recent UNESCO report recorded a much lower percentage of girls (39%) than boys (50%) enrolled at school in the developing world in 1992; and, in 1995, an alarming proportion of illiterate women in these countries in relation to men, 64% (UNESCO 1997). In SSA, the figures indicate both low enrollment ratios and significant gender gaps, with 26% male and 20% female enrollment. Thus, despite improvements in the position of women over the last decade, demonstrated by increasing female enrollment levels, it appears that much more needs to be done to correct global gender imbalances in education. The National Machinery for Women, which exists in some form or another in 90% of United Nations countries, must be strengthened to meet this challenge. These programs appear to be weak, underresourced, and vulnerable to changing political fortunes.

Various factors account for these discrepancies, including the following:

- Social conditioning and gender stereotyping,
- Lack of government resources to support education for all,
- In some cultures, a national bias favouring the education of boys over that of girls,
- Parental preference favouring education of boys over girls resulting in young girls assuming family and household responsibilities early in their lives,
- Curricula and textbooks containing gender-biased language and failing to promote woman role models for girls,
- In some countries, girls' schools are under-resourced with laboratories and equipment compared to boys' schools.

UNCSTD–GWG (1995, p. 7)

These factors underpin the even smaller proportion of female students in disciplines oriented to science and technology (S&T).

The problem is further compounded by the view that at co-ed schools, the boys receive a better quality education than the girls. Wolpe (1988) issued a word of caution in this regard and argued that various factors, such as class, race, and classroom control, influence the practice of teachers and that although the argument might hold for the more elite schools in the United Kingdom, it is not necessarily the norm for all schools. There is no doubting or disputing, though, that education plays a prominent role in the "domestication" of girls, that girls are, generally speaking, poorly positioned for educational opportunities beyond schooling, and that their "lesser" social status is reinforced by social values and traditional attitudes that limit women.

These arguments have clear implications for the nature of the training women receive in the use of ICTs. It appears that there is a need to move beyond the notion of gender sensitivity in training and embrace the underlying principle of gender equity. In other words, women and girls need to have the same educational opportunities as men and boys. At a more subtle level, though, a distinction is drawn between gender equity and gender equality. According to Ramphele (1995, p. 6[2]),

> Equality is non-negotiable with respect to the rights of citizens before the law. All citizens — men and women — have to be treated equally. But equal treatment in all cases, in a society scarred by discrimination, also has the potential of reinforcing inequity.
>
> Equity, on the other hand, is more contextually defined and can mean both equal treatment and preferential treatment. For example, women as bearers of children have certain demands made on their time and bodies. They need preferential treatment to allow them to cope with biological demands. Maternity leave, flexi-time at work, flexible career advancement and so forth are essential. Failure to effect these preferential treatments would perpetuate the under representation of women in the workplace, particularly in the skilled professions.

This distinction between gender equality and gender equity enables a more informed consideration of educational interventions that could both improve women's access to education and ensure that the training is not just geared to men

---

[2] Ramphele, M. 1995. Submission to the Ad Hoc Committee on the Establishment of a Commission on Gender Equity. National Assembly, South Africa. Unpublished address.

but also incorporates concepts, terms, roles, and experiences with which women identify. Huyer (1997) reported, for instance, that women prefer being trained by women as much as possible.

Equally importantly, the problem of women's education has to be addressed at the level of schooling itself. Attempts to establish gender equity in training must be spread. Experiences in this area suggest the following (EOGS 1996):

- Emphasize values, knowledge, and skills, as this attracts more girls;

- Offer optional areas of study, as this allows boys and girls to pursue activities of particular interest to them;

- Demonstrate the fantastic and spectacular features of technology;

- Relate projects to the real world, beyond the school and domestic contexts;

- Place problems in context to avoid abstraction;

- Avoid diffusion of the subject; and

- Seek feedback from students as a means of evaluation.

These experiences allow us to take a sober look at the ways ICTs can be used for women's development.

The new ICTs: learning and development opportunities

Recent work has indicated that the new ICTs are blurring divisions between certain historically demarcated areas of work. These technologies not only create the opportunity to flatten hierarchical organizations (or at least introduce a level of democratic participation for everyone who has access to them) but also blur the boundaries between traditionally compartmentalized disciplines, allowing learners to approach their work and similar phenomena from different perspectives. In addition, they allow global communities of scholars to share paradigms, experiences, and concepts, thus generating new knowledge that is neither discipline specific nor necessarily formal. Partnerships between remote villages and highly urban areas are also possible.

It has been argued that access to information and ICTs improves people's opportunities to fully participate in society. Human-resource development to enable people to use the new technologies is clearly a prerequisite for realizing their value. As argued above, women's schooling and social status generally underprepare them to use the new ICTs. It is imperative therefore to ensure that women receive the kind of education and training that will prepare them to fully participate in ICT environments.

Some issues must be addressed to ensure that women are able to use ICTs for development. It must be noted that women's concerns are hardly represented in policy at the macrosocial level. This is not surprising, as women are seldom found in positions of power that formulate policy (Marcelle 1997). In any attempt to redress the imbalances, it is also imperative for schools to encourage girls to pursue S&T training. Policy is also needed to guide this practice.

A number of factors should be considered in developing any training program to support women's use of ICTs (Huyer 1997):

- High rates of illiteracy among African women constitute the first obstacle to their use of ICTs;

- Language issues are intensified for women, as they have less time, money, and opportunity to learn English — the dominant language of ICTs — and few of the existing information and training documents have been translated into other languages; and

- Women have less access to basic computer-literacy courses, let alone advanced computer training.

As argued by the GIWG (IDRC–GIWG 1995), women face two further sets of crucial ICT issues:

- *The information environment (the message)* — The type of information needed, how accessible it is, and whether it is gender sensitive; and

- *Enabling technologies (the medium)* — The availability, adaptability, and user-friendliness of the technologies used in information systems.

ICTs and the production of knowledge

Women in Africa produce not only new knowledge of agricultural systems but also some of the new technologies used. However, a number of competencies are needed to take advantage of the new ICTs:

- Women require training to enable them to develop information systems and to use these to gain access to information about similar work and initiatives and to disseminate the knowledge and information they themselves produce.

- Women also require training on how to use their knowledge to influence decision-making so they are better protected and receive greater regard for their social contribution and status. This implies training for content development, including how to publish and how to use experiences from other information systems (not only content, but also technical lessons). As Braman (1997, p. 17) argued, the distinction between technology and content is blurring:

  > People training to become specialists in developing content, whether as film producers, journalists, or web page designers, do need to know something about the technologies they are working with. Conversely, those who design, build and maintain the technological infrastructure need to know something about the social effects of the use of those technologies — that is, what kinds of content are carried and what happens when content of different types flows.

  This appears to underscore the need for a multiskilled workforce. One must also take into account, however, the earlier arguments about the importance of respecting and comprehending the nature of local knowledge systems, their structures, their ethos, and their modes of production.

- More information-technology people are required to work with women's groups. Ideally, women should be trained for these positions, through which they can ensure that more information systems and networks are developed by women and serve the interests of women.

  This kind of training is the focus of Women'sNet, a network set up to promote gender-sensitive ICT training, that is, to develop technological skills among women. Its objective is to "empower women through skills training to harness an important networking and information re-source" (SANGONeT 1996, p. 5[3]).

Using the new ICTs

In addition to the obvious hardware and software skills, some less spoken of but equally critical ICT competencies are needed to advance the position of women. These include the complex skills of information literacy, which link the new technologies to the growing framework of lifelong learning and the concept of a learning society.

Information literacy has been variously described and defined. One such working definition was developed in South Africa in an attempt to take account of issues such as prior learning and to link information literacy to knowledge production. The concept, based on inputs from a range of informants, reads as follows: "information literacy refers to the ability of learners to access, use and evaluate information from different sources, in order to enhance learning, solve problems and generate new knowledge" (Sayed and Karelse 1997, p. 2). Although largely premised on the new ICTs, information literacy is best developed through contextual learning. Although the concept encapsulates the ICTs and imparts this training as a matter of course, it applies equally to contexts without the new ICTs. Being self-conscious of the ways we use, process, and generate information and knowledge is equally relevant in settings with or without the new ICTs. In other words, awareness of the value of information itself is crucial. Women must develop an understanding of, and confidence in, their own information and knowledge systems to derive a sense of their own power.

Information-literacy education can demystify both information and information technology. When people become aware of themselves and their role in producing information and knowledge, they can challenge models of learners — in any context — as empty vessels into which information is poured, and, it is hoped, these models will give way to a recognition of every person's role in constructing meaning and reality.

The challenge of information-literacy education is to encourage curiosity and critical thinking, as well as reflexivity. Education has by and large been consumer oriented, concentrating more on selling products and degrees than on processes of learning, but it is these processes that are currently regarded as crucial.

---

[3] SANGONeT. 1996. Empowering women in the information society: building a women's information and communication network for South Africa on SANGONeT. SANGONeT, Pretoria, South Africa. Unpublished.

To achieve a shift to a learner-centred culture, learners must become more aware of how they learn individually and collectively; how they use information to solve problems and generate and communicate new knowledge; and how these processes affect knowledge systems. Training programs should generate such awareness so that women become not only technically competitive but also truly informed about how they can use their experience — their information and knowledge — to improve their position in society.

Managing ICTs

As noted earlier, few women are in senior positions of authority, decision-making, and policy-making. Training programs must redress this legacy of gender imbalance by training women specifically for senior management positions so that the women in such positions can integrate women's concerns into policy, as well as act as role models for girls, which is a crucial component of resocialization. Not just girls, but all people, need to acknowledge and come to appreciate the value of having women in these positions.

When using or introducing the new ICTs, organizations or social groups must be completely conscious of what they are using the new technologies for and how they would like the ICTs to work for them. This does not mean that there could be a blueprint for how the ICTs should be used, as their introduction may generate unpredictable ripple effects. It is, however, a call for the consciousness needed to direct the use of the technologies, attend to the new needs they spawn, and facilitate any changes the organization may wish to make. Leadership, collective or otherwise, is of paramount importance to ensure that the use of ICTs is people driven and empowering for the organization or social group as a whole.

Women's experiences with ICTs

Various initiatives have used the new ICTs to advance the position of women. Before I make recommendations about the ways ICTs are presently used to this end, I briefly outline some of these initiatives below.

Women's Programme of the Association for Progressive Communications

The Women's Programme of the Association for Progressive Communications (APC) has operated for most of this decade (1990s) and has made tremendous strides in bringing ICTs to women and in exploring ways for women to use global information systems. It has facilitated women's access to and use of ICTs across the globe and thereby advanced women's networking. It has not only supported women online — providing help and mentoring facilities — but also conducted a survey to assess progress and to find out what lessons have been learned and what ICT-related needs have been expressed by women. The following are some of its findings (APC 1999):

- Obstacles to access are mainly cost and a lack of training;

- Women desire training opportunities, gender- and culture-sensitive training programs and materials, and mentoring programs;

- Women make increasing daily use of ICTs, mainly e-mail, to communicate and find information;

- Women make less, but nonetheless substantial, use of search engines and the web to access and post information;

- Women repackage information for "unconnected" groups and in this way ensure the flow of information; and

- High-level endorsement for women's use of ICTs is important, as are female role models.

Agencia Latinoamericana de Información

The Agencia Latinoamericana de Información (ALAI, Latin American agency for information), an Ecuador-based organization, promotes the use of electronic networks among mainly rural, indigenous, and women's organizations. ALAI, operating since the late 1970s, promotes women's access to ICTs and encourages critical and strategic use of these resources. It gender-sensitive training programs to encourage and enable women to get involved in the decision-making processes shaping the GIS and the adoption of ICTs. ALAI has also attempted to demystify technology by promoting ICTs as tools to be used to advance an organization's causes. It has not limited itself to online technologies, though, and like the APC Women's Programme (with which it works closely), it repackages information for people without Internet access. ALAI's work has had a ripple effect throughout Latin America, affecting many other women's organizations, many of which are electronically active, developing web pages, and meeting the challenges of the information explosion (Burch 1997).

Women'sNet

Women'sNet is a joint project of SANGONeT (a network of South African non-governmental organizations [NGOs]) and the Commission on Gender Equality, which are both based in South Africa. Women'sNet aims to improve women's access to and use of ICTs to promote gender equality. Women'sNet makes information on developments in gender-equality policy and global practice accessible to governments, policymakers, and women in general. In addition, the project learns from the experiences of similar initiatives, and it offers gender- and culture-sensitive training to women from NGOs and women's organizations. Women'sNet is also interested in empowering South African women to use the new technologies and information effectively to meet their own needs and objectives. Like ALAI, it wishes to demystify ICTs and provide ongoing support and training for women.

The project also aims to network (as is the historic custom among women's groups) with other groups electronically and to engender an ICT culture. Women'sNet strives to ensure that a gender perspective generally informs ICT policy so that gender is institutionalized in this newly developing area early on. SANGONeT already has close ties with the APC Women's Programme, and these ties will be strengthened through Women'sNet, which could deliver services beyond the borders of South Africa.

Using the ICTs to advance the position of women

A call for citizens to get involved in shaping the GIS is coming from a range of quarters. This call is all too easily converted into pressure to become electronically connected and active so as to promote the sharing and flow of information. One of the agendas advancing these interests is concerned with developing new markets for products from the developed world, especially the West. To combat the one-way flow of information, the developing world has to not only market its own knowledge more assertively but also encourage its citizens to critically evaluate the information flooding its markets and become conscious of reasons for adopting the new ICTs. More importantly, women, who are, generally speaking, more disadvantaged in the developing world, must develop these capacities.

Training programs can impart two categories of needed skills. The first category consists of the more easily taught and possibly more transferable technical skills, such as keyboarding, e-mailing, searching, and certain networking and hardware skills. The second, more difficult category of skills relates to the world of information: identifying needs and locating, using, evaluating, processing, and generating information. People seem to learn these competencies, or "literacies," more easily in the context of undertaking meaningful assignments or tasks.

A further aspect of using ICTs for women's purposes is gender sensitivity. To ensure equitable access to educational programs, women's time and availability for training should be taken into consideration. Furthermore, development planners should introduce ICTs in organizations and locations where women are involved so that the ICTs become an accessible part of their lives. Telecentres must take women's access into account and provide spaces that cater to the needs of women.

Developing women's capacities and information literacies

Globalization focuses attention on human-resource development, but the process of globalization must be people driven. As argued above, women have for numerous reasons been marginalized from many aspects of S&T. However, women's experience and knowledge are needed to ensure the holistic development of the GIS.

Many initiatives that aim to educate and train women in the adoption and use of the new ICTs are developing gender- and culture-sensitive approaches and support materials. These initiatives are also advancing a women's collaborative of technical expertise, mentors, and "buddies" to ensure that women have ongoing access to initial and follow-up training. These programs by and large address the tangible skills needed to use ICTs: an understanding of the ICT environment; and working with e-mail, search engines, hypertext markup language, and the web. They impart networking and hardware competencies to varying degrees, and to some extent they consider issues of locating and accessing information. They are only beginning to become engaged with the more complex task of developing a critical-learning and information culture.

Although some programs provide training in accessing information from a variety of sources and channels, few deal with the difficult area of helping learners understand and articulate their information problems and needs. This aspect of information handling is crucial to enable people to decide what information is appropriate to their needs. It also helps individuals and groups become conscious of their needs and of how they are different from or similar to the needs of others.

Training programs seldom cover the more difficult task of critically evaluating information sources, either because trainers consider it "fuzzy" or too difficult or the pressure to deliver other aspects of training is greater. Consciousness and self-consciousness about information are obviously fundamental to shaping both the ICTs themselves and the ways we use them. These abilities clearly cannot wait until the second phase of training but ought to be integrated, in some way, into initial programs and further developed in intermediate and advanced programs. It is important to present them even in initial programs so that these competencies are included in the more "basic" skills and so that people keep them in the foreground of their consciousness and, from the outset, think critically about ICTs as tools to advance social causes.

Training of this nature should ensure that women are equipped to occupy decision-making positions and to inform policy. Without doubt, if women are to benefit from ICTs, then women must be centrally involved in the strategic choices about how to introduce ICTs and what training should accompany their use. Women should also make decisions about content development. This is another area of ICT management in which women need to develop skills.

Gender audits and assessments of women's information needs

Many have called for gender audits, which take into account the fact that women's positions and information needs are different from men's. The Gender Working Group of the United Nations Commission on Science and Technology for Development endorsed this suggestion, arguing that

> the concept of gender differentiation underpins the conviction that "science and technology for development" must systematically and purposefully recognise the gender-specific nature of development and respond to the concerns, needs and aspirations of both women and men appropriately and equitably.
>
> UNCSTD–GWG (1995, p. 3)

Gender audits should highlight the positions women occupy in the information industry and provide the profile of the number of women who act as role models for others wishing to work with the new ICTs. Gender audits must include information on female trainers and technologists. The report should also give a comparative reading of the number of women in decision-making positions who influence policy and strategies related to the adoption of ICTs. In addition, an assessment of women's information needs should move beyond "practical interests" and identify the kinds of information women require to redress inequalities and pursue better lives.

It should be noted, though, that the articulation of needs is not always straightforward. People often have needs they are unaware of or fail to express.

An assessment of women's information needs should therefore go some way to making people aware of the issue of need and make them aware of their own information needs that are in flux. Women's groups should also ensure that support is provided for women to move beyond articulating their information needs to addressing these needs. Investigations and audits of this nature should identify not only areas of training but also training opportunities.

The role of the private sector

The private sector clearly has a significant contribution to make to the development of the African information infrastructure. As noted earlier, most of the investments in this infrastructure have been made by donor agencies and foreign companies. The private sector should not only see this as its social responsibility but also realize that it is in its interest to help create an informed and skilled citizenry. A skilled resource base clearly makes a more valuable contribution to economic growth than an impoverished and uneducated one. A recent study undertaken in South Africa on the private sector's role in developing the information infrastructure reported the following:

> The concept of the sustainable electronic learning centre is based on the premise that if this centre can be shown to be cost-effective and relevant to the private sector, the costs to extend the concept into under-privileged communities will be reduced. This will occur for two reasons:
> - The content costs will have been borne by the private sector;
> - The communication costs, to extend the connectivity of the learning network into the under-privileged areas, because of shorter distances will be reduced.
>
> IDRC (1997, p. 1)

If the private sector can appreciate the value of these initiatives to their workforce and therefore to the private-sector companies themselves, then overtures in this direction must be made. Clearly, gender sensitivity must have a place in any training approach to ensure equality of access to courses, as well as equity in terms of quality of training.

The private sector can contribute in other ways to the development of an information infrastructure in Africa. As argued previously, women need role models in the ICT sector. The role of the private sector is therefore not limited to providing training opportunities for women but may also include ensuring that, through whatever strategies, women occupy decision-making positions in companies.

The private sector, through its research and development (R&D) offices, should also assist with the gender audits and the assessments of women's information needs. Most importantly, though, these offices should learn about the contributions that local communities and knowledge systems make to development. The involvement of private-sector R&D offices in community development programs should be informed by an understanding that economic growth has to be coupled with sustainable development and that as long as women are oppressed and marginalized, development is not going to improve the quality of life in general. The private sector's involvement in telecentres and training initiatives must also be accountable, ensuring that female representatives from the relevant groups are involved in directing these initiatives and that the initiatives themselves are accountable to the communities they aim to serve.

Conclusions

This part of this chapter has argued that women should be involved in every sphere in which the new ICTs are used for social development. I have expressed the concern that ICTs are not necessarily of the same value to each group involved in knowledge production and that ICTs can be used negatively to subordinate and further marginalize women from decision-making power. Thus, although women can use ICTs to communicate, network, and share their ideas and find in these technologies support and strength for their struggles, they have to manage ICTs as tools that, like other technologies, can either perpetuate divides or strengthen social ties.

It has been argued that women have to be involved from the outset in decisions concerning the adoption of the new ICTs and be centrally engaged in developing information systems, both initially and throughout the processes of change, so that their needs and interests are always integrated into systems. Capacity development is the primary area of need for women, who are historically and presently disadvantaged in their access to education and levels of education. However, education in the use of ICTs has to concentrate not only on technical skills but also on empowering women to think critically about the ICTs, information, and its role and value in meeting their requirements. In addition, education must give women the capacity to assume management positions in the information sector. Critical consciousness and self-consciousness must be encouraged to ensure that women value their own experiences and opinions in evaluating information and generating knowledge. Women must have confidence in themselves and their local knowledge systems if they are to participate fully in shaping the GIS and making it work for them and their groups.

Part 2: Francophone Africa[4]

It is becoming easier and easier to selectively access and circulate information, owing to progress made in computers, telecommunications, and audiovisual and multimedia. Information (be it theoretical or practical) may now come from anywhere on the planet and on any topic. ICTs comprise the whole array of technologies for capturing, processing, and accessing information.

This is the era of ICTs, and Africa should insist on being more than a consumer. She needs to spread her knowledge, develop it, and participate in the development and production of ICTs. She needs to contribute her own content, drawn from her own cultures, and use the new ICTs to meet her own specific needs. To do this, she must use all her human resources. She should prepare her children, both boys and girls, to master ICTs.

Today, children in developed countries and even those in the capitals of developing countries are discovering and using ICTs without asking any questions. ICTS are just there as part of their environment. These children are unaware of the power of these new technologies. They are acting exactly as their parents and grandparents did when they encountered domestic appliances and television, that is, just using them, consuming them as a natural part of the environment.

But what do we observe in reality? I have carried out experiments and found that boys are more interested in technology than girls. For a period of more than 2 months, a computer was set up in a classroom with four pupils (two girls and two boys). They were given an initiation lesson, and they all mastered the keyboard and the basic programs within the first few days.

At the beginning, the girls used the machine for word processing and games; they learned how to play "solitaire," a card game, along with the boys. They also learned to design cards and draft electronic messages to send to their friends abroad. They mastered the computer commands perfectly and could do whatever they wanted. But what upset me was that the girls never took the initiative to use the computer, even when they were free, not even to try to understand the new programs I brought them or to play among themselves.

By contrast, the boys wanted to be at the computers all the time. They were fascinated, especially with the games. They also liked to draft and design. However, what brought them to the computer most often were the games. And what type of games? Nothing but violent games, virtual destruction of stuff and human lives. The girls were not at all attracted to these games; on the contrary, they considered them repulsive and a reason to avoid the computer.

---

[4] The author of part 2 is Fatimata Seye Sylla.

At a less technologically advanced level, in a less homely atmosphere, such as the socioeducative centres, the girls are usually directed to socioprofessional activities (tailoring, knitting, cookery, etc.) that do not even involve traditional technologies (television, computer). They make no use of the latest communication techniques, either to exchange ideas and know-how with communities elsewhere or to spread the products of their activities.

At schools, one notices more boys than girls in the technical disciplines. However, when girls venture into technical studies, they perform as well as the boys, if not better. In the physical technologies (building, maintenance, and repair of domestic appliances, mechanics, etc.), girls constitute a minority in the training programs. Given this situation, the principal objective of this study was to develop strategies to encourage African (particularly, Senegalese) women to involve themselves fully and without prejudice in the use, management, and production of ICTs and thereby draw maximum benefits from them for themselves and their society. Other objectives were

- To detect the causes of disparities between women and men in the mastery of ICTs, both in formal and nonformal education; and

- To propose ideas, methodologies, and means to change this situation by emphasizing

  - Production and validation of various types of knowledge, potential use of ICTs in establishing local know-how, and the preparation of specific data for the information needs of diverse groups of women,

  - Identification of the capacities needed to produce, use, and manage ICTs,

  - Preparation of methodologies and training materials of interest to women, and

  - Study of perspectives on the mechanisms and methodologies for making ICTs available, with the involvement of the private sector.

The procedure involved the following steps:

- Collection of reliable data on the socioprofessional characteristics of women, their constraints and difficulties, and their legitimate aspirations in S&T, based on a survey (see the questionnaire in Annex 1), interviews, and documentary research;

- Analysis of collected data to identify predominant elements of daily (socioprofessional) activities of women, thus bringing out the specific centres of interest;

- Analysis of success factors for women in ICTs;

- Use of these success factors and listed interests as a basis for tackling other important issues in human socioeconomic development and for proposing methodologies to encourage women to use ICTs;

- Recommendation of methodologies to produce and validate diverse types of knowledge with ICTs; and

- Recommendation of methodologies to develop educational programs and teaching materials to interest girls in S&T, especially ICTs, from an early age.

The ideas for this study were drawn from several sources:

- The annual report of the UNESCO Regional Office for Education in Africa (UNESCO–ROEA 1996) and UNESCO's (1996) *Statistical Directory*;

- A report of the Senegalese Delegation for Scientific and Technical Affairs (DSTA) on the S&T potential of Senegal;

- A questionnaire survey (see Annex 1), based on a sample of 100 people (52 women and 48 men), all Senegalese, with levels of education varying from primary to postgraduate (it should be emphasized that, in the view of the researcher, the men based their responses on the impact they thought they would have, as fathers, on girls' education and choice of jobs); and

- Personal experiences of women who were highly educated professionals and occupied senior positions.

Causes of disparities

To encourage women to take an interest in ICTs, it is important to attract them by addressing their needs. We therefore need to identify their specific needs in their sociocultural environment and respond to these needs through educational programs, textbooks, computer teaching programs, games, etc.

Sociocultural environment

Although women generally cannot avoid being agents of socioeconomic development, their needs are different from men's. As a result of their roles as mothers, educationalists, and custodians of family values (especially in African society), women generally focus on concrete issues in their daily lives. Their concerns are management of the home and the education of children; at the same time, they are constantly contributing to the development of society in general. The major objective of the socioeconomic activities of a country is the well-being of its people, and women as much as men are actors in this endeavour.

My personal experience and the experience of many women of my generation and level of education provide patent examples. We are female engineers, architects, economists, doctors, police officers, teachers, researchers, etc. We are all senior people in the professional world, but we each have our own households, husbands, and children. As senior professional women, we accomplish our duties appropriately, find personal satisfaction in doing our jobs, and enjoy the respect of our colleagues. We have the same attitude in meeting family responsibilities, which keeps us always occupied in doing something. One thing is certain: women in this position have an incredible capacity for accumulating duties and, what is more, managing to perform them marvellously well. The results of the survey conducted to study women's needs in life in general bring out the same preoccupations, such as aesthetic and functional management of the home, children's education, and personal development through sport, reading, conversation, and parlour games (Scrabble, chess, cards, etc.).

Statistics show that in educational institutions, women are registered in less-technical departments and often become teachers or health professionals. Perhaps they feel predisposed to these disciplines by their role as educationalists and dedicated helpers. Or they may feel that teaching gives them more free time to attend to their primary occupation or that practicing as health professionals outside their homes enables them to assist needy people.

The UNESCO–ROEA (1996) report indicated that, in Senegal, only 34% of those enrolled in technical and professional education were women, about half the number of men. A close scrutiny of the UNESCO (1996) *Statistical Directory* on S&T potential provided no specific statistics on the number of women working in S&T in Africa because three-quarters of African countries (among them Senegal) hardly gave any data on women in the section on the "Number of Scientists, Engineers and Technicians Employed in Research and Experimental Development, with the Corresponding Number of Women." An indication of how much smaller the women's presence is can be seen in the two categories targeted: the women constituted slightly more than 15% of engineering scientists and 21% of technicians (UNESCO 1996). The DSTA's 1994 pilot project on S&T potential involved 216 Senegalese S&T workers and indicated that women constituted only 14% of this group.

Does the physical condition of women, especially those of child-bearing age, constitute a handicap in certain activities? The reply to this question is "no," as all depends, according to the informants, on a woman's will to succeed in a given activity, whether technical, sporting, or purely intellectual. Paradoxically, the survey conducted at the end of December 1997 revealed that 31% of the people interviewed thought for the same reasons that women should take up teaching or work in the health profession. Only 43% would have liked them to undertake studies in technology, especially in computers, which they considered a profession of the future (indicating a real awareness of technical matters in general).

Why then are more women not involved in technical studies? Why don't they use new technologies, especially ICTs, as much as men do? The sociocultural framework has confined the African woman to her role of housewife, and the teaching programs, tools, and methods for children's education in general and those for girls in particular are also greatly responsible for the underrepresentation of women in the S&T branches of study.

Educational programs

The teaching instruments we use at schools contribute to confining women and men to certain distinct roles. The same sociocultural values prevail in the books and scholarly manuals, defining and separating male and female roles from an early age. Even the books and manuals we receive from the West follow the same patterns. For instance, the English textbook we used presented "mummy" as the guardian angel who should take care of everybody in the household.

Examples used in ordinary books and generally in S&T workbooks rarely depict the surroundings in which women evolve or apply to their usual activities. One example of this is the 1993 textbook, *Practical Training Technological Education Teachers Book: Stages 2 and 3*, of the Senegalese National Institute for Study and Action for the Development of Education (NISADE). Of its 11 modules, only 6 contain examples of women's activities, and these concern agriculture (watering), painting (dyeing), livestock rearing (caring for and selling chickens), health (housecleaning, cooking, washing), use of electricity (maintaining a gas cooker, making a *Ban ak suuf* cooker from granite and sand), and provision of water. Examples for boys appear in 11 modules, and 5 of these modules are exclusively meant for them. These are the modules on mechanics, carpentry, masonry, fishing, and management. Out of the 167 illustrations, only 20 depict girls. Yet, NISADE is the body that attaches maximum importance to gender equity in the development of educational syllabuses in Senegal. Indeed, it has made considerable efforts. But one feels that the gender division of labour and the depiction of the respective needs of girls and boys derive from the heritage of our sociocultural values.

With the advent of ICTs, the new educational tools based on these show the same pattern, as they are principally conceived by men, who only perpetuate what they have learned. Even for amusement, they create the violent electronic games they enjoy, which women in general fail to appreciate. Yet, games are methods of cognitive development that women also need for their training.

Women are therefore left out of the circuit, although they are always interested in methods and means to improve their society through management of the immediate environment. Yet, the principal objectives of S&T are family well-being, a more convivial society, ease in meeting one's needs, and continuous improvement in the quality of life. Who better than women can contribute to this enterprise? Women need to be involved in developing curriculums and textbooks and in high-level decision-making.

The next section provides, for the purposes of discussion, a number of ideas and suggestions for having all areas of education consider women without prejudice.

How do we encourage women to be more involved in the world of the new ICTs?

The following are proposed ideas, methodologies, and means of encouraging women to be more involved in the production, use, and management of ICTs. These are arranged in stages of implementation.

Validation of know-how; potential application of ICTs and preparation of data specific to the information needs of diverse groups of women

A campaign on the Internet might call for potential actors to engage in this project. This would lead to the creation of sites and electronic reservoirs with specific information on given subjects. Women would contribute effectively to these sites.

Historically, women have an important heritage. Among the numerous Senegalese heroes are many women who have played important roles in the history of the country, such as Yacine Boubou of Cayor, Alioune Sitoe Diatta of Casamance, Ndiémbett Mbodj and the women of Nder du Oualo, and Mame Diara Bousso of Saloum. We can make important use of these women's stories to promote the values they exemplify.

One of the greatest needs of women is the continual nutrition of children, right from birth. Internet sites should be used to disseminate new recipes for children's nutrition, with variations based on locally available products. The research findings of the Institute of Food Technology would be an important contribution.

In the medical field, rural women have special knowledge of plants and other substance for treatment of sterility, vaginal infections, ulcers, diabetes, rheumatism, mental diseases, etc., and modern researchers are studying this knowledge with a view to making it more widely available. Dr Gbodouso, for example, runs the PROMETRA project of the Association for the Promotion of Traditional Medicines, within the Ministry of Scientific Research and Technology of Senegal. Dr Gbodouso is working with the women of Fatick (the *saltigués*) and the women of Rufisque for the cure of mental illnesses. Women's special knowledge in this area should be in a database accessible to other people in the world. Black Americans are studying and using the *saltigués* findings.

Women like to talk about their interests, exchange ideas, and, more still, help and participate. A site for meetings and the exchange of confidences should be created to enable women to communicate among themselves. Certainly, such

communication would be easier at the local level, using national languages. However, for communication between regions with different languages, one should
think of having accompanying measures and technical means to enable simultaneous translation.

To produce and validate various types of knowledge, one needs to create
and tap Internet sites. Once the contents have been identified for sites on African
history, fashion (tailoring, hairdressing, etc.), eating habits, traditional medicine,
hobbies (music, dance, etc.), art (goldsmith's trade, painting, dyeing, pottery,
weaving), etc., their installation would require the following steps:

- Data collection from recorded interviews (sound), photography, film,
  documentary research, cassette or CD music, etc.;

- Selection of programs and materials to capture, store, and process data
  to be put on the Internet:

  - Materials for collection of diverse types of data (video cameras,
    tape recorders, cameras),

  - Database-management programs for processing all types of data
    (text, sound, video, image, graphic, and spatial) and for accessing
    them through the Internet,

  - Computer materials to capture, store, and process data (one would
    need a powerful multimedia computer equipped with connection
    devices for peripherals to process all these types of data — at least
    two large-capacity hard disks [the second being a security backup],
    a photo scanner, videocassette player, audiocassette player, CD
    ROM player, etc., and, especially, a high central-memory capacity),
    and

  - A modem and a telephone line;

- Capture of data by computer;

- Data validation, with the involvement of the authors;

- Thematic-data processing, by sectors of activity;

- Development of web pages; and

- Installation of the web pages on the Internet through an Internet access server.

Once the site is operational, it needs to be publicized through the media. Women should also update the information (additions, modifications, elimination of obsolete data), and for this, they need the capacity to produce, use, and manage ICTs.

Identification of capacities needed to produce, use, and manage ICTs

PRODUCTION OF ICTs — The producer of ICTs should have the necessary training, that of a high-level technician (engineer) in computer technology or telecommunications. The future producer must, therefore, from the onset of his or her training, master the scientific concepts needed for this profession, at whatever level the preparation starts. Higher education may be unnecessary for first-level technicians, who mount and maintain equipment. Therefore, young girls and women with a secondary education can easily enter training programs for first-level technicians. Preuniversity or university training, preferably in the sciences, is a prerequisite for higher level technicians and engineers.

To be involved in the production of ICTs, women would also need to meet professional requirements, that is, possess the required training. Yet, it has been remarked that women are a minority in the S&T branches at all levels. Thus, we will need other ways and means for training and interesting them in the sciences.

USE OF ICTs — Anyone literate can use ICTs. In fact, illiterate people can use voice commands to operate highly developed ICTs. Therefore, no barrier impedes women's use of ICTs other than a lack of interest or sensitization due to the impact of the sociocultural environment on their activities. We need to tackle this problem at the root, meaning that at an early age children should see behavioural changes in their educators (parents and teachers), and even then new teaching methods and tools (books, manuals, computer tools, television, etc.) are a must.

MANAGEMENT OF ICTs — The profile of the ICT manager corresponds exactly to that of the producer of these technologies at the various management levels. His or her work involves managing a whole information network, allowing or blocking access to certain users. She or he updates (creates, adds, modifies, eliminates) information to be communicated. Because ICT management is subtended by the latest computer programs, the ICT manager must possess the basic notions of

these programs. The ICT manager should ensure that no blockage of the information system arises from material defects or computer program errors. The ICT
manager should be a senior technician with a good mastery of computers. Here,
too, women need to have the same profiles as men to carry out these tasks.

What is the secret of the women already working with ICTs in Senegal?

One way to encourage women to be more interested in S&T training would be to
show them examples of women in the world of ICTs. Talks with women, as well
as the findings of the survey, revealed the following success factors:

- Personal determination (women with an interest in ICTs all affirmed
  their determination to succeed in this field);

- Aspiration to a better life, as ICTs are a field in which workers are
  generally well paid;

- The desire to prove that women can be just as effective as men in this
  area;

- The influence of the environment from an early age, either by parents
  working in the ICT field or by a technologically well-equipped learning
  environment; and

- Admiration for women who have succeeded in the ICT field in other
  countries, as seen in the media.

Preparation of methodologies and training materials that encourage women

Attitudes are changing, thanks to information circulated by the media (radio,
television) on the advantages of training for women. Girls' literacy and schooling
programs have also greatly contributed to these changes. Such information or sensitization should be beefed up to reach the remotest zones, especially the rural
areas. The best methods for doing this would involve the people themselves in the
information, sensitization, and training activities.

School heads in the rural areas can encourage awareness among pupils'
mothers. For example, in a predominantly rural Senegalese region (Diourbel), the
headmistress of a primary school brought together the mothers of the pupils to
discuss the school's daily problems. She managed to convince the mothers to
undertake tailoring, dyeing, and similar activities to meet the school's needs. In

this manner, she made them more interested in their children's schooling. If the aim of this headmistress had been to involve mothers in developing the syllabus for practical work and textbooks to attract girls to technical training, she would have certainly achieved her objective.

The best way to develop methodologies and training materials more encouraging to women would be to start with the biggest possible information campaign to sensitize women to the jobs in the ICT industry that are within their reach. The potential actors (educators, journalists, technicians, parents) should form committees to reflect on topics, images, and slogans to be broadcast through the media with the support of radio and television companies. Intellectual and non-intellectual women and youth should play an important role in this campaign. The youth would be the most effective agents for determining the centres of interest and the instruments for training in the use and mastery of ICTs.

Educational planners should tame computers and multimedia for use as early as primary school, by emphasizing their suitability for educational projects and providing systematic training for teachers. As financial constraints would prevent the equipping of every school, clubs grouping schools could be attached to a centre well equipped in material (ICTs) and human resources. Well-equipped socioeducative centres might further facilitate young women's access to ICTs.

Educators should make a greater effort to ensure that school teaching materials suggest other socioprofessional activities to girls, in addition to those usually reserved for them. For instance, girls are attracted to reading, tailoring, music, and meetings at family ceremonies. Today, it is perfectly possible to think of electronic games for girls preparing to study design, drafting, creation of abstract microworlds (virtual learning environments) based on family life or show business, recipes designed to teach quantification, etc. These materials would enable girls to develop their individual initiative and creativity.

One needs also to think of texts on women's emancipation and of women's role in creating ICT learning. Books and science textbooks should also use examples drawn from women's usual activities to make the lessons more attractive, more familiar, to girls. These methods would interest them in the S&T disciplines and prepare them for training in the production and management of ICTs.

On the issue of teaching materials (books, textbooks, educational computer programs), the findings of the survey decry the high costs and unsuitability of a good number of these, given African countries' purchasing power and sociocultural preoccupations. Africans are consumers, rather than producers, of the new tools (especially educational computer programs), which we get from the West. Another problem is that educational programs change too frequently.

As in the areas of training and employment of women in ICTs, the involvement of the private sector may also be of great benefit in the area of teaching materials.

**Perspectives on mechanisms and methodologies for involving the
private sector in making ICTs available**

The private sector can be involved at several levels is making ICTs available:

- *Production of ICTs* — As African countries have no computer industry
  to produce machines and accessories for ICTs, they can only import
  them, which considerably increases the costs of access to ICTs. Private-
  sector investment in this area (even if it is only in assembling electronic
  components for mounting machines) would contribute greatly to African
  women's access to ICTs and reduce the purchase and maintenance costs
  of material. In assembly factories, the finesse of women's fingers has
  proven a major asset in handling small, fragile electronic components.
  If well trained, therefore, women can be effective technicians.

- *Production of teaching materials* — Having local companies produce
  educational materials and ICT appropriation instruments would reduce
  costs. Local human resources are also often sufficient to prepare textbooks and teaching instruments. Having local companies produce these
  educational materials and instruments would also be very beneficial because it would, in addition to reducing costs, create jobs for youth in a
  technical area. We should facilitate validation of the contents of these
  materials through interaction with local communities (where a large
  proportion of women are sensitized). Feedback and corrections of manuals and instruments would also occur almost immediately, owing to the
  participatory approach and the proximity of producers and users.

- *Training* — The private sector can partially support ICT training institutions. Private-sector firms can pay these institutions to train and retrain
  their personnel. Within the framework of these training sessions, a
  quota[5] should be allocated to women working in the private sector, to
  enhance their competence in ICTs. It would be necessary to further encourage women to undergo this training by attaching special benefits to

---

[5] In terms of the number of women to be trained in each session.

it, like more responsibilities, productivity allowances, excellence prizes, etc. Telecommunications companies should accord preferential rates to educational centres using ICTs and making a special effort to recruit women. Telecommunications companies can also facilitate access to ICTs in homes (reduce purchase costs; develop a subscriber system that would enable the use of ICTs at low maintenance costs or that would avoid the precariousness of equipment, given the lightning evolution of technology).

- *Popularization of teaching materials* — The private sector, especially publishers, could develop online guides for youth by selecting the best educational sites, classified according to women's interest centres. Private-sector firms can contribute to the widest possible diffusion of ICTs among formal and nonformal educational institutions (schools, universities, training centres, clubs, socioeducational centres) by giving them favourable terms on their purchases or by donating equipment to them.

- *Employment* — Women trained in ICTs should be well received in the private sector, and efforts should be made to discourage the prejudices that make private-sector firms prefer hiring men. The private sector should make practicums available to women in the last stages of training. Women employed in the production of teaching units should also be involved in developing educational materials and instruments for ICT appropriation.

Conclusions

All these changes in behaviour and educational methodology are needed to make girls more interested in S&T studies in general and in the new ICTs in particular, and they cannot become a concrete reality without the goodwill of the state to support efforts of researchers and educationalists in their private and concerted initiatives. Nevertheless, state decisions should emanate from the wishes of the population for a better life. It is therefore up to researchers, educationalists, individuals, and organizations to mobilize themselves, sensitize other actors, and gain the support of the private sector and R&D aid institutions around the world.

The media to be used to sensitize people in the remotest parts of the country are definitely radio, television, and meetings, with effective participation of the youth in preparing the content and broadcasting the messages. Youth should be involved at the concept stage in the creation of stimulating games and examples of practical work themes to encourage girls to undertake technical training.

Decentralized communities may provide favourable frameworks to prepare information and sensitization and training methods and to create Internet sites for women's groups. Such sites are becoming more and more numerous in the region with the advent of the Economic Interest Groups (EIGs). These are private initiatives with the status of limited corporations. They work to make a profit and pay taxes, but they pay less than a normal corporation. Women's groups are considered EIGs. In Senegal, the state is already promoting women's private initiatives through the EIGs, and each year the head of state gives a prize to the one that has obtained the best socioeconomic-development results for its members and local area.

The production and validation of diverse types of knowledge should be based on decentralized communities in each region. Each community might create its information network from women's groups. These EIGs (the women's groups) would provide a database, using the findings of their studies to feed the information network in return. The communities would be interconnected. This means that the EIGs from the same community would be able to communicate among themselves as well as with EIGs from another regional community or even another country, once the communication problems are resolved through the promotion of national languages.

To solve the communication problems related to the myriad of national languages in Africa, female intellectuals might translate works between local languages or between local and foreign languages. Oral traditions can be advantageously exploited using ICTs, thanks to the advent of multimedia, which permit the association of sounds (speech, music) with images. Although this method is at the forefront of current technology, it can serve as a soft transition for Africans, especially in the rural and peri-urban areas, where many people are illiterate. The expansion of ICTs in workplaces, educational establishments, hotels, exhibition centres, conference halls, and homes is becoming more and more impressive. It is enabling women, especially those who work in administration, to operate in highly technological environments and more easily master ICTs.

The survey indicated a change in attitudes concerning women's professions. Despite statistics placing women far behind in S&T, one can be optimistic about the effective involvement of women in ICTs in the future.

References

APC (Association for Progressive Communications). 1999. APC Women's Networking Support Programme. APC, San Francisco, CA, USA. Internet: www.gn.apc.org/apcwomen/

Appleton, H.; Fernandez, M.E.; Hill, C.L.M.; Quiroz, C. 1995. Claiming and using indigenous knowledge. *In* United Nations Commission on Science and Technology for Development Gender Working Group, ed., Missing links: gender equity in science and technology for development. International Development Research Centre, Ottawa, ON, Canada. pp. 55–83.

Babb, S.; Skinner, K. 1997. End user computing. Paper presented at the Information Technology National Qualifications Forum, 11–12 Nov 1997. Internet: www.wn.apc.org/nitf/ws971112.htm

Braman, S. 1997. ICT education in the information society. Paper presented at the Information Technology National Qualifications Forum, 11–12 Nov 1997. Internet: www.wn.apc.org/nitf/ws971112.htm

Burch, S. 1997. Latin American women take on the Internet. Internet: www.connected.org/women

Ekong, D.; Cloete, N. 1997. Curriculum responses to a changing national and global environment in an African context. *In* Knowledge, identity and curriculum transformation in Africa. Maskew, Miller and Longman, Cape Town, South Africa. pp. 3–17.

EOGS (Equal Opportunities Gender Strategies). 1996. Staff handbook. Internet: www.rmplc.co.uk/eduweb/sites/trinity/gender.html

Huyer, S. 1997. Supporting women's use of information technologies for sustainable development. Women in Global Science and Technology, Grafton, ON, Canada. Internet: www.wigsat.org/it/womnicts.html

IDRC (International Development Research Centre). 1997. Private sector learning centre partnerships. IDRC, Ottawa, ON, Canada. Internet: www.idrc.ca/acacia/outputs/op-selc.htm

IDRC–GIWG (International Development Research Centre Gender and Information Working Group). 1995. Information as a transformative tool: the gender dimension. *In* United Nations Commission on Science and Technology for Development Gender Working Group, ed., Missing links: gender equity in science and technology for development. International Development Research Centre, Ottawa, ON, Canada. pp. 267–295.

Jensen, M. 1996. Bridging the gaps in Internet development in Africa. International Development Research Centre, Ottawa, ON, Canada. Internet: www.idrc.ca/acacia/studies/ir-gaps.htm

Kettel, B. 1995. Key paths for science and technology: on the road to environmentally sustainable and equitable development. *In* United Nations Commission on Science and Technology for Development Gender Working Group, ed., Missing links: gender equity in science and technology for development. International Development Research Centre, Ottawa, ON, Canada. pp. 27–55.

Kularatne, E. 1997. Information needs and information provision in developing countries. Information Development, 13(3), 117–121.

Lenox, M.F.; Walker, M.L. 1993. Information literacy in the educational process. The Educational Forum, 57(3), 312–324.

Lipani, B. 1996. Changing the learning culture. Sunrise Research Laboratory, Melbourne, Australia. Internet: www.srl.rmit.edu.au/mindware/learning/acea1996.htm

Marcelle, G. 1997. Using information technology to strengthen African women's organisations. Abantu Publications, London, UK.

NRC (National Research Council). 1996. Pacific island knowledge assessment. TechNet, World Bank, Washington, DC, USA. Internet: www.vita.org/technet/kajsum.htm

Rathgeber, E. 1995. Schooling for what? Education and career opportunities for women in science, technology and engineering. *In* United Nations Commission on Science and Technology for Development Gender Working Group, ed., Missing links: gender equity in science and technology for development. International Development Research Centre, Ottawa, ON, Canada. pp. 181–201.

Sayed, Y.; Karelse, C-M. 1997. The segregated information highway: an assessment of information literacy in higher education. INFOLIT, Cape Town, South Africa.

UNCSTD–GWG (United Nations Commission on Science and Technology for Development Gender Working Group). 1995. Taking action: conclusions and recommendations of the Gender Working Group. *In* United Nations Commission on Science and Technology for Development Gender Working Group, ed., Missing links: gender equity in science and technology for development. International Development Research Centre, Ottawa, ON, Canada. pp. 1–27.

UNESCO (United Nations Educational, Scientific and Cultural Organization). 1996. Statistical directory. UNESCO, New York, NY, USA.

————— 1997. Gender sensitive educational statistics and indicators. UNESCO, New York, NY, USA. Internet: unescostat.unesco.org/publications/public.asp

UNESCO–ROEA (United Nations Educational, Scientific and Cultural Organization, Regional Office for Education in Africa). 1996. Development of technical and professional education in Africa. UNESCO, Paris, France.

Wolpe, A. 1988. Within school walls: the role of discipline, sexuality and the curriculum. Routledge, London, UK.

Wolpe, A.; Quinlan, O.; Martinez, L. 1997. Gender equity in education. Department of Education, Pretoria, South Africa.

WTC (World Trade Conference). 1997. Paper presented at AFCOM '97: 6th Annual Conference on African Telecommunications, Informatics, and Broadcasting, 19–23 May 1997, Mbabane, Swaziland. AFCOM International Inc., Fairfax, VA, USA.

Annex 1: Detailed description of the survey and summary interpretation

The questionnaire

TOWN:

SEX:

PROFESSION:

LEVEL OF EDUCATION:

STATUS: Single — Married — Widow — Divorced
            (circle as appropriate)

NUMBER OF CHILDREN:

What are your different favourite games?

What are your main preferred extraprofessional activities?

Are you a little or very interested in technical sectors, such as
        Computers
        Mechanics
        Telecommunications
        Maintenance
        Surgery
        Aviation
        Others

What essential criteria push you to make this choice?

Do you know the Internet?

Have you heard about it?

What is its usefulness?

Is gender distinction important for exercising certain professions, especially technical ones?

If you had a daughter, which profession would you like her to exercise later? Give your reasons.

What do you think of the current teaching materials:
        Books
        Manuals
        Computer programs

What improvements would you suggest to attract more girls?

Identification

The sample for the survey was drawn basically from the Dakar region of Senegal (Dakar, Pikine, Rufisque). The 100 participants (52 women, 48 men) came from numerous, diverse socioprofessional backgrounds, which can be classified in the following 10 categories:

- Building and civil engineering
- Education
- Health
- Artisanry
- Forestry
- Telecommunication computers
- S&T research
- Commerce and industry
- Business management
- Others

The analysis of this sample revealed levels of education ranging from primary to postgraduate studies for the two sexes combined. Finally, the analysis showed that the marital status of the respondents was single, divorced, or married. This information served as a guide for interpreting the responses to the questionnaire.

The questionnaire findings

Preferred games

The majority of respondents declared that parlour games, sports, and dance were their favourite pastimes, as revealed by the following results:

Parlour games	54% of the women
	52% of the men
Sports	21% of the women: basketball
	42% of the men: basketball
	11% of the women: handball

Another section of the sample — 7% of the women and 12% of the men — seemed not to be interested in any amusement.

Preferred extraprofessional activities

Two types of responses emerged for the question on extraprofessional activities: some respondents did and others did not engage in such activities. In the first category of response, 25 extraprofessional activities emerged. Reading dominated for 39% of the women and 21% of the men, along with housework for 29% of the women exclusively.

Interest in ICTs or another technical sector

Women were very interested in aviation (32%), telecommunication computers (29%), mechanics (18%), and computers (11%), etc. In contrast, men came out massively in favour of computers (94%), telecommunications (61%), mechanics (45%), and maintenance (39%), etc.

Essential criteria for choosing this technical sector

Criteria for citing a particular technical sector in the previous question varied according to the respondent's socioprofessional profile. Analysis of the reasons given by the majority of the respondents for their choice of sector revealed that 82% of the women and 88% of the men were interested in technological matters, especially ICTs. The most relevant and most cited criteria among the two sexes can be summarized as follows:

- Compatibility of these technologies with the profession exercised (for people employed) or with a future profession (for those in training);

- Pronounced impact of these sectors on contemporary world development but also, and especially, on the third millennium, with the Internet emerging as a modern communication tool to be well mastered by all; and

- Personal passion for a given technical sector.

The Internet and its impact

The survey revealed that women did not want to be outdone in the use of the new ICTs, including the Internet. The three questions about the Internet received the following responses: of the women interviewed, 36% knew the Internet, 86% had heard of it, and 68% knew of its usefulness; of the men interviewed, 61% knew the Internet, 79% declared having heard of it, and 85% knew of its usefulness.

The importance of gender to the performance of a technical job

Four types of trends emerged from the responses to the question concerning the importance of gender to the performance of a technical job. Principally, women and men did not subordinate job performance to gender considerations, even for technical jobs. Thus, 79% of the women and 73% of the men thought that jobs were "unisex" and that only competence should prevail. Nevertheless, 11% of the women interviewed still considered gender important to the performance of a given job.

Choice of a job for a daughter

Four types of response also emerged in reply to the question concerning the choice of a job for a daughter. Both the women and the men affirmed the right of parents to look into this matter: 64% of the women and 55% of the men said they would like to choose their daughter's future job. Proportions of women and men who were proponents of free choice were more or less equal: 29% of the women and 27% of the men. All of these respondents declared that the choice of profession should be left to the girl, as this would be the only guarantee of success.

Among the proponents of "choosing the daughter's job," parents seemed to have an interest in the following sectors:

- Computers (chosen by 14% of the women and 18% of the men);

- Medicine and telecommunications (chosen by 11% of the women); and

- Maintenance chosen by 12% of the men.

Teaching materials (books, scholarly manuals, computer programs)

The analysis of responses to the question on teaching materials revealed two types of result:

- Some gave no opinion (18% of the women and 3% of the men); and

- Others gave opinions on teaching materials in use, and their evaluation criteria were basically as follows:

  - High cost or rarity of teaching materials, cited by 24% of the women and 43% of the men,

- Complementarity of teaching materials (books, text books, computer programs), cited by 5% of the women and 17% of the men,

- Inappropriateness of the content of teaching materials, given the sociological realities of the environment, cited by 13% of the women and 63% of the men, and

- Usefulness of teaching materials for all curricular or extracurricular learning, or both, cited by 63% of the women and 49% of the men.

Suggestions for improving girls' access to S&T training

Although some of the participants (26% of the women and 26% of the men) offered no suggestions for improving girls' access to S&T training, the majority gave a number of suggestions, which can be summarized basically as follows:

- Providing information to the girls and their families or closely sensitizing them (45% of the women and 37% of the men);

- Breaking sociological taboos and giving girls confidence (16% of the women and 34% of the men);

- Increasing or diversifying short-term professional courses (13% of the women and 17% of the men);

- Reaffirming political goodwill in directing girls to technical and professional training (13% of the women and 23% of the men); and

- Making teaching materials more accessible and reducing the training costs for economically weaker target groups (11% of the women and 14% of the men).

Chapter 6

EXPANDING WOMEN'S ACCESS TO ICTS IN AFRICA

Rachel Solange Mienje Momo

Since the first United Nations World Conference on Women in Mexico, in 1975, women's opportunities for human-resource development have improved globally. Thanks to the efforts of individual countries and the international community, spectacular progress has been made in the fields of health and nutrition, education, childbirth, and rights. However, despite these well-known successes, the appraisal prepared for the Beijing conference revealed that the period 1985–95 showed a certain stagnation, if not a decline, in progress, as a result of the economic, political, and social turbulence of that decade.

In Africa, women's living conditions have worsened, and their incomes have diminished. Depending on the region, they have lost social gains, become victims of poverty and unemployment, experienced new forms of exclusion, and become more vulnerable. As well, institutional, legal, socioeconomic, and cultural constraints, which women have been unable to escape in any country, have denied them access to opportunities that are available to men. Women have understood that the acquisition of knowledge constitutes the first stage in any process of change, be it social, economic, cultural, or politicolegal. Information is the catalyst, the driving force, and the product of such evolutionary processes of change. Good information flow is an integral part of development. To promote sustainable development, therefore, governments should facilitate women's access to information and allow them to contribute to economic growth. Within this framework, it would be essential to free women's productive potential by adopting specific measures to give women access to information, training, technology, and technical assistance.

Information technology, info highways, information products and services etc. are concepts and realities that have become unavoidable for anyone involved in the issues of development. In tandem with these developments, globalization and worldwide processes of economic change are at work in all sectors of activity throughout the world. Developing countries should not be kept out of the information revolution. In fact, the emergence of new information and communication technologies (ICTs), especially those with Internet connections, is a fantastic opportunity that women should seize. Such ICTs are choice tools for development. The Internet itself is likely to become a principal instrument, rather than an accessory, of economic and social renewal.

Development aid, whether bilateral or multilateral, has in every case been changed profoundly, as one must now take into consideration the new ICTs and the lightning progress the Internet is making throughout the world. If African countries do not participate in this world revolution, the gap between African and industrialized countries will widen, and the continent will be even more marginalized. Participating in this revolution implies calling on the active forces of both women and men, without restriction.

Women represent slightly more than half of Africa's population. One cannot therefore talk of development without including women. The awareness created recently among African women, along with their emancipation, has brought them slowly out of the yoke that tradition and society had reserved for them and caused them to become more interested in sectors hitherto considered the reserve of men. Sensitizing women and promoting their access to ICTs would give them the means to assert their emancipation, as well as the wherewithal to ensure their economic independence and take control of their contribution to the economy.

The African woman in her sociocultural context

In Africa, women do not live in isolation. Most women (married or single) live in households and bear enormous responsibilities for their families. They are the backbone of small-scale agricultural holdings; they constitute an important reservoir of wage-earning agricultural labour; and they play key roles as traders in markets and distributors in their communities.

Although women are in the majority, they have less access than men to the various levels of formal education, owing to the constraints of an aggressive social environment. This imbalance at all levels is due to several sociological factors: parents show little interest in having their daughters pursue long-term studies; all over the place, girls are victims of aggression in a society in which traditional values are crumbling; and quickly earned money is becoming the sole norm of social success. Outside of these subjective factors, demands on girls' labour, young girls' having to work, early pregnancies, and promiscuity are factor in girls' school failures. Low levels of schooling, illiteracy, and lack of exposure and access to training disproportionately affect women. In most developing countries, women are less educated than men: in Africa 58% of girls attend primary school, but the figure is 73% for boys.

To alleviate these problems, governments should help to create a generation of literate young girls and women who can use ICTs. Knowing how to read, write, and count contributes greatly to helping women overcome their fears. By simply learning to read a weighing machine and check what is written in the register, they can verify their relations with surrounding institutions. Furthermore, their education should be functional, that is, centred on immediately usable knowledge, such as the ability to keep a ledger (with entries of debits and credits, harvest deliveries, etc.) and to read simple, common-knowledge reading materials.

Training

Women's access to training is limited in the rural areas because all training is given in far-off centres. Women should receive training in their villages, in the language they prefer, and in accordance with a schedule convenient to them. Experience shows that women who receive training in a village are often better motivated and then more willing to take a course at a centre. Women who wish to have a job or create a microenterprise would require training in technical competencies or simple management practices. They should receive this type of training in conjunction with training in credit and commercialization procedures, health, environmental protection, and other related subjects.

Governments can render a precious service to women and young girls (the women of tomorrow) by encouraging national educational institutions to introduce technical subjects into the school syllabuses — subjects such as agriculture, market gardening, livestock rearing, artisanal transformation of agricultural products, elementary accounts, and management. Teachers might use a good portion of the teaching and popularization materials drawn up within such projects, and popularizers might make visits to local schools.

Information

It goes without saying that women who are not informed about a resource or new initiative cannot benefit from it. The old adage that "information is power" is still true, but women are often unaware of the services available to them. The new information technologies can considerably widen access to information and communication and advance and accelerate sustainable development. Notable among this perspective's implications is that women's attitudes toward information and its use will give way to cultural practices in which being informed and informing become simple reflex actions. Although few studies have been done on the relationships between information, development, and science and technology (S&T), the information sector has an influence on what the women of developing countries learn about S&T, and learning mechanisms also become more and more important. ICTs have the potential to, above all, improve women's learning, interaction, and participation.

The policy-formulation process should reformulate and adapt new approaches in favour of sexual equality to encourage women's and communities' total participation in the conception and management of all development initiatives in the ICT sector. This process should also encourage the media to respond more effectively to women's needs and interests and increase women's access to S&T information and other relevant knowledge. As we shall see below, women have specific and fairly precise information needs.

The specific information needs of women

Because of previous results, especially in matters of rights and education, and because of the almost international awareness of the need to improve women's quality of life, women's information needs are recognized in practically all spheres of social life:

- *In education* — African women need at least a minimum basic education that, in the worst-case scenario, would enable them to read and write their names and to distinguish between the necessary and the superfluous and between good and evil. This basic education should also enable women to actualize their traditional knowledge and be more involved in improving their conditions of life. Women who cannot move far should have the opportunity to pursue their education by correspondence. Teachers might also instruct rural women in their own mother tongues. Training centres should facilitate attendance for women who are breast-feeding. This tolerant attitude would encourage many women to participate in training sessions and would help to reduce or even eliminate illiteracy.

- *In health* — Women need to receive general information on the elementary rules of hygiene. Well-informed women can eventually

    - Avoid contracting sexually transmitted diseases (consider the AIDS phenomenon, for example) that are decimating their ranks;

    - Reduce early pregnancies and thus reduce infant and even maternal mortality;

    - Adopt and practice family planning techniques and reduce birth rates; and

    - Treat minor diseases without always resorting to doctors' services, which are in some places difficult to access and expensive.

- *In agriculture* — To ensure food security, women can take measures to improve seed selection and their cultivation, irrigation, and fallowing techniques. They can use information on appropriate technologies to harvest and conserve food crops.

- *In the environment* — Women need information to avoid environmental crises and disasters. With adequate warning, women can take steps to prepare for drought, floods, etc. They can also learn techniques to conserve the environment and the soil and methods to make the environment and the soil more profitable without destroying them (through bushfires, etc.).

- *In law* — Women who know their rights and obligations are better able to defend themselves against all types of violence (sexual, physical, social, professional, etc.).

- *In the economy* — Women need information to improve and reinforce their economic independence through commercial activities, such as information on exchange-rate fluctuations, international market trends, prices of foodstuffs and other commodities on the market, and bank transactions (conditions for obtaining credit, etc.). They might then integrate themselves economically with women of other towns and even other regions.

- *In the professions* — Women can reinforce their positions with appropriate training. Women who know about the new findings in their areas of specialization can enrol for refresher courses and participate in meetings and seminars to improve their work.

- *In society* — Women can create associations and professional groups to exchange experiences and knowledge and thus break out of the isolation they often find themselves in.

- *In culture* — Women need information on their cultures; vestiges of their villages, towns, and country; traditional practices; and modern life. They therefore need libraries.

- *In tourism* — Information on national, regional, and even world affairs is needed for women to put their everyday lives into perspective and to inspire them to improve their own image vis-à-vis other countries.

- *In politics* — Decentralization of authority creates a golden opportunity for African women to show what they are made of. Although women are present and significant in diverse national organs of power, one must admit that their progress has been very slow. If they are better informed, they will express themselves almost everywhere, make themselves heard, and participate in the political destinies of their countries. (I note, in passing, that African women are becoming more numerous in the posts of minister, assistant minister, permanent secretary, etc.)

One can declare, without fear of overestimation, that these information needs are as characteristic of rural as of urban women (World Bank 1994).

Information centres

People should have appropriate, adaptable, and widely available ICTs at their disposal, especially ICTs related to women's information needs. Political reform and the creation of economic alternatives will bring the information and communication era to Africa by dissolving the inequalities and disparities in Africa today.

Because information is power and women constitute more than half of the African population, it is essential to free women's productive potential by taking specific steps to give them access to information. Information centres should be established in rural towns or areas covering more than one village or commune.

Women would meet at these centres to discuss issues, with due consideration being given to their realities, such as poverty, and their needs, such as education, water, health, and appropriate environmental technologies. These centres would enable women not only to resolve their problems by themselves but also to open up to the world and have a larger vision of it. They should develop a sort of drug-like dependency on information. These centres should not only be accessible to women but also reflect their perspectives as much as possible.

The following are some priority actions needed to establish a women's information centre:

- Conduct an area study to collect socioeconomic data and identify information needs (education, family planning, legal matters, etc.);

- Establish the needs of youth and women in the area;

- Define objectives, establish a methodology, and identify beneficiaries;

- Take into consideration the legal requirements for the setup and operations aspects;

- Take infrastructure into account for the choice of techniques, cultural traditions (oral), adapted tools (radio), audiovisual tools (video); and

- Use existing infrastructure (a school, a church, etc.) to make the information centre a concrete reality.

Women's relations with the media

Women have a particularly important role to play in the development of Africa. The image of women presented by the media can either hinder or promote the integration of women into the development process. In the press, women are sometimes presented as sex objects or condemned for their lack of morality. On other occasions, they are presented as strong, productive people who make an appreciable contribution to the well-being of their families and to the development of their country. In summary, women's media image reflects the conflict between society's traditional expectations of women and the new roles they are starting to play in modern society.

Women's contributions range from the sharing of traditional practices within their community to official involvement in the professional information and communication community. Women's information needs cannot be understood or fulfilled unless the women themselves participate in determining and selecting better mechanisms to spread this information.

In addition, educating women in information management, technology, and policy formulation would make them more aware of their stakes in this areas and enable them to seize, organize, and exchange information for their own ends. Moreover, because female journalists, announcers, and radio and television facilitators speak the same language as other women, they would know better how to inform and sensitize their female audience in matters that preoccupy women. The special way in which women communicate would indicate their unique vision of existence.

Women in such professions as doctor, social worker, nurse, and nutritional and agricultural-extension educator could also be trained to use radio and television as essential teaching aids. By appearing on radio and television programs in the dynamic role of experts, the women in such professions would help to shape new attitudes toward women while contributing to the education of listeners and viewers. Furthermore, the development process will proceed better if information in these vital sectors can be spread more widely and quickly, via radio and television.

Within the framework of the Expanded Immunisation Programme, two Radio Senegal facilitators, armed with microphones and accompanied by six doctors and the head of the village health centre, held a meeting with the village women in Nguekhokh, 75 km east of Dakar (MOHSA 1996). This meeting allowed the villagers to talk freely about their health problems (as they were talking directly to the facilitators). They asked questions about meningitis (a serious problem at the time), pregnancy, babies' "running stomachs" (diarrhea), ways to stop children from eating green mangoes, etc. The doctors stayed in the background and only intervened when really necessary. Born of the collaboration between the nongovernmental organization (NGO) Environment, Development, Action (ENDA) – Third World, the United Nations Children's Fund, the Ministry of Public Health and Social Action in Senegal, and Radio–Television Senegal, this initiative was intended to restore dynamism to the Expanded Immunisation Programme, "do real proximity radio and create new reflexes in women so that they switch on the radio to get information" (MOHSA 1996).

With financial assistance from the Agency for Cultural and Technical Cooperation, the Senegalese government intends to create four women-run community radio stations in the regions of Kolda, Podor, Fatick, and Mattan.

Finally, because women make an important contribution to both society and the economy, programs with a focus on their daily lives should be created. One can cite, as examples of topics, information on agriculture, family planning, health and nutrition, trade, and management. In addition to dealing with matters of particular interest to women, a well-slotted radio or television broadcast might help to reduce rural women's isolation. In summary, if ICTs are used to facilitate the integration of women into development, this would benefit both the women and the country at large.

Active participation in the use and management of ICTs

Networks

The network phenomenon is another aspect of communication. A network is defined as an exchange site or an ideas bank, with members spread throughout the country, region, or even the world. The aim of a network is to facilitate the collection and circulation of experiences and information from several people or organizations. More and more women are organizing themselves into networks to assert themselves in the process of development. Their ambition is to enrich and renew reflection and cooperation in areas concerning women (especially health, agriculture, trade, etc.). With this in mind, they are multiplying discussions with others involved in their socioeconomic emancipation by organizing meetings in various residential areas, towns, and countries, as well as meetings of members from neighbouring regions. These multiple networks support the resolve to build dialogue and a common future that goes beyond the usual professional or regional cleavages.

Women are trying, above all else, to stimulate the most varied exchange of experiences and thoughts in favour of development. The Association of African Communication Professionals (AACP), a framework for reflection and study on women and the media, was created in Dakar, Senegal, in 1984. AACP aims to improve the working conditions of professionals by fighting sexual discrimination in the workplace. AACP proposes to present an image of women that reflects their effective participation in social, economic, political, and cultural life and in development in general. The Ivorian chapter of AACP was created in Abidjan, Côte d'Ivoire, by the Minister for Communications, Madame Danielle Boni Claverie, on 5 December 1996.

An example in another area is the African Network for Support to Feminine Entrepreneurship (ANSFE), created in January 1995 at a business forum in

Senegal and organized alongside the Fifth African Regional Conference on Women. ANSFE comprises 469 African members, and its objectives are

- To help its members develop enterprises;

- To promote local products;

- To facilitate access to credit;

- To create conditions that help informal-sector enterprises graduate to small- and medium-scale enterprises (SMEs); and

- To share experiences with women from other countries.

There are dozens of examples of women's networks everywhere in Africa.

Economic independence

Because of ICTs, women have made progress toward a certain economic independence and have better access to resources. This is essential to realizing their projects, which cover their needs and those of their families and take into consideration their choices, ensuring their autonomy in matters of marriage and procreation. More and more women, as a result of their growing participation in the job market, are earning an independent income, even if this income is far from corresponding to their actual economic contribution — discrimination in salaries is still strong.

Women are also beginning to access another resource: international aid and credit. Having noted the essential role of women in the fight against poverty, international institutions are redirecting their aid policies to provide financing for women's activities, especially in the agricultural and small-enterprise sectors, which are considered potential sources of wealth and dynamism. International institutions are following the examples of local banks, which are more and more disposed to financing women's projects, including even those of the poorest women, as their projects are most likely to have an effect on family members and the community.

Some of the resources that women are increasingly accessing are new techniques, competencies, and qualifications in essential sectors for the future, such as agriculture, ecology, management, and microelectronics. Even if this trend concerns only a minority of women, it opens up promising prospects for independence, reduction of workloads, improved results, and diversification of activities.

Women have also made progress in areas such as autonomy and economic power. They are becoming numerous in the middle- and senior-level cadres of the private sector and constitute a real reservoir of talent in economic policy-making. The proportion of women in the ranks of managers and directors of companies has more than doubled in Africa, Asia, and the Pacific, and if only a few are heads of traditional companies, many more are creators of new industries, innovative services, and SMEs — a new type of entrepreneur capable of using new techniques to improve the quality of life, respond to unmet needs and neglected social demands, create new markets and services, and make a profit.

Women and business

The privatization process has affected men and women differently. The conversion of labour from the public sector to the private sector has been detrimental to women all over the world. Nevertheless, they are making surprising breakthroughs by creating and heading up their own modern and prosperous businesses. They are investing in such varied sectors as agriculture, food processing, trade, and artisanship, not to mention industrial cleaning, metal retrieval, ready-made clothes, etc. In my research, many women who created SMEs were inspired by an example from television, the press, or radio. Others say they saw examples on the Internet. Examples of black American women who head up their own business enterprises have influenced more women than one, such as Madame Christine Mugisha, a former English-language teacher at Kabale school, in southwest Uganda, who started a wrapping-paper- and card-making business.

A young Senegalese businesswoman, owner of a tailoring and ready-made clothing shop in Dakar, confirmed that she looks on the Internet for the names of big European shops having sales and travels abroad for these sales, and this is how she is able to buy high-quality goods at competitive prices. I mention in passing that all these female entrepreneurs explore the Internet for joint-venture opportunities and use mobile telephones.

Telecentres

The problem of underemployment and unemployment of women requires the formulation of networks to link women to job opportunities. Women, in search of both an easier mode of communication and financial independence, have also turned to the telecommunications sector.

Witness the proliferation, in both urban and rural areas, of telecentres. Their main service is offering long-distance telephone communications, whose unit cost depends on the country, for example, 100 XOF for 3 minutes in Côte d'Ivoire, Senegal, etc. (in 1999, 637.48 CFA francs [XOF] = 1 United States dollar [USD]). In addition, telecentres send and receive faxes, and some can consult databases, such as the electronic directory. Their principal advantage is that they give assistance to clients, whether literate or illiterate, who may have difficulties using ICTs. Like all SMEs, these telecentres contribute to the development of other small businesses (women's preferred sector), directly or indirectly creating employment for young women and thereby reducing unemployment. Furthermore, while facilitating communications and access to information these telecentres can also serve as multipurpose centres for the surrounding populations, addressing people's educational and health problems, with due consideration given to levels of literacy.

In the final analysis, equipped with computers and a modem, telecentres can serve as access points to the information highway. Moreover, cybercafés are timidly emerging, such as the Metissacana cybercafé in Dakar. The Metissacana, which is co-owned and partly managed by a woman, was created in May 1996. Its motto is "Accessible information for all." Metissacana's objective is to circulate information as widely as possible. It has a database on Senegal, a professional electronic directory, and an art gallery, and it organizes events, artistic galas, and fashion shows. Open 24 hours a day, 7 days a week, the cybercafé has a computer team available to show learner internauts how to navigate the web, use e-mail, and enter the Internet's direct conversation zone.

Women constitute 50% of Metissacana's clients. Although some have never used a computer keyboard in their lives, all the clients are enthusiastic about the idea of exploring the information highway. According to Mr Michael Mavros, one of the three managers,[1] the Metissacana advocates access to the Internet for all. It undertook a demonstration tour of the villages, using a giant screen to show people that they, too, could have access to the Internet. Each day at the Metissacana, the youth and women use e-mail to communicate with their friends and loved ones outside the country. It is faster, more reliable, and often cheaper than the telecopier or post.

Although women are not in the majority among those who have created telecentres, these centres provide women with an excellent opportunity to facilitate and develop communication among themselves.

---

[1] The other two are Oumou Sy and Alexis Sikorsky.

Examples of successful experiences

In 1993, the United Nations Development Fund for Women, the Inter-American Institute for Cooperation Through Agriculture, and the International Fund for Agricultural Development formulated a strategy for information exchange to ensure that women have access to S&T for development, together with ICTs as a major component of S&T. Its ultimate objective is to contribute to the empowerment and development of women. This strategy specifically addresses governments, NGOs, and other organizations whose programs aim to increase the contribution of women to rural economies and agricultural production.

The World Association for Christian Communication has developed another type of communication plan, providing information and information exchange in the following categories: satellite television and women in the media; publishing houses, radio stations, and broadcasts managed by women; and documentation and resource centres, establishment of networks, and new technologies for women working in the development sector. Several media and information services managed by women have already proven their feasibility. ISIS International, the Women's Feature Service, and Women Ink are all international, but numerous other services operate locally.

ICTs are making the importance of networking for women more and more evident. NGONET was created before the Earth Summit to enable women, Southern groups, indigenous peoples, and community-based organizations to use innovative information-exchange processes. The network has proven itself an effective medium for encouraging participation in preparatory discussions, for supervising progress, and for stimulating action, even in forums from which NGOs had been excluded before. NGONET inspired the creation of the aid program for the women's networks of the Association for Progressive Communications, which played a similar role in preparing for the World Conference on Women in Beijing (Stamp 1989).

The case of Burundi

An NGO in Burundi created a women's centre with the following objectives:

- To support activities directed to peace and reconciliation;

- To develop and maintain dialogue among women;

- To develop group work;

- To maintain solidarity to improve the status of women; and

- To sensitize and educate people on family rights.

To achieve these objectives, the centre

- Organizes roundtables, reflection days, and discussions on themes proposed by women from various backgrounds;

- Trains women in matters of associated movements and on techniques for conflict resolution;

- Creates income-generating activities;

- Offers documents describing women's activities in other associations;

- Visits other women's associations on the ground;

- Facilitates contact with NGOs to obtain assistance when necessary;

- Trains trainers on family rights; and

- Works with female lawyers.

The centre's perspectives are to widen women's experience by creating peace clubs, meetings, and forums (with videos, television and radio, etc.); and to look for contacts with other organizations for fruitful exchange.

The case of Burkina Faso

The NGO Réseau de communication et d'information des femmes (RECIF, communication and information network for women) was established in response to the marginalization of women in Burkinabe society. Having started with only 5 members, RECIF has more than 50 today.

RECIF's objectives are the following:

- To facilitate access to information;

- To ensure training to strengthen women's capacities; and

- To offer women a forum to exchange ideas.

Its activities are the following:

- Training more than 600 women in diverse economic and social activities and experience sharing;

- Publishing a newsletter that is translated into the country's two principal languages;

- Offering a forum to enable women to valorize their knowledge; and

- Using ICTs (radio, video, and audiocassettes) to disseminate specific information;

With cooperation and partnership assistance, RECIF created a documentation centre, which serves one-third of the country. The centre uses diverse information channels, such as e-mail, theatre, newsletters, and television.

The case of Uganda

In Uganda, former soldiers created an information centre to promote ideas on improving rural living conditions. The centre has enabled the wives of former combatants to become traders. People in Uganda are generally without television but have access to information on the radio. NGOs operating in Uganda provide newspapers and organize seminars on health, appropriate technologies, education, etc. According to one Ugandan, the Ugandan people would like to have a centre where the population could access information and share experiences. To this end, it would be important to identify the population's needs. The government and politicians should be more involved if the Ugandan people are to achieve these objectives.

Conclusion and recommendations

ICTs facilitate exchange among women from diverse social groups; allow rapid access to information needed for exchanging, buying, producing, and selling products; and lead to increased productivity gains.

Through accessing, possessing, and using ICTs, women will play a bigger role in the redistribution of resources and wealth, and globalization is expected to bring about improved market operations and economic effectiveness within and between countries.

We have no choice but to recognize that the future of the planet, to a great extent, depends on women. Access to ICTs improves their living conditions through improvements in education, health, and employment and accords women important, urgently needed decision-making powers, rights, and freedoms. The African Women's Centre should use the opportunity offered by the United Nations Economic Commission for Africa to specifically improve the plight of African women. The Centre should develop a database on women and put all existing information on women on the Internet because there have been several successful experiences in rural areas all over the world. The centre might be linked to other networks around the world to avoid duplication, overlap, and other wastes of time and to build on the information already at the centre.

In areas without electricity, such as in Kenya and Nigeria, solar panels can be used to provide lighting and to pump water, thus giving women more time to pursue distance education and to improve their own living conditions.

Women's ability to exercise their responsibilities, use their capacities, and realize their projects will depend on efforts to reduce poverty and exclusion and ultimately on efforts to create a coherent global society with solidarity among people throughout the world. To this end, I recommend that the various components of society, such as government, foreign partners, the private sector, and civil society

- Define quantifiable goals in the ICT sector within an institutional framework (ministries of communications, education, etc.) to create a certain division of labour in society at the largest consultative levels;

- Ensure technical assistance;

- Develop appropriate interfaces, technologies, and tools;

- Become an active part of the consultative process and contribute their active participation;

- Formulate educational and training programs to eliminate illiteracy among young girls and women;

- Establish equal access to ICTs for women and men;

- Formulate relevant educational and training services for women and young girls in the ICT sector;

- Sensitize women to all the means of communication at their disposal and to ways to use and adapt them to their needs;

- Promote the image of women as people who can successfully use ICTs;

- Encourage women's entry into the ICT field;

- Sensitize women to the need to acquire competencies in the use of computers and information systems; and

- Facilitate and encourage the creation of telecentres with Internet access.

References

MOHSA (Ministry of Health and Social Action). 1996. Expanded Immunisation Programme. *In* Orientation Plan for Economic and Social Development. MOHSA, Dakar, Senegal.

Stamp, P. 1989. Technology, gender, and power in Africa. International Development Research Centre, Ottawa, ON, Canada.

World Bank. 1994. Exploiting information technology development: a case study of India. World Bank, Washington, DC, USA.

Chapter 7

ICTs as Tools of Democratization: African Women Speak Out

Aida Opoku-Mensah

The winds of political change that blew across the African continent in the late 1980s and early 1990s brought, by and large, the demise of military dictatorships and one-party states. This new political climate offered renewed hope for the governance process, with the prospect of creating democratic cultures with dynamic civil societies and vibrant and pluralistic media. Given a well-informed citizenry capable of participating in governance, Africa's odyssey into the democratic era would be complete.

However, the democratization process in Africa has only just begun, and in most cases African countries have yet to achieve the full emancipation of their citizens, although in others the reemergence of civil-society groups promises new forms of political, economic, and social governance. The strengthening of information and communication channels in all countries will become an urgent, if not critical, ingredient in this process. Evidently, information and communication technologies (ICTs) can support popular participation, particularly that of women, in governance.

Democratization and the emergence of civil societies in Africa

Increasingly, the democratic dispensation in Africa is imposing new demands on governments to foster a more pluralistic and open society and promote a greater role for various groups in public decision-making. Democratization affects political, economic, social, and cultural governance, embraces a diversity of views and opinions, and guarantees all citizens access to and participation in decision-making. Diversity, or "pluralism," in civil society underpins sustainable, people-centred development and democracy. Unless people scrutinize the decisions that affect their lives, these decisions are unlikely to be sustainable. Freedom of expression is a vehicle of the democratization process, and it ensures political expression, economic participation, and social well-being. The principles of freedom of expression have become globalized. Faxes, e-mail, and communications satellites have made it impossible for political authorities to deny their citizens access to external information. However, women have not yet achieved the status of full and equal partners in key decision-making, particularly in politics and governance. If women are to become active participants in governance, they need to have access to credible, relevant, and understandable information. Citizens' poor access to information and their lack of influence in decision-making processes can undermine the progress of many emerging African democracies.

Promotion of women's participation in electoral and political processes

Eritrea, Uganda, and Tanzania have introduced gender quotas for parliaments, and major political parties in Botswana, South Africa, and Zambia have instituted minimum thresholds. Recent multiparty elections throughout the subcontinent have had mixed results. In Angola, Cape Verde, Guinea, Guinea-Bissau, and São Tomé and Principe, the proportion of women in parliaments has fallen. By contrast, it has risen in Ethiopia, Mozambique, and South Africa.

African women seeking political office face many constraints, which are for the most part not unique to Africa. Among the common hurdles are the following:

- Political parties rarely support female candidates;

- Women have difficulty obtaining campaign funding;

- Few women have political-campaign skills;

- Women do not vote for women;

- Women are taught to avoid confrontation;

- Women in public are expected to follow, rather than lead; and

- Women and men are heirs to customs, traditions, and legal systems that discriminate against women.

On average, women represent a mere 10% of all elected legislators world-wide, and they remain underrepresented in most national and international administrative structures, both public and private. Recently, for instance, an exit poll conducted by the University of Namibia at regional and local elections found that about one-fourth of the respondents would not vote for a woman candidate because "they were not suitable" (NCR 1997).

In the Kenyan elections of December 1997, a woman stood for President. The number of women aspiring to Parliament in Kenya has more than tripled since 1992. These candidates were backed by an increasingly sophisticated network of women's organizations determined to feminize Kenyan politics. The major symbol of women's political advancement has been Charity Kaluki Ngilu, a 45-year-old business executive and mother of three, who gave President Moi a good run for his money. Phoebe Asiyo, a member of Kenya's last Parliament, attributed the sharp rise in female political activity in Kenya to education and communications (Useem 1998). Despite these women's efforts, few of them have been voted into Parliament. Although the number of women standing for election in Zambia increased from 14 in 1991 to 61 in 1996, their presence in Parliament only increased from 7 to 15.

Close-up of women and political empowerment in Africa

Women in Botswana, South Africa, Uganda, and very recently in Kenya have approached the issue of political participation with various strategies, but a common goal has been the empowerment of women at the political level (UNIFEM–AAI 1995). To varying degrees, many African women's organizations are making a difference:

- *Emang Basadi, Botswana* — Emang Basadi, meaning "stand up women," in Setswana, was formed as a nongovernmental organization (NGO) in 1986. Botswana is a country of 1.2 million people, a multi-party and parliamentary democracy. Parliament has 40 elected and 4 appointed members and is complemented by the House of Chiefs. Although women make up slightly more than half the population, only two women sat in Parliament before October 1994. No woman has ever been in the House of Chiefs. Only 65 local government councillors out of 358 are women, and only 1 of the 17 cabinet ministers is a woman.

  Although women carry out a large portion of the grass-roots political activity, they have been effectively excluded from positions of power and influence. Because of this, Emang Basadi published the "Women's Manifesto," a 20-page document in English and Setswana that cites the underrepresentation of women in all sectors of the economy (UNIFEM–AAI 1995). Under "Women and Democracy," the manifesto demands that the government and all political parties "ensure equal participation and representation by women in all national and local legislative and decision-making bodies so that they have a say in the making of laws, policies and programmes that affect their lives."

Emang Basadi's political-education project brought women's issues into the political manifestos of the country's two largest parties for the first time since Botswana's independence in 1966. Furthermore, the Botswana government met Emang Basadi halfway in its demand that the government appoint women to four special parliamentary positions, and the proportion of women in Parliament grew from 5% to 11% after the 1994 election. This was an improvement, although it fell short of the 25% goal.

- *Uganda Women's Caucus* — Unlike Botswana, Uganda suffered two decades of political strife and turmoil after achieving its independence. In 1994, the Constituent Assembly began work on a new Constitution for the country. A minimum of 15% of those elected to Parliament and the Constituent Assembly and one in nine local-government council members were to be women, according to an affirmative-action measure of the Nghonel Resistance Movement government. To increase women's political clout and broaden the base of support for women's issues, women in the Constituent Assembly embarked on a series of strategic alliances with youth, workers, and disabled delegates. To increase the skills of its members, the Women's Caucus embarked on a series of training exercises through advocacy workshops, and it organized training workshops on managing campaigns, constituency- and coalition-building, and parliamentary procedures.

The most innovative tool of the Women's Caucus has been the Gender Dialogues, in which both men and women are invited to debate and hold discussions on common issues. These initiatives have ensured that the new Ugandan Constitution would be gender neutral and would prohibit any laws, customs, or traditions undermining the dignity or well-being of women.

- *Women's National Coalition, South Africa* (Taylor 1997) — In the 1990s, women from various organizations came together to form the Women's National Coalition in South Africa to mobilize women to develop and promote a charter of women's rights. The South African Parliament has now accepted this "Charter on Effective Equality of Women in South Africa." In addition, women insisted on being active participants in the multiparty Convention for a Democratic South Africa (CODESA), the first formal negotiations forum for the National Party government, the African National Congress, and other parties, which began its work at the end of 1991. CODESA negotiated the political transition from apartheid under National Party rule to multiparty elections, as well as an interim Constitution during 1991–94. As a result of women's participation in this forum, they now constitute one-third of all representatives in Parliament. In addition, the new South African Constitution entrenches gender equality and makes provision for a Commission on Gender Equality.

Ellen Johnson-Sirleaf, a candidate for the presidency of Liberia in 1997, stated that

> Women's vision for their societies often differs from men's because they understand clearly the impact of distorted priorities on their families and communities. The vision of women is one of inclusion not exclusion, peace not conflict, integrity not corruption, and consensus not imposition.
>
> Johnson-Sirleaf (1997, p. 25)

With access to communication channels, women can express themselves more and contribute more meaningfully to the democratization process. ICTs can undoubtedly enhance people's participation in the democratic process and, in many instances, are already doing so. However, although ICTs can provide new opportunities for social and political dialogue, they can also further disenfranchise already marginalized regions and peoples as the gap widens between the information rich and information poor — those with and those without access to information technologies. Africa in particular is in danger of being further disenfranchised in this process.

Ultimately, democratization relies on effective and dynamic public debate, with a critical mass of expertise and knowledge to interpret and provide indigenous analyses of issues. Many African countries lack the institutions and expertise to subject communication policies to informed and constructive scrutiny. Countries must strengthen such capacities if they are to adjust to the economics of the new communication environment. In South Africa, widespread competition in the Internet market has led to low prices and a rapid diffusion of services. In Ethiopia, those favouring privatization as a means to generate greater accessibility to information say that government monopoly of Internet services is incompatible with moves to spread Internet use.

Promotion of women's use of communication resources in society

Currently, communication resources in Africa do not take women's needs into account, nor have the current policies of deregulation and liberalization of communications addressed issues of communication for empowering women. Furthermore, in many African countries, the mass media are the voice of the powerful. Government-owned media are the mouthpieces of the ruling party, offering the majority of people little opportunity to articulate their views and opinions. Consequently, the women's movement in general has long been critical of the mass media, charging that they are deeply implicated in reinforcing patterns of discrimination against women in society. An analysis of gender roles and stereotypes in the media indicates that few reports deal with issues of special concern to women or reflect a gender perspective.

With the advent of ICTs, women need to discuss the use of gender-sensitive information to decide whether to create their own closed spaces on the Internet or to assert their presence in mixed spaces. Without this kind of action, we can expect that the new medium will be yet another means to perpetuate negative stereotypes, another male enclave discriminating against women and marginalizing them. What is important is that people can participate in creating the messages transmitted through the new ICTs. Because communications is at the heart of empowering people, women must ensure that the new technologies facilitate their empowerment. Increasingly, computer literacy is becoming an indispensable tool for organizing and mobilizing communities throughout the world, and women need to be directly involved in the use of this new medium.

Experience shows that women have created and used alternative communication channels to support their efforts, defend their rights, diffuse their own forms of representation, and question dominant models of mainstream culture. One outstanding example is the Radio Listening Clubs in Zimbabwe. This project started in 1988, with funds from the Friedrich-Ebert-Stiftung. Some of the partners are the Federation of Africa Media Women Zimbabwe (FAMWZ), the Association of Women's Clubs, and the United Nations Educational, Scientific and Cultural Organization (UNESCO). There are 52 Radio Listening Clubs in Zimbabwe. Members, mostly women, assemble at a local centre and listen to a half-hour radio program, recording it with a portable cassette recorder. Thereafter, the members debate the recorded broadcast. They raise other issues of concern and record them in the same manner, setting their own news agenda. Back at the studios of the Zimbabwe Broadcasting Corporation, the coordinator identifies the officials or others who should respond to these recordings and compiles a program to broadcast the responses. Through the Radio Listening Clubs, rural Zimbabwean women have been able to articulate their views and opinions on legislative processes affecting their well-being.

The importance of the Radio Listening Clubs was noted by Jennifer Sibanda (1997[1]):

> Currently, the notion of ICTs as tools for democratization presents more challenges than benefits. For the rural African women with no electricity or piped water a computer is unrealistic. So the challenge would be, how do we fit such people into the information superhighway? The answer lies in reinforcing projects such as the Radio Listening Clubs where rural, ordinary women have created their own voice. We need to integrate radio and the Internet to create space for such women. But then again, rural Zimbabwean women speak only Shona and/or Ndebele not English. Language, therefore limits the participation of such women in the information revolution.

FAMWZ might facilitate debates and discussions of the Radio Listening Clubs by accessing the Internet and adapting information for members' use.

In other dimensions, women are finding ways to use ICTs for their advocacy efforts. For example, groups in Mexico have found that electronic networking has facilitated their work in fighting the North American Free Trade Agreement. Other groups help women gain access and training. For example, the Women's Online Network is an online advocacy and action group sponsored by women's organizations. In Africa, groups such as Abantu for Development, SANGONeT, Environment, Development, Action (ENDA), and the African Women's Network of the Association for Progressive Communications (APC) have been conducting training for women's groups.

---

[1] Interview with J. Sibanda, Director of the Federation of African Media Women in SADC (Southern African Development Community), Harare, Zimbabwe, 16 Dec 1997.

New technologies have characteristics similar to those of the alternative media, and they are suited to the needs of women's networks because they are decentralized and horizontal. The essential difference between these and the mainstream media is their relation to space. The challenge is to maintain the Internet as an open communication system with democratic access to information, as opposed to maintaining a centrally controlled medium. For women's organizations, this may mean establishing and defining their own spaces or influencing the character of online culture in favour of gender balance and nondiscrimination.

Women and ICTs

Women in continental Africa are far more likely to walk on dirt track than to surf along the electronic information superhighway. Despite the hype and hyperbole regarding global information development, there still exist significant geographic disparities in the rate of development of these electronic and communication networks. African's supply of the three basic constituents required for the introduction and development of these technologically intensive projects — telecommunication networks and computer systems; knowledge and skills for design, utilization, modification and adaptation of these systems; and integration of science and technology developmental objectives in national planning policies and programmes — is still woefully inadequate.

Marcelle (1997)

ICTs actually process information, rather than merely storing or transmitting it. Computers (the key hardware) and their nonmaterial software systems form the essential core of ICTs. Ultimately, women's roles as processors and users of information are an important issue in realizing the potential of ICTs as tools for democratization in the information age. In Uganda, the Forum for Women in Democracy (FOWODE) uses the Internet to access critical and relevant information for female Members of Parliament (Mps), which they can use to support their contribution to parliamentary debate and to investigate the issues when a new bill is before the House.

Through the Internet and e-mail resources, such as discussion groups and newsgroups, FOWODE can link up with other organizations in the region, discuss critical regional issues, and inform MPs about regional dynamics and politics. For instance, when war broke out between Eritrea and Ethiopia in 1998, President Museveni visited Addis Ababa to consult with President Meles Zenawi. Through a listserv, FOWODE members could follow discussions between the leaders of the region and even issue a statement before President Museveni arrived home.

FOWODE staff print out discussions of interest to MPs, solicit their responses, and feed these into the listserv. Also, staff members respond to an MP's request for specific information, which can involve research on the Internet on a particular issue. MPs now have training programs to help them use computers, conduct their own searches, and participate in listservs.

A need for this was expressed in the remarks of Elizabeth Chipampata, MP for Kalulushi, Copperbelt Province, Zambia, speaking at the Panos Internet & Telecommunications Workshop for MPs, 5–6 January 1998:

> The use of the Internet as a source of information for women within the democratization process is a positive idea. As a female Member of Parliament, it would assist me to research and access information on various issues concerning women and obtain information from other parliaments around the world. If I owned such a facility it would greatly enhance my work. The knowledge and skill I acquired on the use of the Internet has been helpful in informing me about what is happening in other countries and enlightened me about various issues. I am grateful for this experience.

Nevertheless, it has not been easy to ascertain whether, in aggregate terms, women have benefited from the information revolution. In some sectors, particularly manufacturing, some women are now threatened with imminent technological redundancy, especially older women. By contrast, the spread of information-processing work, especially in banking, finance, and telecommunications, has opened up new opportunities for computer-literate women who are young enough to learn new skills. Information technology heralds new self-employment opportunities for women and men; yet women, more than men, fail to achieve their potential in self-employment because of their lack of access to training in business and marketing skills. Against this background, it is futile to formulate a general strategy to give women access to education and training.

In a recent survey, the Women's Networking Support Programme (WNSP), a project of the APC Women's Programme, quoted Dale Spender (*Nattering on the Net*), who maintains that women's marginalization from the new technologies has "less to do with women and more to do with computers," as computers are the domain of wealth, power, and influence. Spender warned that "women cannot afford to permit white male dominance of these technologies because a very distorted view of the world is created when only one social group, with one set of experiences pronounces on how it will be for all" (APC 1997). Relevant and useful resources on women will never appear unless women work to create them (often under difficult conditions). Moreover, as women's knowledge is presently encoded in books, it may be endangered by a shift from print to electronic media.

The new ICTs have considerable potential to aid in the advancement of women. Reasonably affordable computer communication media, such as e-mail, the Internet, hypertext, and hypermedia, make it infinitely easier to network, do research, train, and share ideas and information. In Africa, women's participation, both at the personal level and at the national level, can lead to positive results. The Community of Living Water, an organization based in the Western Cape of South Africa, works with a group of women called Masizakhe (meaning "building together") in the area of Kayamandi. The purpose of the project is to support women's organic gardening. It has used ICTs in two ways: to deliver information on organic-gardening techniques and resources and to teach English-language skills via CD-ROM. The group has used two websites in particular — one maintained by Ohio University; and Time–Life's electronic encyclopedia of gardening. Women initially develop reading skills with CD-ROMs and then supplement these skills with adult-educational information on the Internet. This has sparked a community initiative to donate used clothing to finance the women's enrollment in additional adult-education courses on SANGONeT, the local network.

However, the obstacles are still formidable. Unequal access to computers at school and at home and highly male-dominated computer languages and operating systems are just some of the factors deterring women from entering into cyberspace. In Africa, high illiteracy rates, language and time constraints, and cultural and traditional inhibitions make women's access to computers all the more difficult.

The notion of women using ICTs to network on a national, regional, and continental basis provides solidarity and breaks the sense of isolation in Africa where women are marginalized and geographically dispersed and lack access to the processes of governance. Electronic solidarity campaigns have been mounted in Africa to advance the rights of women, and e-mail has proven an effective tool for mobilizing solidarity and influencing public opinion. Female MPs have used e-mail to gain solidarity with other female MPs in South Africa and in countries in West Africa, for instance.

ICTs and women's rights

We have to acknowledge that women's low status and the discrimination against them which limits the scope of their rights in most of our countries is not an accident. The causes of women's subordination and unequal gender relations are deeply rooted in history, religion, culture, in

laws and legal systems, and in political institutions and social attitudes.
The solutions therefore, require a comprehensive approach to address
long-term systemic discrimination and oppression.

Amoako (1997[2])

A society's ability to develop depends on its ability to access information,
so information and access to ICTs are no longer a luxury but a human need and,
by inference, a basic human right. Thus, ICTs and women's rights are inextricably
linked. The 1995 World Conference on Women in Beijing reaffirmed the univer-
sality of human rights for women, and the People's Communication Charter was
developed to strengthen current provisions in international law on information,
communication, and culture.[3] Article 6 of the Charter states that

> People have the right to acquire the skills necessary to participate fully
> in public communication. This requires basic literacy in reading and writ-
> ing, training in story-telling, as well as media literacy, computer literacy
> and critical education about the role of communication in society.

Article 15 adds that

> People have a right to universal access to and equitable use of cyber-
> space. With the increasing importance of cyberspace for many social
> activities, people's rights to free and open communities in cyberspace,
> their freedom of electronic expression, and the protection of their privacy
> against electronic surveillance and intrusion should be secured.

Such fundamental freedoms are not only something important in their own right
but also the basis for political, economic, and social development. Unless people
have the right to communicate, political, economic, and social development can
be impeded or delayed.

For this reason, the International Development Research Centre developed
the Acacia Initiative to widen access to ICTs in Africa. Telecentres provide public
access to telephone, fax, e-mail, and the Internet. Telecentres with 8–10 telephone
lines each are transforming people's communication opportunities in Uganda's five
districts. Elizabeth Amuto, a community development officer in Nabweru, one of

---

[2] Dr K.Y. Amoako, Executive Secretary, United Nations Economic Commission for
Africa, opening comments at the Conference on Gender and Law, 29 Oct 1997.

[3] The People's Communication Charter was developed by the Centre for Communication
and Human Rights (Netherlands), the Third World Network (Malaysia), the Cultural Environment
Movement (United States), and the World Association of Community Broadcasters – World Association of Community Radio Broadcasters (Peru and Canada).

five districts with a functioning telecentre, reported that it was a welcome relief
or people, especially women:

> Currently, people have to go to Kampala for information, it costs money
> to travel and then they may find the person is not there or they don't
> have the information. The "telecentre" will save us time and money.
>
> Opoku-Mensah (1998b)

Amuto added that the telecentres are for women because lack of information has
hampered their income-generating potential:

> We have plenty of women's projects in this area but many remote vil-
> lages can't get information on when there is an exhibition where they can
> bring their handicrafts.
>
> Opoku-Mensah (1998b)

Nabweru currently has just one phone line to serve 58 000 people, and this is
typical of phone access outside the capital. The whole of Uganda has 70 000
telephone lines, almost three-quarters of which serve subscribers in Kampala.

With funding from the United States Agency for International Development
(USAID), the Women's Law and Public Policy Fellowship Program of George-
town University (Washington, DC) has, since 1993, sponsored and administered
the Leadership and Advocacy for Women in Africa (LAWA) project. The LAWA
project recruits, selects, and trains female lawyers from Ghana, Tanzania, and
Uganda who are interested in advancing the cause of women's rights upon returning to their country. Selected participants come to Washington for 16 months of
advanced legal study and work assignments on legal and policy issues affecting
the status of women.

All of the LAWA fellows receive Internet and e-mail training, and USAID
has made funds available to enable the women to purchase computers and start up
e-mail accounts upon returning home. Of the 15 fellows who have returned home,
only 3 women based in Uganda have succeeded in activating accounts, which can
be difficult. One of the alumnae, Gloria Ofori-Boadu of Accra, Ghana, did her
graduate work on legal obstacles to women's empowerment in Ghana. She and her
colleagues have been attempting to set up a microcredit initiative, modeled on the
Grameen Bank, to work with Ghanaian female small-traders. Gloria has not had
direct access to e-mail because she has not yet been able to afford or obtain a
separate phone line. To use e-mail, she drives 20 km to the university library,
presents a copy of the information to be sent, either in manuscript or diskette
form, and pays 1 United States dollar (USD) per page to send a message. She
pays 50 cents per page to receive a message. She has to wait 2 days to pick up

replies, but in any event most e-mails sent from the university library never arrive at their destinations because the library personnel key in the wrong addresses.

In the second half of 1996, LAWA placed Regina Rweyemamu, a magistrate from northern Tanzania, with the US Federal Judicial Training Center and the International Women Judges Foundation (IWJF). Regina has worked to develop a judicial training program for Tanzanian judges, and IWJF wants to work with her to further develop and present her program. But it will be impossible to run a program with Regina if she cannot get online.

Ultimately, LAWA expects all of its alumnae to succeed in activating accounts, because it is too important not to. They need to be able to share information about litigation and legislative strategies to combat domestic violence; change sexually discriminatory inheritance, contract, and family laws and practices; and learn about new developments in AIDS prevention (a subject several of them are working on). Funding is expected to be an ongoing problem. Although the costs of access are falling, they are still likely to be higher than these women can easily afford for the foreseeable future.

Creating content and disseminating information on women's rights

> Women are taking new steps and increasingly moving in new directions by networking electronically. ... these days it is not unusual to see women's networks and organizations making the most of new information and communication tools to get their message out and make their voices heard.
>
> IWTC (1996)

There are some positive advantages to be derived from the number of ICT initiatives in Africa, although these initiatives are often uncoordinated. Experience shows that with access to ICT resources, women's groups tend to bridge the information gap among themselves and share their knowledge. For instance, the Zimbabwe Women's Resource Centre makes information available to women through rural libraries.

In the survey conducted by the WNSP, a Kenyan woman wrote specifically about her experience with an APC training session in South Africa:

> My experience with e-mail was very basic. The workshop enabled me to articulate a proposal for increasing connectivity among adult educators on the continent and amongst members. It gave me enough knowledge of e-mail to be able to train other people in basic elements of e-mail. As a result, we held a workshop and connected a number of organizations.
>
> APC (1997)

The way that women use technologies and organize their user groups is often more cooperative and collaborative than that of men, who have a far more individualistic approach. Whereas men tend to explore the technology out of curiosity and fascination, women, because of time constraints, technophobia, and limited access, tend to use computers out of necessity, with a genuine willingness to communicate effectively with others. As a result, women are creating special spaces for themselves and seeking to share ideas and exchange views with diverse groups.

According to Marie-Hélène Mottin-Sylla of ENDA–Dakar's Synergie, Genre et Développement (SYNFEV, Synergy, Gender and Development),

> The freedom to have access to spaces other than the bedroom and the kitchen, and to fully and safely be able to act in other public spaces is key to women's participation in the world's future. Unless African women can participate fully in cyberspace, they will face a new form of exclusion from society.
>
> Pruett and Deane (1998, p. 2)

The South African Women'sNet

A critical aim of Women'sNet, set up in 1998, is to enhance the ability of law- and policymakers and civil society to influence various political and decision-making processes that seek to redress the unequal status of women in South African society. Thus, the initial target groups for this network were

- Gender specialists in legislatures, local and provincial governments, and government line departments;

- People working on women's and gender issues in nongovernmental organizations (NGOs);

- Membership-based women's organizations;

- Women's studies departments and gender units in educational institutions; and

- People working on women's issues at the community level.

Once a significant number of organizations working with women at the community level had begun to participate in the network, the target group was expanded to include women with direct access to the network through NGOs or community-based organizations (CBOs), such as small- and micro-enterprise support groups; resource, training, and advice centres; health and reproductive-rights services; and child-care support groups.

Information on how and where to make a submission to a parliamentary committee, for example, would accompany a government gazette announcement inviting public submissions on a particular bill. Updated information, such as an online calendar of events, would have a format that allowed it to be effectively reproduced as a printed document. Information might also be edited and presented in a format for community radio stations, the most accessible medium of communication in South Africa.

To minimize the gap between those who already have access to technology and to basic computer-skills training and those who have historically been denied such access, a critical component of Women'sNet is to empower women through skills training. As Anriette Esterhuysen (1997[4]) remarked,

> Women in Africa are marginalised, geographically dispersed and lacking in access to the processes of governance. To achieve political emancipation women need to acquire the skills that enable them [to] access, publish and propagate issues, opinions and experiences from their own perspectives. Emancipation is a political process that requires organizing, strategizing, accessing information, lobbying and advocacy. ICTs offer networking, creating peer support, campaigning and sharing of information — spaces that women can control and use to further their interests.

Women'sNet skills training focuses on the technical skills needed to use the electronic network, as well as a basic introduction to information-network development. It has provided this skills training in a series of workshops, including the following:

- A training workshop for an information-management team;

- A national workshop to launch the Women'sNet and provide electronic networking and skills development;

- Provincial workshops on networking and skills development;

- Workshops to train trainers; and

---

[4] A. Esterhuysen, Executive Director of SANGONeT, Johannesburg, South Africa, telephone interview, Dec 1997.

- Maintenance and occasional skills training on request.

The APC Women's Programme has been developing gender-sensitive training materials on electronic networking, which SANGONeT will be able to draw on and adapt for developing a local manual.

Africa-wide database at the United Nations Economic Commission for Africa

The African Centre for Women (ACW) is a division of the United Nations Economic Commission for Africa (ECA). Established in 1975, ACW is the regional women-in-development structure in the United Nations system in Africa. ACW services national, regional, and subregional structures that are involved in the advancement of women. ECA's strategy places a new and greater emphasis on gender issues as crosscutting concerns in the priority areas of focus, which are the following:

- Economic and social policy analysis;

- Development management;

- Food security and sustainable development;

- Information for development; and

- Regional cooperation and integration.

National women's organizations should be encouraged to work with the ACW to establish a continental database of initiatives and organizations using ICTs. Abundant information should also be available on how women can access this database to enhance their networking goals and learn about best practices in Africa.

Sharing experiences

NGOs — linked through functionally relevant networks — have the potential to play a crucial two-way role of strengthening the work and organizational skills which grassroots communities require for their food self-sufficiency, and articulating grassroots concerns at the policy level. NGOs, therefore, potentially have a developmental function both in directly enhancing the food security context of the poorest populations as well as placing their food security concerns and needs on the national development agenda.

Ephraim Matinhira,[5] quoted in Richardson (1996)

Dale Spender claims that literally thousands of women's groups are now online, although it seems that most of them are located in — and limited to — North America. An exception is the Virtual Sisterhood, described as a "network for women around the world to share information, advice and experiences" (APC 1997). It claims to have links with women's networks in a wide range of countries in Asia and Latin America.

Internationally, APC is among the most actively involved in supporting women through electronic communication. Women in Latin America, as well as Canada and the United States, have been using the APC networks for information exchange, and the WNSP has provided training workshops for women in Africa and Asia.

Karen Banks of GreenNet made the point that women's ICT activities take on a dynamic of their own:

> They help women to develop confidence and experience in expressing their viewpoints publicly by allowing space for experimentation and enabling them to find allies across communities, nations and regions.
>
> IDRC (1999)

A woman in South Africa, for example, was recently working on a campaign for women's reproductive and health rights and posted a message on the APC African women's mailing list concerning campaigns and information from other African countries. Women from two other African countries provided information on precedent legislation that could help her advocacy campaign in South Africa. In another case, a Senegalese woman promoting women's participation in African governments was unable to find information locally on the number of female government ministers in Africa. She contacted the international APC women's network through its mailing list. As a consequence, a woman in Geneva with access to United Nations agency information was able to fax information to help her Senegalese colleague.

---

[5] Regional Administrator, Food Security Network of SADC (Southern African Development Community) NGOs.

Training partnerships in Africa

Training women in Africa will require a collaborative approach from donors and
international, regional, and national organizations. A few collaborative training
initiatives are described below.

Setting up networks in francophone Africa: SYNFEV, ENDA's program on communication for women

After the Beijing World Conference on Women, SYNFEV proposed a workshop
to facilitate the development of electronic communications for women's groups
in francophone Africa. With the assistance of APC, SYNFEV was able to identify
a donor, the World Association for Christian Communication (WACC), to financially support this project. Participants each left the workshop with a modem,
installation and configuration disks, and addresses for local Internet or network
access. An electronic network on the theme was put in place to further the process
of communication. SYNFEV also set up an electronic conference on rights and
health for francophone African women, "femmes.afrique" (the primary theme of
SYNFEV's organizations). Currently, SYNFEV is working to increase its capacities to search the World Wide Web for other sites with information relevant to
femmes.afrique, to diversify its sources of information.

WACC has also agreed to financially support a project to provide technical
on-site assistance for electronic communications for women in Burkina Faso,
Cameroon, Côte d'Ivoire, Mali, and Togo. In each country the technician does the
following:

- Checks the technical situation of the organization's electronic connection and reviews and completes the user's training;

- Organizes a session on sensitizing the country's women's organizations;

- Installs two modems and trains users from two women's organizations;
  and

- Participates in visits to sensitize local organizations involved in the provision of Internet access (administrative services, Internet service providers [ISPs], support agencies for women's development), with the
  goal of facilitating future establishment of national-level projects for
  training and equipping other women's groups.

However, it is still difficult for participants to effectively use interactive services, such as the World Wide Web and Gopher, owing to unreliable phone lines. Moreover, repairing modems and other equipment is difficult in most of the countries.

Members of the group are still not posting information, which reduces the network's level of interactivity. This is still a new tool for most women, and they are not used to sharing information in this way. However, Mottin-Sylla (personal communication, 1998[6]) said she received

> lots of Christmas messages from women all over the sub-region. This shows that there is room for a culture of electronic networking on issues once they start to share information. It's just a matter of time.

Connecting a coalition for reproductive rights: the Reproductive Rights Alliance, Johannesburg, South Africa

The Reproductive Rights Alliance is a network of organizations and structures "committed to creating and promoting a liberalised, safe and legal framework for reproductive health and well-being" (IDRC 1999). It was formed in early 1996 to organize support for reproductive rights and comprehensive reproductive heathcare services in South Africa and, more specifically, to work to have legislation passed to allow safe abortions. It brings together some 27 organizations with a history of activism on the issues of reproductive freedom, rights, and health.

As a networking body, the Alliance has planned to strengthen the work of individual organizations in the field by disseminating information and lobbying for the pro-choice position. The Alliance raised funds to help its members and management committee get online — where necessary, purchasing modems, supplying software, and taking out subscriptions to ISPs to enable its members to make effective use of an e-mail communication system.

In February 1996, the Alliance set up a listserv through SANGONeT. Some of the women who joined the listserv were new to computing and even newer to e-mail, having received modems from the Alliance. Some of the participants commented that they did not include electronic communications in their daily routine. People with busy programs were used to spending time on the telephone, faxing, or attending meetings but were unaccustomed to taking time to check their e-mail and participate in the listserv. However, those with many years of experience using e-mail participated in the listserv more freely and actively.

---

[6] Marie-Hélène Mottin-Sylla, SYNFEV, ENDA–Dakar, Senegal, personal communication, 1998.

Some of the criticisms of the listserv were that too few people participated actively (about 20–25% used it consistently to discuss substantive issues) and that it was a one-way communication stream from the Alliance to its members. The major problem was in sending documents. People were unable to decode them. The Alliance used WordPerfect 6.1, which may have added to the difficulties encountered in reading the files in MSWord.[7] The Alliance therefore had to send documents by fax or resend them in ASCII, as well as by e-mail. This was identified as a training issue but was never effectively addressed.

A further plan of the Alliance is to reach rural organizations dealing with reproductive rights. It would use e-mail to do this, as far as possible. However, most of the contacts are through government organizations or NGOs, which tend to lack infrastructure. Although money alone is not the issue, the lack of infrastructure, such as computers, and the knowledge to use them may present problems for the Alliance.

North–South partnerships

Supporting women's electronic networking in Africa: WNSP

The WNSP works with a community defined as groups of female networkers who are leaders in their own right in the fields of journalism, health, and reproductive rights, ISPs, information brokerage, and environmental sustainability. They work as intermediaries, providing linkages for their communities in and through national and international initiatives and forums. They are motivators, animators, and focal points of networks in their countries and regions, and they use ICTs to facilitate their work with their communities.

The WNSP's objectives are to equip women's groups in Africa, Asia, and Latin America with the necessary access to training, technology, and information to

- Facilitate local, regional, and international communication and information exchange;

- Empower women with an information tool they can use to increase their own visibility and highlight their own achievements as primary agents of development;

---

[7] Mention of a proprietary name does not constitute an endorsement of the product but is given only for information.

- Provide access to communication channels and facilitate information exchange for women and men around the Beijing process;

- Respond to women's training needs and support the involvement of a core group of female technicians and information-management specialists (IDRC 1999).

APC set up the WNSP in 1993 in response to several convergent needs and demands from women and women's organizations working within and outside APC and its network alliances. Generally speaking, the WNSP has had the most impact in Ghana, Kenya, Morocco (and the Maghreb), Mozambique, Senegal (and francophone West Africa), South Africa, Tanzania, Uganda, and Zambia.

ICTs and governments: strengthening women's political and public participation

Making government information available to citizens is important, if not critical, to governance. By giving society access to such information, a government invites wider participation. Tools such as the World Wide Web and e-mail can be useful in furthering both central- and local-government communication, which can create a culture of open governance.

For instance, in the United States, the League of Women Voters, the Public Information Exchange, and the Project Vote Smart began the Voter Online Information and Communication Exchange to provide information on local, state, and national candidates via a web page. Public libraries had project terminals, and the web page was available to anyone with a computer and modem. Citizens could find candidate profiles for local, state, and national campaigns, in addition to information on polling places, voting, candidate voting records, campaign contributions, and third-party ratings of candidates.

With the introduction of telecentres in some African countries, there is no reason why women's groups cannot create online sites to enhance women's access to voter information. Such telecentres would respond to some of the difficulties in the electoral process cited by Prisca Nyambe (personal communication, 1998[8]):

> During the 1991 Zambian elections, one of the difficulties in the electoral process was communicating vital information to voters, especially women

---

[8] P. Nyambe, human-rights lawyer with the International Criminal Tribunal for Rwanda, based in Arusha, Tanzania, personal communication, 1998.

in rural areas who knew nothing about civic education, voters rights, etc. If at the time computers were strategically placed throughout the country people could have obtained relevant information for their political emancipation. It is not only critical that voters have access to information during elections, but there must also be consistent information flows from voters to politicians and vice versa — otherwise the process becomes meaningless. The use of ICTs can address this.

Integrating ICTs into governance — South Africa

The South African government is planning to integrate information technology into much of what it does. At the Africa Telecom '98 conference, it launched a new scheme to provide 24-hour access to government departments through public information terminals (PITs). Research conducted by the Department of Communications had shown that just as people like to do their shopping after working hours and during the weekend, they also want to deal with government departments most during those hours. Under this scheme, the public uses a PIT for such time-consuming tasks as applying for a driver's licence, a passport, or even a government tender — at the public's convenience.

According to Andile Ngcaba, Director-General of South Africa's Department of Communications, who conceived of the project, "PITs can ease backlogs in medical care, as well as provide other valuable government information usually not found, and offer citizens access to the Internet, e-mail and teleshopping." So far, five prototype terminals have appeared in post offices, supermarkets, and other public places, at a cost of 40 000 USD per unit. "The next generation of PITs," Ngcaba said, "will have small cameras integrated into the technology with digital signatures for people to fill and sign most government forms straight from the machine" (Opoku-Mensah 1998a).

ICTs and local government

African countries are making efforts to decentralize their governments and to strengthen local-government administrations. Strategic ICT interventions might be of help in this endeavour. Women's groups could work with local governments to expedite women's access to government services and information, promote their participation in political debate and government decision-making, and enhance government accountability. If ICTs are to be used for these purposes, stakeholders need to develop goals, identify constraints, as outlined in Tables 1 and 2, and proceed to the issues of how to present and access information.

Table 1. Policy goals for governments.

Policy goal	ICT implementation	Measure of success
Promote women's participation in political debate and government decision-making	Provide information on town meetings, agenda, and minutes on issues of concern to women's groups	Women's increased participation, electronic or otherwise, in local government affairs
Enhance government accountability	Provide electronic access to government officials via e-mail	Results of a survey of women to measure quality of responses to complaints and comments

Table 2. Constraints for NGOs.

Constraint	Potential resolution
Lack of women's access to ICTs	Provide Internet connections at focal points: telecentres, public libraries, hospitals, community centres, and Internet kiosks owned and operated by women
High costs of owning computer equipment and high fees for Internet access	Provide free access for disadvantaged citizens, subsidize access for associations and NGOs, provide discounts to SMEs owned by women
Computer illiteracy among users	Provide free or low-cost computer training and more user-friendly software
Limited knowledge and use of the English language	Enlist NGOs to act as intermediaries, providing translations and disseminating information

Note: NGO, nongovernmental organization; SMEs, small- and medium-scale enterprises.

Conclusions and recommendations

In summary, a mixture of political, technological, and economic changes has enabled a new model of communications to emerge. It is decentralized, pluralistic, and democratic, empowering rather than controlling, and it fosters debate among citizens, communities, people, and government. This model envisages increasingly horizontal communications, allowing people to communicate with each other easily and inexpensively, and involves the steady disintegration of the top-down approach, in which governments own and control the flows of information.

Communications will have radically new effects on the social well-being of African countries over the next few years. Global economic liberalization of telecommunications, the rapid deployment of the Internet in most developing countries, mobile telephony and other new technologies, along with a changing political environment, have all coincided to make the last years of the 20th century a definitive moment for countries attempting to adapt to these developments and exploit them. If such changes are to accommodate politically and economically marginalized people and improve their lives, then both governments and people will have to make deliberate decisions that reflect the diversity of views within their societies.

Recommendations

Based on the examples and models put forward above, I make the following recommendations.

Policy dialogue with governments

Two main sets of actors greatly determine the information-technology landscape in Africa: national governments and specialized agencies in the United Nations system, primarily the International Telecommunication Union and UNESCO. The feminist movement needs to exert its influence on how the state diffuses best or accepted practices. New networks, such as Women'sNet and the Reproductive Rights Alliance in South Africa, should engage the government in communication-policy dialogue in the legislative and decision-making processes.

African governments need to involve women and women's organizations in devising strategies to develop the Internet and telecommunications. To arrive at more rational and humane policies, governments must involve women's organizations more closely in consultations and decision-making sessions.

Partnerships with local governments

If ICTs are to have a greater impact on the democratization process, then local governments must come into the loop (see the earlier section "ICTs and Governments: Strengthening Women's Political and Public Participation"). CBOs must in particular try to forge alliances with local-government authorities to introduce the use of ICTs in communities.

Women's groups as information facilitators

Connecting individual rural women directly to the Internet is impractical in Africa. However, women's groups can use Internet systems and ICTs to provide better services to a range of groups, from small-scale farmers, to petty traders, to housewives. Women's groups are in a unique position to act as information facilitators and to serve as bridges for people without access to ICTs. For example, the Zimbabwe Women's Resource Centre, FOWODE (in Uganda), and the South African Women'sNet offer information to people without access to computers or to ICTs in general.

Exploring appropriate technology

Africa can find ways to adapt to ICTs without thinking in terms of high-tech equipment. For instance, the use of alternatives to full Internet connectivity, such as protocols like FIDO, is still quite popular in Africa. Offline facilities or low-tech tools, such as radio, fax, or personal communications, that are combined with computer facilities can be particularly useful for rural African women's organizations. Uganda's Bushnet is an ISP using high-frequency radio communications to provide links between its servers and its subscribers. A centrally managed polling station has a computer, a high-frequency radio, and a modem and is linked to the Internet through another Ugandan ISP. Through high-frequency radio stations owned by its customers in remote areas, Bushnet brings Internet services to parts of the country that no other ISP can reach. But this service doesn't come cheap! The full high-frequency radio station costs 6 600–7 500 USD, and the connection fee, which includes training and online support, is more than 1 000 USD. To send messages four times a day would cost 100 USD. This is considerably more expensive than Uganda's conventional ISPs, which charge 50.00–65.00 USD a month. However, countries would find it a challenge to decide how to bring down the price, given the limited infrastructure in rural areas.

Monitoring and evaluating the impact of ICTs on women

Efforts should be made to monitor and evaluate women's use of ICTs for sustainable development and democracy. These efforts should focus on the following:

- Assessing women's needs:

    - Identifying needs and opportunities for increasing women's access,

    - Identifying needs and opportunities for increasing women's control of ICT resources and benefits,

    - Relating women's needs and opportunities to the country's general and sectoral development goals, and

    - Determining how women have been consulted;

- Monitoring the impact of ICTs on women's activities:

  - Assessing how ICTs have affected women's activities, and

  - Assessing the positive and negative impacts of ICTs on women; and

- Measuring the impact of women's access and control of ICTs:

  - Assessing how women can acquire roles in the generation and dissemination of information, and

  - Assessing women's access to and control of ICT resources and how the benefits can be increased.

Data from monitoring and evaluation should determine the impact of ICTs on women in empirical terms.

African economies and democracies are in transition, and the interface between their economies and their democracies will be the greatest challenge facing this continent. ICTs will be crucial to managing this interface. ICTs also offer African countries an opportunity to leapfrog into a technological era that can transform the continent.

References

APC (Association for Progressive Communications). 1997. Global networking for change: experiences from the APC Women's Programme survey. APC Women's Programme, London, UK.

IDRC (International Development Research Centre). 1999. The Acacia Initiative. IDRC, Ottawa, ON, Canada. Internet: www.idrc.ca/acacia

IWTC (International Women's Tribune Centre). 1996. The Tribune, 55.

Johnson-Sirleaf, E. 1997. Empowering women for the 21st century: development and leadership. *In* Aderinwale, A., ed., The challenges of politics, business, development and leadership. ALF Publications, London, UK.

Marcelle, G. 1995. Using information technology to strengthen African women's organisations. Abantu for Development, London, UK.

NCR (Namibia Country Report). 1997. Reports submitted by states parties under Article 18 of the Convention on the Elimination of All Forms of Discrimination Against Women:

initial report of states parties: Namibia. United Nations Development Programme, New York, NY, USA. CEDAW/C/NAM/1, 10 Feb.

Opoku-Mensah, A. 1998a. Need a passport? Panos Features, 30 Jun.

———— 1998b. Telecentres excite Ugandans — but what about the poor? Panos Features, 4 Aug.

Pruett, D.; Deane, J. 1998. The Internet and poverty: real help or real hype? Panos, London, UK. Panos Briefing No. 28. Internet: www.oneworld.org/panos/briefing/interpov.htm

Richardson, D. 1996. The Internet and rural development: recommendations for strategy and activity. Food and Agriculture Organization of the United Nations, Rome, Italy.

Taylor, V. 1997. Social mobilization: lessons from the mass democratic movement. Mega Print, Cape Town, South Africa.

UNIFEM–AAI (United Nations Development Fund for Women; African–American Institute). 1995. African women in politics: together for change — three struggles for political rights (Botswana, Uganda and Zambia). UNIFEM, New York, NY, USA.

Useem, A. 1998. Greeting Madame President. Africa Today, Jan.

Chapter 8

ENHANCING WOMEN'S PARTICIPATION IN GOVERNANCE: THE CASE OF KAKAMEGA AND MAKUENI DISTRICTS, KENYA

Shanyisa Anota Khasiani

The end of the Cold War in international politics has had impacts on nations and peoples around the world. It has led to shifts in political alliances from the Cold War balance of power at all levels; it has led to shifts in international finance from support for undemocratic regimes to strict conditionalities for pluralization of sociopolitical and economic relations. The new development paradigm emphasizes partnerships between the state, the market, and civil society. For the majority of the population in Africa, this is a new beginning and the advent of a new political emancipation.

This new paradigm and the new order have been accompanied by some obviously negative processes: inflation, economic marginalization of subgroups, and increased poverty. However, the emerging revolutions, including increased democratization, economic liberalization, and competitive politics, are also providing windows of opportunities, which are in turn shaping people's needs. This has also brought existing gaps into sharper focus, particularly gaps in existing civic knowledge and in the skills needed to use information and communication technologies (ICTs). These gaps are setting a new agenda for development work.

In Kenya, the lack of civic knowledge, which is worsened by a lack of skills and access to ICTs, has resulted in voter apathy and the failure of the Kenyan people to participate effectively in the electoral process and governance. Kenya held its first multiparty election, under colonial supervision, in 1963. The seventh general election, in 1992, was the first multiparty election held in the independent Republic of Kenya. Following this election, numerous allegations were made concerning election anomalies and malpractices, such as violations of election laws and bribery, which undermined the principle of free and fair elections and ultimately those of efficient management practices, such as good governance, transparency, and accountability. The 1997 election was thus organized amid country-wide demands for a level playing field and minimum constitutional reforms.

The situation for women is particularly grave and justifies the establishment of community-based information and documentation centres. Women constitute the majority in Kenya's population and play a pivotal role in the economy. Most live in rural areas, where they form the backbone of the small-scale sector. Many households depend on women's incomes. Women, therefore, contribute significantly to Kenya's gross domestic product, its employment generation, and its supply of foreign revenue. Women also produce and maintain the country's labour force.

Despite the numeric advantage of Kenyan women and their significant contribution to the economy, they fail to have access to key development resources and are consequently poor. Although Kenya has a development-policy commitment to balancing access to development resources for women and men, this has not translated into reality. Despite government policy pronouncements, the difference between women's and men's access to development resources is intensifying, with levels for men closer to the targets than those for women.

Table 1 shows the gender-based disparities in all policy areas. In 1996, 64% of trained secondary-school teachers were men. Most of the untrained teachers were also men (77%). Women's representation in modern-sector employment only rose from 12% in 1964 to 21% in 1990. The same pattern appears for gender representation in the civil service and the media. In 1989, women made up only 22% of extension workers; by 1994, this proportion had dropped to 20%. Men also dominated in teaching at training colleges (data not shown). Gender disparities also appeared in the legal sector in 1994: only 23% of the high-court judges and magistrates were women. Most of the Members of Parliament (MPs) and representatives in the local authorities were men. In 1969, women constituted only 7% of the MPs; after the 1997 general election, the proportion that was female dropped even further, to 3%. The number of women in civic positions increased after the 1997 elections, but men still held 86% of these positions.

Such gender-based disparities are unjustified in a country where women form the majority of voters. Women's lack of involvement in professional and political life in Kenya is perpetuated because few women are aware of their civic,

Table 1. Women's and men's access to development resources in Kenya, 1960–97.

Development areas	Women	Men
Education and training		
Trained teachers in secondary schools (1996) (%)	35.7	64.3
Untrained teachers in secondary schools (1996) (%)	33.0	77.0
Illiterate people		
1960 (%)	96.0	70.0
1990 (%)	53.0	27.0
Labour, employment, human-resource development, and civic service		
Proportion of employment in modern sector		
1964 (%)		
1990 (%)	12.0	88.0
Proportion of employment in civil service (1991) (%)	21.0	70.0
	23.0	77.0
Information and media (1994)		
Number of provincial information officers (n)	3	5
Number of deputy editors of rural press (n)	3	8
Number of editors of rural press (n)	0	11
Agriculture and extension work		
Proportion of extension workers		
1989 (%)	22.0	78.0
1994 (%)	20.0	68.0
Judiciary (1994)		
Proportion of judges and magistrates (%)	23.0	77.0
Members of Parliament		
Proportion of Members of Parliament		
1969 (%)	7.0	93.0
1997 (%)	3.0	97.0
Civic seats (1997)		
Proportion of counsellors (%)	14.3	85.7

Source: FASI (1999).

social, and economic rights. Because of their lack of civic awareness and their poverty, women are convenient targets for those who try to buy their votes during political campaigns. Women are also ill-equipped to perceive the connection between their choice of leaders and the resulting social and economic policies affecting their lives.

In this chapter, I describe the Women and Governance project in Kakamega and Makueni districts of Kenya and assess the role of ICTs in this project. I show that community-based resource centres, equipped with ICTs, can

- Play a key role in informing Kenyans, especially women, of critical issues in the electoral process;

- Enhance women's interaction;

- Be used for generating, storing, and exchanging strategic information; and thus

- Enable women to make informed decisions and participate effectively in the electoral process.

In this chapter, I assume that 'women's lack of access to information is a reflection of the disparity in women's and men's access to development resources. Although women have demonstrated their capacity for leadership and have transformed communities, they have been considered inefficient in their roles, being dismissed as "immature," as "lacking the capacity to be scientific," as "followers of men rather than leaders," or as "unable to take stress." Such perceptions have limited women's ability to acquire new skills and responsibilities and use their potential to the maximum. In particular, their failure to acquire the new and dynamic ICT skills has confined women to the indigenous sector, variously described as traditional, rural, backward, or informal, and kept them away from the modern, urban, progressive, formal sector. Another assumption of this chapter is that women can use ICTs to work together, gain peer support, campaign effectively, and share, control, and use information to further their interests. ICTs will thus also enable women to be proactive and introduce their own perspectives when publishing and propagating issues, opinions, and experiences. The Women and Governance project helps women gain control and fluency in the use of contemporary tools for production, processing, dissemination, and use of information and enhances women's civic awareness.

The information in this chapter was obtained from primary and secondary sources and consultative meetings. A needs assessment was conducted among women in Kakamega and Makueni to generate primary data. A stakeholders conference provided additional information. The conference brought together women from Kakamega and Makueni; a number of ICT service providers; representatives of government and nongovernmental organizations (NGOs); and development experts in the fields of ICTs, civic knowledge, women in development, and information, education, and communication (IEC). The chapter also draws on information from a curriculum- and materials-development workshop, which brought together women from Kakamega and Makueni and specialists in materials development, civic knowledge, and ICTs.

Pitfalls in the evolution of civic knowledge in Kenya

Following the reintroduction of a multiparty system in Kenya, in 1992, civic education emerged as an issue of interest to the *Wananchi* (a common term used in Kenya to refer to the ordinary people), particularly the women. Women in Kenya, more than any other group, emerged as strong and organized. They demanded a voice; they demanded a mainstream position for their interests on the new political agenda; and they demanded equal participation with men in the democratization process.

A flurry of activities revolved around the sensitization of leaders to gender-based issues. Workshops were organized to discuss strategies for mainstreaming the issues affecting women. The objective was to have more women in decision-making positions. The ultimate goals were to improve the citizens' knowledge of their democratic rights and responsibilities, enhance their understanding of the impacts of the social and political situation in the country on their lives, and enable them to manage their own governance process.

One of the main constraints on women's participation in the democratization process was found to be a lack of civic awareness. At that time, no one had begun to generate, design, or package civic information to enhance women's full political, economic, and social participation. The research established that appropriate civic information would give women greater confidence to seek leadership positions at both local and national levels. Civic activities focused on educating women on their civil and political rights and creating a pool of leaders with civic knowledge, particularly in the areas of women's empowerment, democracy and governance, and gender.

The strategy was to increase women's participation in all spheres of development, especially leadership and decision-making. In 1992, 18 women vied for parliamentary seats, and 6 were elected. The strategy had limited impact. This situation persists today: women's representation in politics and decision-making is still low. Women have failed to translate their numeric strength into political power, and this is attributable to structural imbalances in Kenyan society that discriminate against women and make their search for leadership difficult. Cultural stereotyping of women in general and of female leaders in particular is negative and buttresses and perpetuates inequality, even in areas where laws have been passed to prevent this. Gender inequality continues in Kenya, even as we approach the new millennium. If we are to change the tide, the challenge will be to change the laws, the electoral system, the economic structures, and the ways women view themselves and are viewed by men. The struggle for both de facto and de jure equality is not feminist chauvinism but an integral part of women's human rights.

The strategy adopted at the dawn of competitive politics in Kenya, in 1992, was to train community educators and leaders so they would themselves be knowledgeable and skilled trainers. This was a feasible strategy to create a better informed community and increase the participation of women in governance. However, it was too narrowly focused on governance and civic issues in electoral politics and left out development conditions of ordinary life.

Following the 1993 World Conference on Human Rights in Vienna, Austria, women's rights began to be defined as "human rights." This became the clarion call. Meetings and civic training stressed that economic, social, and cultural rights are interrelated with, and inseparable from, civil and political rights. Civic training was expanded and focused on creating awareness in the following areas:

- Gender and equity issues;

- Legal issues (particularly those pertaining to women);

- Voter education;

- Human rights (women's rights);

- Responsible citizenship; and

- Reproductive health.

However, civic education in Kenya continued to lack consistency and regard for development. Preparations for the 1997 general election were dominated by the need to educate voters and have them understand the electoral process. After the elections, the focus shifted to the constitutional review process. Women established lobby groups, such as the Kenya Women Political Caucus, for specific constitutional issues. After some time, the focus of civic concern would shift to something else.

Spontaneous responses to sensational, often short-lived issues have characterized the evolution of civic education in Kenya. The responses have been emotional and reactionary. Civic education has therefore not been consistent or harmonious. It has not been directed to persistent issues. It has not established a program with a system of relevant, cumulative knowledge, experiences, methodologies, and solutions. Activists have made numerous haphazard, often contradictory resolutions and formulated action plans to carry forward the spirit of empowerment. But this is worsened by the restrictive environments created by government, which, at best, has withheld its support for civic education and, at worst, interfered in it. This mood persists. Despite a legal amendment to allow the Electoral Commission to carry out voter education, the government refuses to allot sufficient funds for this activity, ostensibly because it is not a national priority.

The Women and Governance project has set itself the task of finding answers to the many questions that remain unanswered: How is it possible to be certain about the state of civic knowledge in Kenya, given the diversity of experience? What has been done with this information? How has this information been stored? What retrieval mechanisms have been established? How is the information disseminated? What are the information gaps? What possibilities and challenges would be faced in any attempt to fill such information gaps? What areas of capacity-building are required to ensure more effective civic education? What has been the impact of the activities directed to civic education and knowledge (involving many donors, NGOs, churches, community-based organizations, and people)? Have educators empowered women to generate, store, access, use, and manage their own information? Whose needs has civic information responded to?

The Women and Governance project

Target areas

The Family Support Institute (FASI), an NGO, has been implementing the Women and Governance project in Central Isukha, which is in Kakamega District, in Western Province; and in Nguumo, which is in Makueni District, in Eastern Province.

Central Isukha

Central Isukha has six sections: Virhembe, Mukulusu, Shagungu, Shinyalu, Shiswa, and Kakamega forest. These cover an area of 620 km^2 and have a total population of 42 126, giving an average density of 679 people/km^2.

Central Isukha is traversed by one main *murram* road (a terraced earth road), from Khayega market to Kakamega town. Some parts of Central Isukha have access to electricity through the government-funded Rural Electrification Programme: the environments along the main road, the District Officers' Centre, Shibuye Girls Secondary School, and Lirhanda Girls Secondary School. Parts of

Central Isukha also have access to piped water, owing to the Integrated Rural Water System of the Ministry of Water Development, the efforts of NGOs, and bilateral water programs.

Central Isukha has a post office and some telephone facilities and other communication services supplied through the post office. However, it has no community-based resource centre and therefore lacks the related services, such as libraries and networking facilities.

Ongoing activities in this locality include those of women's groups, mainly supported by the Ministry of Culture and Social Services (MCSS), bilateral or multilateral donors, and nongovernmental agencies. These activities include civic training conducted by community-based civic educators and coordinated by the Catholic Justice for Peace Commission. The Family Planning Association of Kenya (FPAK) provides education for women's groups, using folk media and drama. FPAK also uses puppet shows to train women in family planning and AIDS awareness and prevention. MCSS supports women's activities in the areas of farming methods (to increase crop yields), estate management (house building and renting), a handicrafts industry, revolving loan funds, social welfare, and adult literacy. In addition, the line ministries, NGOs, and community members implement sectoral activities. But the donor and NGO presence is more limited in Central Isukha than in other parts of Kenya.

Nguumo

Nguumo covers an area of 3 410 km^2 and has a total population of 151 310, giving an average density of 44 people/km^2.

Nguumo is on the Nairobi–Mombasa road and has access to electricity through the government-funded Rural Electrification Programme. Water is available through the Integrated Rural Water System of the Ministry of Water Development, the efforts of NGOs, and bilateral programs.

Nguumo has a community-based resource centre, established by the African Medical Research Foundation (AMREF) with funding from the International Development Research Centre (IDRC) and the Swedish Agency for Research Cooperation with Developing Countries. The resource centre, which serves 12 villages and focuses on community-based health information systems (HIS), was the output of an applied research project on health information and primary health care. It used a geographic information system to develop an intersectoral database for subdistrict-level planning and management. Various HIS components were tested by the Integrated District Diagnosis project, which was implemented in the former greater Kibwezi division between 1989 and 1992. The communities run the project with the help of AMREF and in close collaboration with the government. The project trains local community members, who generate survey and qualitative information and prepare and produce manuals on the use and development of community-based health information in rural areas and on health-care management. Eco News Africa, with funding from IDRC, and other donors will establish a community-based high-frequency and FM radio station for exchange of information and experiences among community members in Kibwezi and two other communities in Tanzania and Uganda.

FASI's Women and Governance project is building on these initiatives. Its Civic Education project is also expected to act as a catalyst for activities of other NGOs and government departments. The government has stepped up efforts to raise the status of women through general awareness, civic education, and the participation of women's groups in promoting equal rights and women at all levels.

Target population and communities

Rural women's group members and their leaders in the communities in the two localities make up the target population for the project. Kenya has more than 30 000 women's groups with memberships totaling more than 1 million. Central Isukha has 1 000 women's groups, with 30 000 members altogether. The catchment area for the Central Isukha project has 500 women's groups, with a total membership of 15 000. In Nguumo, the project targets another 500 women's groups, also with a total membership of about 15 000.

Until recently, women's civic participation was mainly restricted to electoral politics. Even within the electoral process, women are seriously manipulated through bribery, violence, and intimidation, owing to their illiteracy, civic ignorance, poverty, and cultural marginalization. The introduction of multiparty politics has provided the opportunity to enhance women's civic knowledge and increase their participation in governance (broadly defined to include electoral politics and development conditions of ordinary life).

Objectives

The general objective of the Women and Governance project is to build on the existing infrastructure in community-based resource centres so that the women in the two rural localities (Central Isukha and Nguumo) will be able to access, generate, and use civic information to enhance their participation in governance. The specific objectives of the project are to

- Increase women's awareness of their civic rights and responsibilities;

- Increase the pool of informed women who can participate in the electoral process as candidates and voters;

- Increase women's representation in decision-making positions in the public and private sectors;

- Increase community members' control of the electoral process and promote the principles of free and fair elections;

- Create awareness of the virtues of accountability, transparency, and good governance;

- Increase women's access to ICTs and their ability to use them for their own daily needs and thereby improve their capacity for development-related decision-making;

- Increase the opportunities for communities to update their information on governance; and

- Increase the opportunities for communities to use ICTs to upgrade their traditional information systems and networks.

Activities

Several activities will be implemented under this project:

- Undertaking a needs assessment in the target districts to determine the status of civic-information resources and ICTs;

- Convening a consultative meeting for stakeholders to review and share information on existing civic materials and ICT resources, to assess their adequacy, to identify gaps, and to develop an action plan;

- Generating additional civic-education materials, securing ICTs, and establishing a training program to respond to identified needs;

- Establishing resource centres in the project areas, equipped with comprehensive civic-education materials, ICTs, and training programs;

- Recruiting resource people skilled in ICTs, managers skilled in management of community-resource centres, and women's group leaders from communities in the target areas to participate in the project;

- Facilitating the resource people's training of two resource-centre managers and volunteer trainers (women's group leaders) in the management and use of community-based information centres and ICTs;

- Facilitating the resource-centre managers' and volunteer trainers' training of women's group members from the local communities in civic education and the management and use of community-based information centres and ICTs; and

- Conducting exchange tours between the women from the two project areas so that they can share information and viewpoints.

Women's common conditions and issues in Kakamega and Makueni

For women in Kakamega and Makueni, governance is still an ideal that they are striving to achieve. The women experience common problems related to socio-economic and cultural governance and to political governance.

Socioeconomic and cultural governance

The women in the two project areas experience similar conditions: deprivation, exploitation, exclusion, and poverty. A needs assessment conducted among women in Kakamega and Makueni showed that socioeconomic and cultural governance (defined as access to and control of resources, improved social status, and participation in economic decision-making to ensure equity) remains elusive (Table 2).

More than one-half of the women in the project had only primary education; less than one-fifth had secondary education; and nearly one-third had never been to school. This reflects high levels of nonenrollment and school dropout among girls. They are not of the favoured gender and are not supported or targeted for skills development. This was further confirmed in the observation that more than one-third of the women in Kakamega and Makueni are unable to read or write in any language.

Table 2. Socioeconomic characteristics of women in Kakamega and Makueni districts.

Characteristics	Proportion of respondents (%)		
	Total	Makueni	Kakamega
Education achieved			
None	28.5	31.0	26.0
Primary	54.5	51.0	58.0
Secondary	17.0	18.0	16.0
Literacy			
Can read	62.0	62.0	62.0
Cannot read	38.0	38.0	38.0
Distance to water			
<1 km	40.5	1.0	80.0
1–2 km	31.5	43.0	20.0
3–4 km	16.0	32.0	0.0
≥5 km	12.0	24.0	0.0
Type of cooking facility			
Wood fuel	97.5	97.0	98.0
Paraffin	51.5	1.0	2.0
Charcoal	2.0	2.0	0.0
Occupation			
Unpaid family worker	76.5	88.0	65.0
Skilled public-sector employee	1.5	2.0	1.0
Skilled private-sector employee	0.5	0.0	1.0
Business person	16.5	6.0	27.0
Unskilled private-sector employee	1.0	0.0	2.0
Retired	0.5	0.0	1.0
Service worker	3.5	4.0	3.0
Sources of income			
Salaried employee	6.5	6.0	7.0
Business	8.5	6.0	11.0
Farming	39.0	44.0	34.0
Husband's salary or business	37.0	40.0	34.0
None	9.0	4.0	14.0
Business ownership			
By respondent	14.0	5.0	23.0
By spouse	2.5	1.0	4.0
Not applicable	83.5	94.0	73.0
Name on land title			
Respondent	5.0	8.0	2.0
Respondent's husband	54.5	62.0	47.0
Father-in-law	24.5	5.0	44.0
Mother-in-law	2.5	5.0	0.0
Son	0.5	0.0	1.0
Father	0.5	1.5	0.0
Not applicable	12.5	19.0	6.0

(continued)

Table 2 concluded.

Characteristics	Proportion of respondents (%)		
	Total	Makueni	Kakamega
Who decides on sale of crops			
Respondent	18.5	21.0	16.0
Husband	67.5	63.0	72.0
Father-in-law	2.5	1.0	4.0
Mother-in-law	0.5	6.0	1.0
Other	2.5	1.0	4.0
Not applicable	8.5	14.0	3.0
Who decides on sale of animals			
Respondent	15.5	21.0	10.0
Husband	52.0	38.0	66.0
Father-in-law	1.5	3.0	0.0
Both husband and wife	0.5	0.0	1.0
Mother	0.5	0.0	1.0

Source: FASI (1999).

Access to water in Kakamega and Makueni is a problem. In Kakamega, water sources are near and can be easily accessed by women; however, the water sources are unprotected and often contaminated, resulting in waterborne sicknesses. Managing the health care of the household members creates more work for the already overburdened women.

The water problems in Makueni relate to the long distances women have to travel for water, which leaves them with little time for other welfare activities. This adversely affects the girls' performance at school. Long distances to water sources also explain why water is a scarce resource. Rationing water within households undermines personal and household hygiene and renders household members vulnerable to disease. Furthermore, women have to perform in multiple roles, as collectors of water and firewood and providers of health care, and have little community support. Having these multiple roles undermines their ability to meet their other responsibilities, especially child care.

Most women in Kakamega and Makueni are engaged in unpaid family labour, mainly farming, which is unreliable because it depends on weather conditions. Most women also engage in their farming activities without owning any land. Men, mainly husbands and fathers-in-law, are the legal owners of the land the women live on and farm. Consequently, women grow crops and keep animals on this land but do not make decisions regarding the sale of crops or animals. In both districts, women only make decisions regarding the sale of animal products, such as milk, eggs, and hides. Women in the two districts are also vulnerable because they depend on their husbands' salaries and therefore their livelihoods and welfare are pegged on someone else's decisions — the husband could choose to leave his job, or he could genuinely lose it. Some women engage in trading activities, selling groceries, vegetables, cereals, animals, second-hand clothes, household goods, and fruits. These businesses are controlled by the women themselves; this reflects their potential to control their own income-generating resources. However, female farmers and traders have poor markets. Most women sell their goods in the local markets. Distributors' exploitation of rural producers is a particularly serious problem in Makueni. Women also expressed concern about having goods to sell but no access to markets.

Political governance

Political governance encompasses the decision-making and policy implementation of a legitimate and authoritative state, which represents the interests of society and allows citizens to freely elect their representatives. Women in Kakamega and Makueni have yet to achieve this.

These women nevertheless know the qualities of a good leader. A good leader, for these women, would be presentable, courageous, honest, sociable, a good example to others, God-fearing, patient and fair and would initiate development and mobilize community members. The women in each of the project districts identified the same qualities, differing only in their ranking of these. Additional qualities included being cooperative, creative, self-respecting, and educated, having stable families, owning some property, and being knowledgeable (Table 3).

Just less than one-half of the women in the two districts thought that men had these qualities and therefore would be good leaders. A discussion group of men reported that people generally assumed that men would be better leaders; they used citations from the Bible to confirm that men are better leaders because they have interests outside the home, whereas women's interests are confined to the home. The majority of the women, especially those in Kakamega, did not consider women to be good leaders. One woman reported that although she thought men were better leaders they had not been leading the country very well. More than one-half of the women in both districts thought that a combination of women and men would provide good leadership.

These women had been increasingly participating in the electoral process, as candidates, observers, managers, campaigners, and voters. More participated in

Table 3. Women's participation in the electoral process.

Characteristic	Proportion of respondents (%)		
	Total	Makueni	Kakamega
Do you belong to a women's group?			
Yes	58.0	68.0	47.0
No	42.0	32.0	53.0
What position do you hold in the group?			
Ordinary woman	27.0	32.0	23.0
Chairperson	4.5	5.0	4.0
Secretary	3.0	3.0	3.0
Treasurer	2.0	2.0	2.0
Committee member	5.0	8.0	2.0
Other	0.5	1.0	-
Not applicable	57.5	49.0	66.0
What are the qualities of a good leader?			
Presentable	23.5	18.0	29.0
Courageous	17.5	12.0	23.0
Honest	29.5	29.0	30.0
Sociable	32.0	27.0	37.0
Good model	21.0	17.0	25.0
Democratic	11.0	17.0	5.0
God-fearing	28.0	22.0	35.0
Patient	11.0	12.0	10.0
Cooperative	10.5	13.0	8.0
Creative	6.5	10.0	3.0
Of good conduct	18.0	12.0	24.0
Advising	8.0	7.0	9.0
Mobilizes community	18.0	29.0	8.0
Initiator of community development	34.0	47.0	22.0
Self-respecting	7.5	11.0	4.0
Knowledgeable	8.5	6.0	11.0
Who is a good leader?			
Men	41.5	47.0	36.0
Women	7.5	11.0	4.0
Both men and women	51.0	42.0	60.0
What positions did women vie for in the 1997 elections?			
Parliamentary	23.5	44.0	3.0
Councillor	47.0	2.0	92.0
Both	5.5	10.0	1.0
Don't know	24.0	44.0	4.0
What other elective positions did women vie for?			
Party leader	8.0	12.0	4.0
Administration (chief or subchief)	7.0	13.0	1.0
School committee	75.0	83.0	68.0
Women's group committees	69.5	61.0	78.0
Church committee	67.5	51.0	84.0
Other community committees	32.0	18.0	46.0

(continued)

Table 3 concluded.

Characteristic	Proportion of respondents (%)		
	Total	Makueni	Kakamega
Did you vote in 1992 election?			
Yes	56.0	82.0	72.0
No	44.0	18.0	28.0
Did you vote in 1997 election?			
Yes	79.5	82.0	77.0
No	20.5	18.0	23.0
Did you receive anything in order to vote?			
Yes	38.5	25.0	52.0
No	61.5	75.0	48.0
Did you attend campaign meetings in 1997 election?	54.5	55.0	54.0
Yes	45.5	45.0	46.0
No			
Did you ever attend civic training?			
Yes	5.0	2.0	8.0
No	95.0	98.0	92.0

Source: FASI (1999).

the 1997 general election than in the 1992 one. In the 1997 election, women in Kakamega mainly vied for civic positions, whereas women in Makueni mainly vied for parliamentary positions. Significantly more women voted in 1997 than in 1992. This appeared to be related to their knowledge of the voting process and their understanding that voting was their right and that their vote would make a difference. More of these women attended campaign meetings and listened to the candidates. They hoped to elect leaders with good qualities. The increased civic awareness was attributable to the civic-education activities that followed the 1995 Beijing World Conference on Women. In addition to being active in the parliamentary and civic elections, women in Kakamega and Makueni were also participating more in the election of committee members in local organizations, such as schools, women's groups, and churches.

However, these women faced many obstacles in their attempts to participate in the electoral process. Some of the women who attended campaign meetings found that the meetings were violent and that the language of the candidates was offensive. Such behaviour prevented the women from effectively participating in governance. As well, because of the women's poverty and the general failure of elected leaders to deliver on their promises, one-third of the women accepted bribes for their votes, mainly money, but also food and clothing. The women blamed this bribery on their elected leaders, who failed to offer women a chance to discuss their problems concerning wife beating, water supply, land, firewood, health facilities, illiteracy, education, credit, income, markets, etc. After the election, the leaders "disappear," and when asked why, they blame the government. Other obstacles to women's effective participation in the 1997 general election included illiteracy, inadequate resources to facilitate communication, especially transportation, and cultural barriers, especially harassment from men and their failure to stand behind their wives.

Women's sources of information

Kenyan women still depend on traditional sources of information and lack control over the most effective sources (Table 4).

Radio and television

Radio and television are major sources of information in Kenya. In 1993, just more than one-half of the Kenyan population had access to a radio (NCPD–CBS 1993). The proportion of the rural population with access to a radio was 48%. The needs assessment for the Women and Governance project established that two-thirds of the women in Makueni and slightly more in Kakamega belonged to households with radios. However, the men in the households owned the radios, and the women had limited access. Fewer households had audiocassette players. These too belonged to the men, and few women listened to them. In Kenya, very few households had televisions (11%), especially in rural areas (3%) (NCPD–CBS 1993). In Kakamega and Makueni, fewer than 10% of the households had televisions, but slightly more women watched TV, suggesting that people need information and that some people who do not own a television watch TV in places where it is available.

Roads, post office, telephone, fax, and computers

Transport and communication networks are very limited in Kenya, especially in rural areas. Kakamega and Makueni have few all-weather roads. Respondents in Kakamega had a post office, but those in Makueni did not. Limited, mostly public, telephone facilities were available in the project areas. One-third of the women could reach a telephone, and fewer than one-half of them had used a telephone. In both Kakamega and Makueni, very few women had heard of a fax or used one. Even fewer women in the study areas knew about e-mail. Only two women in the sample (one in Kakamega and one in Makueni) knew about e-mail or how to use

Table 4. The main sources of information for women.

Characteristic	Total	Makueni	Kakamega
	Proportion of respondents (%)		
Do you listen to the radio?			
Yes	62.0	57.0	67.0
No	38.0	43.0	33.0
Do you listen to audiocassettes?			
Yes	27.0	21.0	33.0
No	73.0	79.0	67.0
Do you watch television?			
Yes	10.5	10.0	11.0
No	89.5	90.0	89.0
Have you heard about computers?			
Yes	54.5	54.0	55.0
No	45.5	46.0	45.0
Have you used computers?			
Yes	0.1	0.1	0.1
No	99.0	99.0	99.0
Do you know about e-mail?			
Yes	0.5	0.1	0.0
No	99.5	99.0	100.0
Have you heard about fax?			
Yes	10.0	8.0	12.0
No	90.0	92.0	88.0
Have you used a fax?			
Yes	2.5	2.0	3.0
No	97.5	98.0	97.0
Do you have telephone in this location?			
Yes	47.0	2.0	88.0
No	53.0	98.0	12.0
Do you have a post office in this location?			
Yes	47.5	2.0	93.0
No	52.5	98.0	7.0
Is there a community centre in this location?			
Yes	6.5	9.0	4.0
No	93.5	91.0	96.0
What types of roads do you have in this location?			
All-weather roads	22.6	23.0	21.0
Tarmacked road	12.5	24.0	1.0
Earth road	88.5	90.0	87.0

(continued)

Table 4 concluded.

Characteristic	Proportion of respondents (%)		
	Total	Makueni	Kakamega
Main source of information			
Radio	53.0	39.0	67.0
Television	3.0	3.0	4.0
Newspaper	0.5	1.0	—
Chief's or District Officer's *baraza*	32.0	46.0	18.0
Relatives or friends	8.0	10.0	6.0
Women's groups	1.0	1.0	1.0
Church	2.0	—	4.0
What type of information do you obtain from this source?			
Health			
Farming	77.0	88.0	71.0
Microenterprise	73.5	79.0	68.0
Politics	7.5	4.0	11.0
Marketing	37.0	30.0	44.0
Education	6.0	6.0	6.0
Employment	36.0	34.0	39.0
Other	10.0	12.0	8.0
	1.0	—	1.0
How do you store the information?			
Audiocassette	1.0	1.0	1.0
Videocassette	1.0	2.0	—
Written and filed	27.5	6.0	49.0
Computer diskette	—	—	—
Other	70.5	91.0	50.0

Source: FASI (1999).

facilities for e-mail. A larger proportion of the women in Kakamega and Makueni, however, had heard about computers or seen them. Only one women in each district had ever actually used one.

Community-based information centres

Fewer than 10% of the women in the project knew about the community-based information centre in their district. Lack of community-based information centres or of information about them in the study areas precluded women from accessing the information services offered at the centres, such as libraries, televisions, cinema, video, social-networking venues, and training.

The radio was the main source of information for the women in Kakamega and Makueni; it was used by more than one-half of these women. The Chief's or

District Officer's *baraza* was the main source of information for one-third of the women. Relatives and friends constituted an important information source. Other sources of information were the church, government officers, and community-based training initiatives. Leaders and members of women's groups supplied information, particularly on politics, to other women. Information was also obtained from letters, telephone calls, and telegrams. These sources supplied information on health, farming, education, politics, employment, marketing, and small enterprise. Most information was not stored. Sources of information were limited by the facilities, such as poor telephones, electricity, and related technology, including computers. What few facilities there were belonged to men, and the women, who were occupied with household chores, were unable to use them. Even where facilities such as telephones were available, women were unable to use them.

Discussion and conclusion

IEC and advocacy

Women have demonstrated their capacity to contribute to development and even to manage their own development. However, for women to be efficient and effective, they need IEC and advocacy to encourage their use of ICTs. This project developed IEC and advocacy materials to demystify ICTs and demonstrate women's need of ICTs to participate effectively in electoral politics and to respond to their own daily needs. The project trained the women to use computers, e-mail, and the Internet for the following tasks:

- To store, transfer, and retrieve information related to their lifelong-learning activities in health, education, business, farming, elections, etc.;

- To easily and quickly get in touch with each other across the country and talk to each other, interact, and develop plans, decisions, and strategies to improve their women's participation in electoral politics (for example, knowing which female candidates to vote for during the election, etc.);

- To conduct personal business, such as searching for employment, looking for markets for farm products or crafts in other countries and regions, and receiving orders;

- To prepare training materials, such as posters, and improve or change them to suit women's needs; and

- To provide training, communication, and duplication services for a fee (this will sustain the project).

Targeting women

Women were the primary target of the Women and Governance project because they were numerically dominant in the two districts and project locations and in the various age groups. Poverty had pushed most men out of Kakamega and Makueni to search for employment in urban areas, and this left the women to head the households and manage the rural farms and small-scale enterprises. Furthermore, women are the custodians of indigenous information so critical to family and community welfare, particularly in the areas of health, environmental management, and religion. As communities urbanize and modernize, this type of information will disappear, unless women are integrated into modern systems of information production, transfer, and consumption.

Priority areas for intervention

Civic education

Poverty in Kenya has been feminized. This poverty has largely resulted from women's failure to access key resources. Marginalization of women is related to their low representation in decision-making bodies, especially Parliament and local government. Although women in Kenya have an increasing level of civic awareness and are participating more in the electoral process, they remain poor and geographically isolated and fail to network, engage in peer support, or formulate a common political agenda. Women's use of ICTs would bridge their geographic isolation and promote interaction, networking, sharing, and formulation of common strategies to address their interests.

Small-scale enterprises

Small-scale enterprises have the greatest potential to generate employment in Kenya, especially among women. A substantial number of women in the target areas are engaged in small-scale enterprises. They have limited markets and are being exploited. They should be introduced to ICTs to enable them to transform this sector with information on supplies, quality control, raw materials, pricing, markets, and technologies. Such information would enable these enterprises to contribute more to the growth of the region and to women's management of this sector.

Challenges to the Women and Governance project

Information packaging

Africa is presently a net consumer of information packaged in other societies. Access to such information could improve productivity. In addition to using existing information packages, the project will assemble and package information on indigenous systems of production and services familiar to women and make it more generally accessible to women.

Addressing the cultural dimension

Women are familiar with the indigenous communication systems dominant in the rural areas and have some control over them. These systems also have a lot of gender biases and prejudices embedded in them. We need to identify and understand these biases and prejudices and to sensitively repackage the information so that it portrays women positively.

Community-based information centres

Community-based information centres are designed to deliver a wide range of information services within communities. This initiative is highly technological and targets women as a disadvantaged group but also encompasses the social, economic, recreational, and governance activities in every sector of society. This involves ICT diffusion, which in turn involves computerized equipment and microelectronic product design and related know-how. Successful use of ICTs also requires technical change to enable us to adapt a number of given technologies, make continuous improvements, and meet a widening range of needs.

Infrastructure

The average teledensity in Kenya is 1 line per 100 inhabitants and is especially low in the target areas. These areas also lack proper access to postal services, electricity, and all-weather roads. No ICT service providers are currently operating there. Alternative sources of energy, such as solar, will be used in areas without electricity (Summit Strategies 1998).

Telephone lines, power, and roads for access are the needed infrastructure for e-mail and the Internet in Kenya. The representatives of Kenya Post and Telecommunications, Kenya Power and Lighting, the Ministry of Transport and Communications, and ICT service providers are therefore treated as partners in the implementation of the project. They also participated in the stakeholders conference (FASI 1999b).

Policy

In 1997, the Kenyan government published its Postal and Telecommunications Sector Policy Statement, defining the framework for developing the postal and telecommunications subsectors. The key statements were that Kenya would construct more telephone lines to increase the teledensity in rural and urban areas, facilitate private-sector participation in the telecommunications sector, and change the status of the Kenya Posts and Telecommunication Corporation (a monopoly operator) (Mureithi 1998).

References

FASI (Family Support Institute). 1999a. Report of the needs assessment of Central Isukha location in Kakamega District and Nguumo location in Makueni District for the Women and Governance project. FASI, Nairobi, Kenya.

———— 1999b. Report of the Stakeholders Conference on "Enhancing Women's Participation in Governance Through Access to Civic Information and Information and Communication Technologies (ICTs) in Kakamega and Makueni Districts: Where Are We Now? Where Do We Go from Here? How Do We Get There?" FASI, Nairobi, Kenya.

Mureithi, M. 1998. Information and communications — the potential for take off. *In* Wamuyu, G.; Shaw, R., ed., Our problems, our solutions. An economic and public policy agenda for Kenya. The Institute of Economic Affairs, London, UK.

NCPD–CBS (National Council for Population and Development; Central Bureau for Statistics). 1993. Kenya Development and Health Survey. Macro International Inc., Calverton, MD, USA.

Summit Strategies. 1998. Status of existing Kenya telecommunications networks. Brief notes for Oxfam. Summit Strategies, Boston, MA, USA.

Appendix 1

CONTRIBUTING AUTHORS

Nancy J. Hafkin
Coordinator
African Information Society Initiative
United Nations Economic Commission for Africa
P.O. Box 3001
Addis Ababa, Ethiopia
Tel.: +251 1 51 11 67
Fax: +251 1 51 05 12 (or +1 [212] 963-4957)
E-mail: hafkin.uneca@un.org (or nhafkin@hotmail.com)

Nancy J. Hafkin has a PhD in African history from Boston University, with a dissertation on the political economy of northern Mozambique from the mid-18th to the beginning of the 20th century. She is the editor, with Edna G. Bay, of *African Women: Studies in Social and Economic Change* (Stanford University Press) and *African Women*, a special issue of *African Studies Review*. She taught African history and women's studies at the University of Massachusetts – Boston from 1969 to 1977 and then joined the African Training and Research Centre for Women of the United Nations Economic Commission for Africa (ECA) in Addis Ababa, Ethiopia, as chief of research and publications. After 10 years there, she joined the Pan African Development Information System, also at ECA. Since 1975 her major focus has been on the link between information and communication technologies (ICTs) and development through ECA's African Information Society Initiative.

Cathy-Mae Karelse
Director
INFOLIT, Adamastor Trust
14 Greenwich Grove
Station Road
Rondebosch 7700, South Africa
Tel.: +27 21 686 5070
Fax: +27 21 689 7465
E-mail: cmk@grove.uct.ac.za (soon to become cathymae99@hotmail.com)

Cathy-Mae Karelse has been involved in information work for the past 15 years, occupying positions in various nongovernmental organizations, with portfolios related to information and development. Over the past 5 years, she has focused more keenly on ICTs and gender, with specific emphasis on how people can use information-literacy competencies to become more empowered to participate in shaping the information society.

Shanyisa Anota Khasiani
Director
Family Support Institute
Professor
Population Studies and Research Institute
University of Nairobi
P.O. Box 30913
Nairobi, Kenya
Tel.: 226350
Fax: 247412
E-mail: fasi@africaonline.co.ke

Shanyisa Anota Khasiani has published widely in the areas of internal and international migration, including refugee movements in Africa, fertility, and family planning, and she identifies women's advancement and gender as her areas of primary focus.

Gillian M. Marcelle
47 Thackeray Ave
London N17 9DT, UK
Tel.: 00 44 181 808 9421
Chairperson
Information Society Gender Working Group
Johannesburg, South Africa
Tel.: 00 27 12 841 2491
Fax: 00 27 12 841 3365
E-mail: gmarcelle@yahoo

For more than 11 years, Gillian M. Marcelle has pursued a varied career in telecommunications and ICT policy, as a consultant to nongovernmental organizations, the private sector, and national governments. She has held academic posts,
as well as positions with British Telecom and the UK's telecommunications regu-
lator, Oftel. She trained as an economist at the University of the West Indies,
St Augustine, Trinidad, and later obtained postgraduate qualifications in international economics from the Kiel Institute of World Economics, West Germany, and
in business administration from George Washington University, Washington, DC.
She is pursuing a DPhil at the University of Sussex, in the United Kingdom,
where her research focuses on technological capability-building processes in the
African telecom sector. She has published on innovation policies of developing
countries, telecom liberalization, and gender and development, and she is an
Honourary Fellow of the British Telecommunications plc. Telecommunications
Engineering Staff College.

Rachel Solange Mienje Momo
Director
Documentation Centre
African Regional Centre for Technology
Fahd House, Djilly Mbaye Avenue
BP 2435 Dakar, Senegal
Tel.: (221) 823 77 12
Fax: (221) 823 77 13
E-mail: arct@sonatel.senet.net

Rachel Solange Mienje Momo obtained her Diploma in Documentation in 1991 from the School for Librarians, Archivists and Documentalists of the University of Dakar. Since 1992 she has been the Director of the Documentation Centre of the African Regional Centre for Technology. She was active in the reorganization of the documentation centres of several UN organizations in Senegal, notably, the United Nations Industrial Development Organization (UNIDO) and the United Nations Educational, Scientific and Cultural Organization (UNESCO). She was equally effective in consultations on the new information technologies on behalf of UNIDO–Vienna, the World Intellectual Property Organization – Geneva, the International Development Research Centre (IDRC), and ECA. As well, she has participated in several international conferences and presented papers on the information system of the African Regional Centre for Technology and its impacts in several areas of development in Africa.

Hilda M. Munyua
Information Specialist
CAB International
Africa Regional Centre
ICRAF Complex
United Nations Ave, Gigiri
P.O. Box 633, Village Market
Nairobi, Kenya
Tel.: 254-02-521450
Fax: 254-02-521001 or 522150
E-mail: Hmunyua@cgiar.org

Hilda Munyua is on the boards of InterLink Rural Information Service and the Kenya Voluntary Women Rehabilitation Institute. She has been actively involved in managing and disseminating agricultural information to users since 1979. She has wide experience in information management, training, and project development and management.

Aida Opoku-Mensah
Program Officer
The Ford Foundation
P.O. Box 2368
Lagos, Nigeria
Tel.: +234-1-262-3970-2
Fax: +234-1-262-3973
E-mail: a.opoku-mensah@fordfound.org (or aidaom@hotmail.com)

From 1996 to 1998, Aida Opoku-Mensah was Regional Director of the Panos Institute's southern Africa office in Lusaka, Zambia. She has also served as a Visiting Lecturer at City University, London, and is the Director of Southern Africa Regional Programmes at the Panos Institute in London. Her many publications include *Signposts on the Superhighway: African Environment (A Handbook of Environmental Resources on the Internet for African Journalists)* and *Up in the Air: The State of Broadcasting in Southern Africa (Analysis and Trends in Six Countries)*. She is a PhD candidate in the Department of Politics and the African Studies Unit of the University of Leeds, United Kingdom, and has an MA in communication policy studies from City University, London, United Kingdom, a BA in linguistics and Swahili from the University of Ghana, and a Diploma in International Relations from the University of London.

Josephine Ouedraogo
Director
African Centre for Women
United Nations Economic Commission for Africa
P.O. Box 3001
Addis Ababa, Ethiopia
Tel.: 251-1-51 12 63
Fax: 251-1-51 44 16
E-mail: OuedraogoJ@UN.org

Josephine Ouedraogo is a sociologist with professional experience in managing and assessing field projects and conducting surveys on economic and social issues related to local development. She is from Burkina Faso and is a former Minister of Family Affairs and National Solidarity of Burkina Faso.

Fatimata Seye Sylla
Director General
Solutions 3+
51-53 Bld Djily Mbaye
BP 21145
Dakar, Senegal
Tel.: 221 822 81 05
Fax: 221 821 23 59
E-mail: fsylla@telecomplus.sn

Fatimata Seye Sylla has an engineering degree in computer science from Le Havre Institute of Technology in France, a degree in education from the Massachusetts Institute of Technology, and a management certificate from the West African sub-regional School of Management in Dakar, Senegal. As a teacher and researcher, she has for several years conducted a research project that introduces computers into the Senegalese educational system. As a teacher and consultant in computer science, she has worked as a manager for the Senegalese government, UNESCO, the United Nations Fund for Population Activities, United States Agency for International Development, IDRC, and various private-sector organizations. She has conducted research and worked in the fields of ICTs, education, globalization, and gender.

Appendix 2

ACRONYMS AND ABBREVIATIONS

AACP	Association of African Communication Professionals
ACW	African Centre for Women [ECA]
AIF	African Internet Forum
AISI	African Information Society Initiative
ALAI	Agencia Latinoamericana de Información (Latin American agency for information)
AMREF	African Medical Research Foundation
ANSFE	African Network for Support to Feminine Entrepreneurship
APC	Association for Progressive Communications
ASARECA	Association for Strengthening Agricultural Research in East and Central Africa
ATRCW	African Training and Research Centre for Women
CABI	CAB International
CBO	community-based organization
CGE	Commission for Gender Equality [South Africa]
CODESA	Convention for a Democratic South Africa
CSIR	Council for Scientific and Industrial Research [South Africa]
CTA	Technical Centre for Agricultural and Rural Co-operation
DSTA	Delegation for Scientific and Technical Affairs [Senegal]
ECA	United Nations Economic Commission for Africa
EIG	Economic Interest Group [Senegal]
ELCI	Environmental Liaison Centre International
ENDA	Environment, Development, Action
FAMWZ	Federation of Africa Media Women Zimbabwe
FAO	Food and Agriculture Organization of the United Nations
FASI	Family Support Institute
FINESA	Farm Information Network – East and Southern Africa
FOWODE	Forum for Women in Democracy [Uganda]
FPAK	Family Planning Association of Kenya
FRN	Farm Radio Network [Zimbabwe]
GIS	global information society
GIWG	Gender and Information Working Group [IDRC]
GK97	Global Knowledge Conference (in Toronto, 1997)
GWG	Gender Working Group [UNCSTD]

HIS	health information systems [Kenya]
HITD	Harnessing Information Technology for Development [United Nations]
HLEG	High-level Expert Group [ECA or European Commission]
ICT	information and communication technology
IDRC	International Development Research Centre
IEC	information, education, and communication
IFAD	International Fund for Agricultural Development
IIA	Internet Initiative for Africa [UNDP]
InfoDev	Information for Development Programme [World Bank]
IOC	Indian Ocean Commission
ISP	Internet service provider
ITU	International Telecommunication Union
IWJF	International Women Judges Foundation
LAWA	Leadership and Advocacy for Women in Africa [Georgetown University, Washington, DC]
MCSS	Ministry of Culture and Social Services [Kenya]
MP	Member of Parliament
MTN	Mobile Telecommunication Network [South Africa]
NFU	National Farmers Union [Mozambique]
NGO	nongovernmental organization
NIS	national innovation system
NISADE	National Institute for Study and Action for the Development of Education [Senegal]
OECD	Organisation for Economic Co-operation and Development
PADIS	Pan African Development Information System
PICTA	Partnership for Information and Communication Technologies in Africa
PIT	public information terminal [South Africa]
R&D	research and development
RECIF	Réseau de communication et d'information des femmes (communication and information network for women)
S&T	science and technology
SACCAR	Southern African Centre for Cooperation in Agriculture and Natural Resources Research and Training
SDNP	Sustainable Development Networking Programme [Mozambique]
SHD	sustainable human development
SMEs	small- and medium-scale enterprises
SSA	sub-Saharan Africa
SYNFEV	Synergie, Genre et Développement (Synergy, Gender and Development) [ENDA–Dakar]
TEEAL	The Essential Electronic Agricultural Library [Cornell University]

UNCSTD	United Nations Commission on Science and Technology for Development
UNCTAD	United Nations Conference on Trade and Development
UNDP	United Nations Development Programme
UNESCO	United Nations Educational, Scientific and Cultural Organization
UNIFEM	United Nations Development Fund for Women
UNU–INTECH	United Nations University Institute for New Technologies
USAID	United States Agency for International Development
USD	United States dollar(s)
UWONET	Ugandan Women's Organization Network
WACC	World Association for Christian Communication
WID	women in development
WLL	wireless in the local loop
WNSP	Women's Networking Support Programme [APC]
WTO	World Trade Organization

About the Institution

The International Development Research Centre (IDRC) is committed to building a sustainable and equitable world. IDRC funds developing-world researchers, thus enabling the people of the South to find their own solutions to their own problems. IDRC also maintains information networks and forges linkages that allow Canadians and their developing-world partners to benefit equally from a global sharing of knowledge. Through its actions, IDRC is helping others to help themselves.

About the Publisher

IDRC Books publishes research results and scholarly studies on global and regional issues related to sustainable and equitable development. As a specialist in development literature, IDRC Books contributes to the body of knowledge on these issues to further the cause of global understanding and equity. IDRC publications are sold through its head office in Ottawa, Canada, as well as by IDRC's agents and distributors around the world. The full catalogue is available at http://www.idrc.ca/booktique.